Communitybuilding
In the Classroom

Vanston Shaw

In consultation with Dr. Spencer Kagan

Kagan

Kagan
1160 Calle Cordillera
San Clemente, CA 92673
1(800) WEE CO-OP
www.KaganOnline.com

ISBN: 1-879097-14-1

Communitybuilding in the Classroom

Vanston Shaw

Table of Contents

Part II: Structures

Chapter 6: Structures

Part III: Lessons

Chapter 7: Lessons

Part IV: Conclusion

Chapter 8: Toward Community and the Inclusive School

————————VANSTON SHAW: *Communitybuilding in the Classroom*————————
Publisher: Kagan Cooperative Learning • 1(800) Wee Co-op

Contents: 3

Structure	Lesson Number																																				
---	1	2	3	4	5	6	7	8	9	10	11	12	13	14	15	16	17	18	19	20	21	22	23	24	25	26	27	28	29	30	31	32	33	34	35	36	37
Brainstorming						X																															
Choral Response																																					
Community Circle	X	X		X						X	X																										
Corners	X							X		X	X																	X		X							
Formations														X	X				X																		
Inside-Outside Circle										X				X	X				X							X		X						X			X
Line-Ups				X						X						X								X											X		
Numbered Hds Together					X	X	X	X	X	X			X			X				X	X	X	X	X	X	X	X					X	X	X		X	
Pairs	X				X	X	X	X	X			X	X								X	X	X		X	X											
Pairs Compare															X	X	X																				
Roundrobin/Roundtable	X		X				X	X	X	X		X	X	X	X	X	X	X			X				X	X	X		X	X		X	X			X	X
Similarity Grouping													X			X											X						X				
Talking Chips							X					X														X								X	X		
Team Projects							X												X	X						X			X					X			
Team Discussion		X		X																	X				X		X		X		X		X	X			
Three-Step Interview		X	X		X	X	X		X			X	X		X												X	X			X						
Think-Pair-Share	X	X		X	X	X	X				X	X		X		X	X	X		X		X	X	X	X	X				X		X		X	X		X

VANSTON SHAW: *Communitybuilding in the Classroom*

Publisher: Kagan Cooperative Learning Co. • 1(800) Wee Co-op

Index of Structures

Foreword
by Spencer Kagan

Vanston Shaw has written a remarkable book. Some books are cute presentations of nifty things to do tomorrow in your classroom. Some books provide inspiration and a rationale for educational change. Some books provide a theory of classroom behavior which explains why students and teachers behave the way they do. *Communitybuilding* does all three: not only do we get an integrated theory and a rationale for change, we get step-by-step lessons which make that change easy. It is important to understand how we reach community in a classroom by satisfying the needs for inclusion, influence, and openness. It is empowering to have the step-by-step structures and lessons to put that theory into practice.

For some time I have traveled the United States and Canada lecturing and providing workshops on cooperative learning. Unlike some other prominent leaders in the field, I have said that teambuilding, classbuilding, and social skill development are all essential elements in the cooperative learning classroom. I have been advocating increased use of these positive contextual elements, because far more students lose their first job for lack of social skills than for lack of technical skills. This is true, and the schools need to respond. But my personal commitment to creating a classroom community is not primarily to solve a social problem. Rather, my core values as an educator include creating a classroom in which each individual student feels known, accepted, appreciated, and, yes, loved by his teacher and classmates. Only in that kind of an environment can each student be fully what it is in him to become.

Our society has changed. In 1960, only one of ten students was born to an unmarried mother; today it is one in four. In 1940,

70% of all families had one breadwinner and one homemaker; today the figure is 20%. We once had stable, extended families with long-term neighborhood and community ties. Families today are mobile units moving every few years. For many students today grandparents, and even one of their parents, instead of a daily source of contact are an occasional phone call. Students, feeling the void, struggle for inclusion, attempting to get from their peers what their are lacking at home -- values, belonging, acceptance and affirmation. But peers do not necessarily give acceptance and affirmation for positive behaviors. In response to this radical transformation of our socialization base we as teachers must respond by providing the missing positive socialization experiences. *Communitybuilding* shows us how.

I spent a number of years as a psychotherapist trying to undo the effects on individuals of living in unloving environments -- whether homes or classrooms. As I listened and worked with each individual trying to become self-affirmative, I realized my job would be like that of the buggy whip maker if only schools and families were affirmative environments. Prediction: After *Communitybuilding* becomes incorporated in the everyday life of schools, from K to College, the need for psychotherapy will decrease dramatically.

As I have trained teachers in teambuilding and classbuilding structures, a remarkable paradox has become apparent. Across the United States and Canada, over and over teachers report to me that the more teambuilding and classbuilding they do in their classrooms the better their students perform academically. Make no mistake, it really is true. Teachers are saying things like, "This is the third class I am teaching in cooperative learning. The first time I tried cooperative learning I did it just like you taught, including teambuilding and classbuilding, and my students were quite successful. The next time, I did only a little teambuilding and classbuilding and my students did not do as well -- they were not as excited about their teammates or the content, and did not score as well on tests. Now I am using plenty of teambuilding and classbuilding again, and the change is remarkable. Not only is the tone of the class more positive, but test scores are up."

This is truly remarkable: Time away from academic tasks leads to better academic performance. In trying to understand this paradox, three solutions suggest themselves. First, as Maslow pointed out, there is a hierarchy of needs. If the need for belonging is not taken care of, we get stuck trying to fill that need and cannot go beyond. For many students 90% of their energy is caught in trying to achieve social acceptance from their peers, leaving only 10% for academics. When some time is spent on teambuilding and classbuilding, basic needs are filled, and a tremendous amount of energy is released for academics. Students who are not worried about whether they are accepted by their peers are freer to study.

A second explanation is based on the nature of attention. We can only pay attention to our external environment for so long before we must turn our attention inward and acknowledge what is there. The teambuilding and classbuilding activities correct the imbalance inherent in a classroom where students are expected to just "take in." The activities involve movement, laughing, emotions, and fun. Putting fun into the classroom; letting students express their personal emotions, provides release. If I just "take in," at some point I get full, and can't take in any more. I need to put out. Over and over again in classrooms and workshops, when students seem tired or bored or just overwhelmed with information -- I pull out a five minute teambuilding activity. After a few minutes of Balloon Bounce or Team Balances, the students return to their desks bright-eyed, with full attention, ready to process new information. Yes the teambuilding and classbuilding take time, but what is better: spending 100% of the time on academics as students sit half attentive with a glazed-over look, or 80% of the time on academics, with the students interested, bright-eyed, and 100% attentive?

A third explanation of why taking time for teambuilding and classbuilding has a positive impact on academics is based on generalization theory. The more I love class, the more I love everything associated with it, including the teacher, and my math, science, and reading. Communitybuilding activities create the environment in which students are set to love learning.

Communitybuilding includes more than classbuilding and teambuilding. In this book Vanston Shaw goes beyond territory I have explored, including lessons on relationships skills. He shows us that Active Listening, Conflict Resolution Skills, and Affirmations are easily taught. They are skills which pay big dividends for classroom climate and productivity as well as in jobs and personal lives. Through our Cooperative Learning Company we sell 20 different posters. Each year our most popular poster is "8 Modes of Conflict Resolution." There is a strong message here. Once upon a time when we looked out at our students, we could count on finding a John Boy Walton in every seat. Today when we look out there, we see a room full of Bart Simpsons. Vanston Shaw has seen the change, and has responded. His response, *Communitybuilding*, will provide for students positive socialization experiences lacking in our modern urban homes. When generally put into practice *Communitybuilding* will be like the stone thrown in the center of the pond. Ripples will travel far beyond today's classrooms.

Spencer Kagan, Ph.D.

Acknowledgments & Dedication

This book would not have been possible without the vision and support of **Spencer Kagan** who saw the promise of the communitybuilding concept and encouraged me to write this book. He introduced me to the structural approach which I saw as helping teachers make sense of cooperative learning. Spencer contributed many ideas and concepts which are incorporated into this book and worked with me through several revisions to make the book clearer and more concise.

I am indebted to **Roger Johnson**, who originally introduced me to cooperative learning as a way to organize classrooms and improve my skills as a teacher.

I am indebted to **Jeanne Gibbs**, author of *Tribes: A Process for Social Development and Cooperative Learning*[1] for the process she developed when she wrote her book. Tribes presented me with the ideas for stages of group development and the teacher as a caretaker of the classroom environment. Jeanne gave me an approach to teaching which changed the way I worked with children and adults. She is also a great friend and human being.

I would like to acknowledge **Laurie Robertson** for her suggestions on content, **Jeanne Stone** and **Jill Carroll** for their editing expertise, **Catherine Hurlbert, Ruth Gardner,** and **Ben Taylor** for their formatting expertise, and **Celso Rodriguez** for his artwork.

I would like to thank the following teachers who field tested the lessons in this book and gave me valuable feedback: **Tom Meyers**, Rose Avenue School (Modesto City, S.D.);

Gordon Chan, Beyer High School (Modesto City, S.D.), **Bill Richards**, Waterford Elementary School District; **Michelle Cahall**, Placer County Office of Education (Special Education Department); **Fred Saltzman**, Calla High School (Manteca High S.D.); **Sandra Young**, Cunningham Elementary School (Turlock Elementary S.D.); **Laurie Taylor**, Rio Altura School (Riverbank S.D.); **Nanci Navarro**, Osborn School (Turlock Elementary S.D.), and **Roxie Seward**, Modesto High School. These cooperative teachers gave me a reality check in the early versions of the lessons presented here. Without their help and encouragement, this book would not be what it is.

Special thanks go to my past colleagues at the Stanislaus County Office of Education who provided support and encouragement when I began this book. These include **James Norby**, Special Education Program Administrator for his encouragement, **Jerry Trow**, past SELPA Director for allowing me the freedom to experiment, and **Debbie Neidigh**, a secretary who was always there to make my job easier.

Special thanks to the staff and parents of Aspen School in Los Alamos, New Mexico for their acceptance and support, especially **Del Dyche**, Principal of Aspen School.

Thanks to my son, **Seth Vanston Shaw**, for always asking when it would be finished. It's for all the children and their teachers that this book is intended.

A special thanks to the woman who nurtured me through all those early mornings and late nights and put up with me and this book; my friend, confidant, lover, soul mate, and spouse, **Nuria San-Mauro**.

1. You can order *Tribes: A Process for Social Development and Cooperative Learning* from Center Source Publications, 305 Tesconi Circle, Santa Rosa, CA. 94501, (707) 577-8233.

I would like to dedicate this book to my friend, **Robert Rudholm**. Robert was my mentor when I first started teaching 20 years ago. He taught me that how we relate with our students and others is as important as what we teach. He is a master teacher who has given me a tremendous amount over the years as we worked together with special education students and later co-presented workshops for teachers. Robert is a beautiful human being who has touched many lives, including mine, in a positive way.

I hope that *Communitybuilding in the Classroom* assists teachers in developing learning communities within their classrooms and schools. Through developing a sense of a learning community within our schools I see the possibility for more positive learning environments for both students and educators. We all need to work together and know that we are "in this together."

Vanston Shaw

Vanston Shaw
September, 1992
Santa Fe, New Mexico

———— **VANSTON SHAW:** *Communitybuilding in the Classroom* ————
Publisher: Kagan Cooperative Learning • 1(800) Wee Co-op

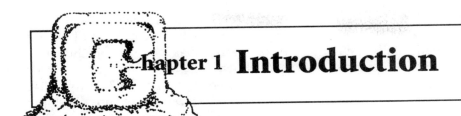

Are you interested in taking cooperative learning teams in your room further than you have before? Have you ever had the feeling that cooperative learning had potential for assisting you and your students to make positive changes personally and improve the total classroom climate? Have you felt that cooperative learning should help build a sense of community within the classroom but didn't know how to proceed? This book is designed to answer these concerns. It is for you, the teacher who would intentionally like to create a sense of community within your classroom. It's for you who want to stretch your skills in facilitating the process of cooperative learning and would like ideas and lesson formats to help you do this.

Each of us is attracted to cooperative learning for different reasons. Some hear about the academic benefits, others the social benefits, still others are attracted because they want to find a more comfortable way to teach. Why you are involved with cooperative learning may not be as important in the long run as the fact that you are making a commitment to change. Traditional lecture style and highly competitive classrooms have been the primary structure of instruction in American education. Cooperative learning provides a positive addition to our repertoire of classroom structures. This addition is re-quired not only because our students need to know how to learn collaboratively, but also for us as educators. It allows us to consciously explore the group dynamics of teaching, to empower our teaching. Above all, cooperative learning empowers our students with new skills both in how to learn and how to relate.

This book is designed for you, the cooperative learning practitioner interested in structuring your classroom learning environment to empower the class as a whole, the teams within the class, and each individual student. The premise of this book is that cooperative learning is a powerful tool to teach students the relational skills they will need to function in the 21st century. This book will focus on relational skills as they influence the class, team, and individual.

"What you do speaks so loudly, they can't hear what you say."

The Classroom as a Community

Why is it that we want to use cooperative learning structures within our classrooms? To improve academic achievement, improve student's interpersonal and communication skills, higher level thinking processes, self esteem, liking for school? It's been for all these reasons and more. Many of us are attracted to cooperative learning because we want our classroom and school to be more than a place where students are taught basic academic skills. We want a classroom and school where there is a sense of community, a community of learners.

This sense of community is important because we know intuitively, and research has consistently shown, that where there is a strong sense of community, trust, high self-esteem, and good instruction, students have higher achievement. Having a cohesive classroom can give many students the sense of support they need to do their best. It can develop the social support systems students require to have a strong sense of self worth. This improved self-esteem assists students in developing a sense of purpose in life and allows students to better resist the temptation of making poor choices.

> *As the teacher you are the creator and curator of the classroom environment.*

One goal of this book is to assist you in this community building process by sharing structures and lessons which develop relationship skills and lead toward that elusive sense of community for the class, team, and individuals. Developing a sense of community doesn't always happen in a classroom and is more the exception than the rule. As we proceed through this book, I will share lessons for classbuilding, teambuilding, and relationship skill building with suggestions on how to sequence these lessons. However, lessons alone are not enough. As the teacher, you are the creator and curator of the classroom environment. The tone you establish for these lessons is as important as the lessons themselves.

Issues of Group Development

Much of the literature about cooperative learning centers on the potential for academic growth and, in some instances, stress-es the need to teach social skills. Very few approaches discuss the process of what happens to a group as it comes together and students learn these cooperative skills, or which skills should be taught first. I've adapted the idea of stages of group development from the work of Will Schultz and from Jeanne Gibbs, *Tribes: A Process for Social Development and Cooperative Learning.* I have found that gaining an understanding of the stages or issues of group development allows you to plan activities in a developmentally appropriate sequence rather than at random. Thus, you can use the lessons presented here throughout the year, lead students through the successful resolution of the issues of group development: inclusion, influence, openness, and community.

You may notice I use the term "issues" rather than "stages" of group development. "Stages" implies a developmental sequence in which the individual, team, or class must successfully master one level before attempting the next. Although it is possible that the issues of inclusion, influence, openness, and community might be achieved in such a sequence, it is more likely that there will be more fluid movement between issues, and that various individuals and teams within your class will experience them at different times and to varying degrees. My desire is for you to become aware of these issues of group development so that when you see an individual or team responding in a certain way, you can thoughtfully consider how best to respond. This response can be founded on the knowledge that the issues of group development are very much like shifting sand. You need to know this because an appropriate response can make the difference of whether you take your class two steps closer to a sense of community or a step back.

Inclusion

When students first walk into the classroom at the beginning of the year they experience many anxieties. "Are my friends going to be in my room? Will the teacher like me? Will I like the teacher? Am I going to be able to make friends?" These are just a few of the questions students have when they start a new school year. Cooperative learning by its very nature is inclusive. However, many students have been trained in such competitive classroom environments that they do not necessarily take to cooperative learning like

> *Issues of inclusion are resolved when individual students feel they are part of a team and class.*

"ducks to water". Many of us have experienced our classroom as a group of ducks who couldn't swim.

The inclusion stage of group development revolves around ideas of self presentation, building trust, and building a feeling of safety within the group. Inclusion happens in all groups we enter, whether in the classroom or in the faculty room. It's important for us to be aware of this stage because you and every student in your class will experience it repeatedly throughout your lifetimes. You can structure lessons and activities to build a sense of trust and safety, and to allow your students to deal safely and successfully with issues of inclusion. You do this by structuring opportunities for students to present who they are to their classmates and teammates.

Inclusion occurs at a class and team level. As the teacher, how can you assist students to come together successfully as a class and as a team? The classbuilding and teambuilding lessons centering on "getting acquainted" will be particularly helpful.

When a group first comes together it wrestles first with the stage of inclusion. During inclusion we want to introduce ourselves as unique individuals. Generally, inclusion is a time when we are seeing how we fit into the group. Once group members begin to feel comfortable in the group, then the stage of influence comes to us with cheer and often times a bit of anguish.

One important concept to keep in mind is that inclusion and the other issues of group development occur in a cyclical fashion. Individuals, teams, and your class may move from inclusion to influence and then back to inclusion. These issues of group development are a process which cycle back and forth depending on what is happening within the group at a given time. You are dealing with the inclusion stage as soon as your students enter the room. Once your students have developed a sense of inclusion, they enter the stage of influence where students deal with issues of leadership and power within the group.

Influence

Much of the drive students feel to join groups in school relates to their personal need for influence or power. Most of us subconsciously relate our personal power to how much influence we have on others. If you were to ask high schoolers to name students who had influence with other students in school, many would probably identify student body officers. How do these people

> *Issues of influence are successfully resolved when all students feel they have impact, & none feel dominated.*

get elected to positions of authority? By building networks of friends and others who will vote for them. They are learning early how the adult world operates. Those with power are those who influence others and have a network of friends and supporters. The same could also be said for gang leaders.

The stage of influence can best be described as the period in which team members feel comfortable and safe enough (a sense of inclusion) to want to assert their point of view within the team. Individuals want to influence the other members of the group to adopt their point of view, to see it their way. This can be a period of turmoil within a team. This is the time when problems in teams emerge and disagreements arise. Influence is the stage where decision making skills must be taught so that teams can learn win-win problem solving strategies as presented in the "Experiencing Mutual Support" and "Valuing Individual Differences" lessons. This is also the time when it is important to teach the "Active Listening" lessons from the relationship skills section.

Openness

Openness is the third stage of group development, a stage which must be nurtured and allowed to grow. As the teacher you foster openness by sharing those parts of yourself you feel safe sharing with your students; they will learn to reciprocate. Not all of us want to be open with our students. It's a risk. I recommend you only open yourself as much as you feel comfortable. These are the same guidelines students have. Openness can happen only as we feel safe to unfold and share those parts of ourselves we often hide.

As teachers you have experienced this stage when students share their feelings about the birth or death of a sibling or friend, abuse, or sorrow of a friend moving away. This is the time when students communicate from their hearts. Sometimes this stage of group development will happen spontaneously. The approach outlined in this book is designed to lay the foundation for students to experience openness, *not by chance, but by*

design. As the teacher you must be aware that feelings may be shared which may be uncomfortable for you or your students. The discomfort is there because we do not usually share our true feelings. This is a

Issues of openness are resolved as students feel trustful to share personal information.

stretch for many of us. It is one of the opportunities waiting for us; a doorway to open and walk through. Students need opportunities to share their feelings in a safe environment. You can provide these opportunities and model appropriate communication skills.

Openness corresponds to the teaching of relationship skills. When we teach active listening and how to use affirmations, we are providing an opportunity for students to open and share more of who they are. Students will only feel safe to share if inclusion has been built and the issues of influence have been resolved. Openness is a prerequisite to developing a sense of community.

Community

Community is the end result of a cooperative learning classroom where the issues of group development have been successfully resolved. When classbuilding, teambuilding, and relationship skill building have occurred, you can sense the feeling of community. Even the student who has been the "ugly duckling" is accepted and your classroom is humming with productive energy. It's the feeling you have when "you know" why you chose teaching as your career.

A colleague of mine, Vicki Stewart, was team teaching several years ago in a special education class. She and her teaching partner, Julee, had been using the Tribes process for most of the year with their twenty-four students. One morning Judy became very ill during class. Since they had neither phones nor intercoms in the room, Vicki went to the office to arrange for someone to take Judy to the emergency room. Judy remained in the classroom at her desk. The students, who had been diagnosed as having severe disabilities in language processing, sensed something was wrong. While Judy sat at her desk, extremely ill, the students formed a circle around her and sang songs they had been taught. It was a moment both teachers will always remember. It was a moment of community within the classroom where even the most severely involved students could relate to the gravity of the situation and respond with support and comfort.

> *Community is reached when the issues of Inclusion, Influence, and Openness are successfully dealt with.*

Once again we must remember the issues of group development are a spiral, ever turning; your class may again enter the influence stage, and you'll see the need to return to inclusion activities. These issues of group development are a process constantly in flux. Understanding the issues of group development and using the lessons in this book provide you an opportunity to lead your class intentionally toward a sense of community - a way of being with one another which is empowering to you and your students.

A Rationale For The Stages/Issues

Remember that inclusion, Influence, Openness, and Community are not linear; you do not always go directly from one to the other. Your students may spiral from one to the other and back again. Community may be reached for an afternoon only to disappear and then reappear when you least expect it.

Much of the cooperative learning training available to teachers and administrators focuses on teaching academic and social skills instruction, and ignores the issues of group development. This may be because many trainers aware of various models for group development, don't want to "scare" teachers and administrators away from cooperative learning by stressing the "process" involved with implementing it. Others may feel it's not important to worry about group development because it will occur whether we plan for it or not.

Understanding group development theory is necessary for teachers for two reasons. First, if a classroom teacher is unaware of group development theory they may react inappropriately to events taking place in the classroom. For example, it's the beginning of the school year and student Johnny Jones is having trouble "fitting into" the class. Always the clown, he distracts from the lesson, and as a consequence is continually sent to the office. Parent conferences are held, but the clowning continues. If you approach this issue from a group development perspective, you might conclude that Johnny doesn't feel included in the group and is making his own inclusion by acting the clown. Instead of sending him to the office, which only heightens his lack of inclusion, you might use lessons which provide Johnny more inclusion in the classroom. Many teachers have done this intuitively for years. However, it's time for each of us to do it at a conscious level, to take the mystery out of why some teachers always seem to know just what to do with students like Johnny.

Another possibility: if Johnny begins acting out as the year progresses, he may feel he doesn't have any influence in the class or his team. He exerts his influence by clowning around and attracting attention to himself. In this case you may want to structure opportunities for Johnny to experience influence in more positive ways. This could be done by structuring team roles where Johnny has a defined role in the team. Once again, you may sometimes intuitively give a student who needs it more responsibility. Applying the issues of group development makes what was intuition a conscious, decision-making process. This approach increases our opportunities to create a classroom which is effective for more of our students.

Secondly, no course in social psychology is required to credential us as teachers and administrators who work with groups our whole careers. Knowledge of group development and its issues/stages can make life much easier for both teachers and administrators. It can assist us in understanding group dynamics, and give us insight into effective strategies to use when what we are doing isn't working.

I recently worked with a teacher who was using cooperative learning and enjoying it. However, when we discussed forming long term teams she hesitated and indicated that she only kept her students together in small groups for four to five weeks because they started to become restless. The students bickered and were not as easy to manage. If all we are looking for are the "easy lessons" in life then we will tend to stay on the surface and never dive down to experience the wonders under the surface. One reason for forming long term teams (for one quarter, semester, or year) is to guide students through these issues of group development. The teacher enjoyed using cooperative learning and saw some of its benefits. What she didn't see was the potential to take it further, to go deeper below the surface.

This book is designed for you to use as a tool to assist you in taking your students to deeper levels of awareness about how to work in teams, how to relate more effectively, and how to become a supportive class and team member.

Class, Team, and Relationship Skillbuilding

This book is organized around the themes of *classbuilding, teambuilding, and relationship skill building*. These themes are strongly related to the issues of group development. Through structural classbuilding, teambuilding, and relationship skill building lessons students can, with relative ease, successfully resolve the issues of group development, minimizing the turmoil which might otherwise occur.

For example, when students wrestle with issues of inclusion, we engage in certain classbuilding and teambuilding activities. These need to be explicitly designed to promote getting acquainted, creating a positive class and team identity, and promoting mutual support. Similarly, when students deal with issues of influence, passage through the stage is eased tremendously though the classbuilding and teambuilding activities designed to promote a respect to individual differences and relationship skill building activities which teach students assertive communication and conflict resolution skills.

The synergism of teambuilding, classbuilding, and relationship skill building interacting provide opportunities for a class to experience a sense of community. Developing a sense of community is a process which requires consistent effort on all three levels; the class, team, and individually. Each relies on the others to create the context of community.

Cooperative Learning Approaches

I was drawn toward the structural approach to cooperative learning because it makes sense. It allows classroom teachers to build cooperative lessons in a systematic way. It gets down to the basics of lesson design and interacting with students. It gives us, a framework which is understandable.

I received my early training in cooperative learning from Roger and David Johnson. The *Learning Together*[1] approach gave me the theoretical basis for cooperative learning. Then, as I was looking for ways to structure social interaction I began applying the *Tribes*[2] process. *Tribes* gave me the concept of stages of group development and its importance to successful cooperative learning. Most recently, I began working with Spencer Kagan and was introduced to the power of the structural approach. The concepts of classbuilding and teambuilding as used in this book were borrowed from *Cooperative Learning* by Spencer Kagan.

Although this book is a synthesis of the work of several leaders in the field of cooperative learning, the vehicle for this integration is the structural approach to cooperative learning. The goal of the book is to understand how aspects of classbuilding, teambuilding, and relationship skill building intertwine to take students and teachers toward a sense of community.

Classbuilding

When you structure your classroom to promote a feeling of mutual connectedness and support among all students, you are classbuilding. Elementary teachers often begin their day with an activity where stu-

dents share something important to them. This creates an opportunity for students to find out about one another in a safe way. As students move through our school system these opportunities to express what's important decrease. Our curriculum becomes more and more *content driven*; we do not make time for individual experiences. During those tumultuous teenage years, when students have the most need to feel connected we structure fewer opportunities for this to happen. Students take a back seat to *pushing through* the curriculum. It's as though the psychological and social needs of students don't count.

Classbuilding is connected most closely with the inclusion stage of group development. As you read the section on classbuilding you'll gain awareness of how classbuilding and inclusion are intertwined. Dr. William Glasser[3], a noted author and speaker about educational issues, developed a hierarchy of needs which he believed all individuals go through. The second need in the hierarchy is the need to belong, the need to feel connected to something larger than ourselves. While the need to belong can be partially met by the process of classbuilding, more intimate connections must also take place in a smaller group setting via teambuilding.

Our Class!!!

Classbuilding

Teambuilding

Our need to belong to a larger unit such as the class meets some of our needs. Along

---

1. Circles of Learning. Roger and David Johnson.

2. Gibbs, Jeanne. *Tribes: A Process for Social Development and Cooperative Learning.* Center Source Publications: Santa Rosa, CA, 1985.

3. Glasser, William. *Control Theory In The Classroom.*

---

with belonging is the need for intimacy. We need more intimate connections which allow us to enjoy a closer sense of connectedness with our peers. This is where smaller support groups, such as a team, comes into play. Teambuilding is the process of developing our identity in relation to a smaller group than the class. The team is a family within the classroom in which closer relationships can develop than if all work were carried on only in the context of the total class.

Remember our high school days: we belonged to different groups within the social milieu of the school. Some were "jocks," others belonged to the "key club," "Chicanos," or to two or three groups at the same time. Many schools have a group for those who don't belong to any other group. Students naturally seek out affiliation with one group or another. The need to affiliate is there, whether we choose to recognize it or not. Creating small cooperative teams can assist students to meet this need for affiliation and focus the team energy toward academic achievement. Many students use a tremendous amount of emotional energy to seek out connectedness. By providing students connections within the framework of the classroom, then we can redirect some of this energy towards learning and academic achievement. One reason gangs attract so many young people is that they can get their acceptance and fulfill their need for belonging at the same time. If we could assist students to make some positive social connections through cooperative learning perhaps fewer of our students would feel the need to join gangs.

Teambuilding is closely associated with the influence issues of group development. During teambuilding students want to influence the decisions their team makes. This is where we need to structure problem solving, consensus developing, and conflict resolution skills.

Something that we may want to share with students is that lessons which promote teambuilding and cooperative learning are training them in strategies they can use to be successful in the "real world" of adult life. Learning how to be supportive of teammates and keep a working relationship going even when you may not like your teammate, are skills related to success in employment settings. Teambuilding is a major effort of many corporations. Cooperative learning is career training. Teambuilding and classbuilding develop students' ability to relate appropriately to one another across a range of settings.

Relationship Skill Building

One component in most cooperative learning models is the teaching of social skills. Social skills are taught so students will be able to function as members of the class and their cooperative learning team. Relationship skills can assist the team in completing assignments and main-

——————**VANSTON SHAW:** *Communitybuilding in the Classroom*——————
Publisher: Kagan Cooperative Learning • 1(800) Wee Co-op

Chapter 1: 8

taining a positive working environment. Relationship skills include sharing information, using first names, taking turns, using affirmations, avoiding put-downs, active listening, encouraging others, assertive communication, and conflict resolution skills. These are all important skills for students and adults to use in group settings. Teaching these skills is extremely important if you want your cooperative learning teams to be the best they can.

Relationship skills are also "real life" skills which assist you and your students to be successful outside school. Let students in on the secret that these skills can help them control their own lives. William Glasser, in his book *Control Theory in the Classroom*, discusses the "needs that drive us all." The needs he identifies are: (1) to survive and reproduce; (2) to belong and love; (3) to gain power [or influence]; (4) to be free; and (5) to have fun. Relationship skills directly relate to all of these. If we relate effectively we can make our needs known and have a greater chance of meeting our survival needs. With good relationship skills, such as the ability to share our feelings, we have a greater opportunity to become intimate with friends. We gain the power to influence others if we have skills to resolve conflicts effectively. Students need to know that relationship skills are not only for use with their cooperative learning team. They are necessary for success in life.

Effective relationship skills allow students to reveal parts of themselves which until now they haven't felt safe to share. In the process students become more fully who they are, and realize their potential, and become more empowered.

Relationship skill building relates closely with the openness stage of group development. This is where students choose how much about themselves they want to share

with others. Relationship skills cannot occur in a vacuum. They need to revolve around real issues and concerns to be most effective. As students learn how to share feelings and be open with one another they form a healthy personality, able to share and interact honestly with others.

Preview:
The book in a Nutshell

Part 1: 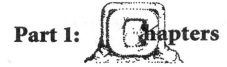 Chapters

Chapter 1 - Introduction

This chapter has given you an overview and rationale for what is to come. It discussed the issues of group development: inclusion, influence, openness, and community. It relates these to the main themes of this book which are classbuilding, teambuilding, and relationship skill building.

Chapter 2 - Getting Started

This chapter is designed to give you suggestions and considerations about how to start using the lessons in the most appropriate manner, some of the preliminary knowledge you'll need to get started, such as how to establish class rules right at the beginning of the year. It discusses when to use classbuilding, teambuilding, and relationship skill building, the concept of the "teacher as facilitator," and various strategies for forming short term teams. The last part of this chapter provides tips on how to begin and end the lessons, anticipatory set, discussion questions, processing and reflection questions, and the use of affirmation starters to finish lessons.

Chapter 3-5 Classbuilding, Teambuilding, and Relationship Skill Building

Classbuilding, teambuilding, and relationship skill building are the focus of each of these chapters. They each give background on the chapter content and refer to detailed lessons you can implement with your students.

Part 2:  Structures

Part II reviews the cooperative learning structures used throughout the lessons. It's important to become familiar with these structures because they become the spring board for you to move beyond the lessons contained here and to create your own lessons, tailored specifically for your students. For more information on these structures you may refer to *Cooperative Learning* by Spencer Kagan.[4]

Part 3: 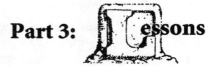 Lessons

Thirty-seven multi-structural lessons present a variety of ways to approach classbuilding, teambuilding, and relationship skill building. The lessons are arranged in three sections: A. Classbuilding; B. Teambuilding; C. Relationship Skill Building. As a teacher you must use your own judgment to select the lessons which are best for your class at a given time.

This part takes us beyond the classroom. It gives some ideas on directions teachers can pursue to further increase their skills in using classbuilding, teambuilding, and relationship skill building with their faculty. Where will this lead us as educators? What possibilities will open to us if we persevere in

Part 4:

Toward Community and the Inclusive School

applying the social context of cooperative learning while students are taught academics?

～ ✸ ～

---

4. Kagan, Spencer. *Cooperative Learning.* Resources for Teachers, Inc.: San Juan Capistrano, CA, 1992.

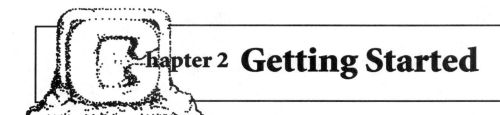

Chapter 2 Getting Started

Teacher As Facilitator

For many, traditional teaching translates into standing in front of the room lecturing 80% of the time, and asking questions answered by individual students, or having students work independently at their desks on dittos, workbooks, or textbooks. Teaching using cooperative learning is very different. You may still lecture; however, the lecture will be interrupted from time to time to facilitate small group work so students can process important elements of what you have said. This processing or discussion may take place in dyads, triads, or groups of four. The important point is that the students are actively involved processing the information you convey.

As educators, we are products of a system which obviously worked for us. As a result of our own experiences as students, most of which were in traditional classrooms, some of us believe that the traditional approach is the "best" way to learn. It was good enough for us as students - it should be good enough for our own students. But there may have been a better way for us to learn, and many of the students in our classrooms today are not learning well through the methods by which we were taught. These methods should be acknowledged, but other approaches which might work better for more students should also be considered.

"To facilitate," taken from Latin, means "to make easy." How can we structure our classrooms so learning can occur in a manner most compatible with student and teacher needs?

I recently saw a television commercial which showed a person driving a car. He had numerous electrodes attached to his body. The announcer's voice explained how at his car company they use "Konsea engineering" to design a car to meet the needs of the human being. Data has been collected from electrodes attached to the brain and muscles of drivers, and as a result, their automobile has been designed so that it makes driving as pleasurable as possible. I believe that if we applied Konsea engineering to teaching we would discover cooperative learning is one approach which makes learning more enjoyable for students and teachers.

To *facilitate* a lesson means a dramatic departure from the example of the teacher lecturing and students working in isolation. Facilitation implies involving students in their own learning. It implies transferring responsibility for student learning from the teacher to the student. You still teach and may even lecture. However, cooperative learning tasks are designed so that students work on tasks together in teams and are at the same time individually accountable. You are actively involved because you are moving around the room as the teams are working. You may be observing different groups work to ensure they are on task and are moving in the right direction. You may be monitoring teams by collecting data on whether students are using the relationship skills taught in an earlier lesson. You may be intervening from time to time to assist teams in resolving curriculum or team issues.

Facilitation in cooperative learning means:

- **Monitoring Teams**
- **Leading Discussions**
- **Structuring Reflection Time**
- **Empowering Students as Problem Solvers**

As a facilitator you are still the teacher. Teaching though, is expanded to include structuring the learning environment to make it maximally conducive to student learning.

Teaming Strategies for Short Term Teams

At the beginning of the year or when you first begin to use cooperative learning, I recommend you use many short-term groups whether you are doing classbuilding, relationship skill building or teaching academic content. Using a variety of groups permits you to observe, and the students to experience, as many different teaming arrangements as possible. This promotes classbuilding, which by its very nature requires students to interact with many of their classmates, and also permits you to proceed with short term teams for academic content. You will be able to observe which student combinations might work better than others.

Pairs Share

Have students pair-up during a lecture when you want to have students actively involved with the information. Simply stop lecturing and ask students to turn to a student near them and discuss how they feel or what they think about that last point you just made. This will also give you an indication of the amount of trust within your classroom. You can have some students form triads if you have an odd number of students in the room.

Study Buddies

Assign pairs to discuss questions you pose and work together. These pairs can be different than other cooperative teams. They may meet only for pairs work. One aspect of reflecting mentioned in this book is the need for students to actively discuss all content presented. The more opportunities we can structure for students to interact with the content, and with each other about the content, the greater the probability they will remember and be able to apply the information later on. Study buddies quickly involves all students with the information you present.

Random Groups

To form random groups first decide how many students you want in a group. Divide that number into the total number of students you have in class.

Then have students count off to form groups. For example, if you have 32 students in class and you want groups of four, 32/4 = 8, so have the students count off by eight. If you have one or two left over, you will have one or two teams of five. With three left over, add a team of three.

Line-ups[1]

I like to use line-ups not only to help form teams, but also as a classbuilding activity and energizer. A variety of line-ups allow students to present different information about themselves, and to discover new information about their classmates which helps to build inclusion. They get students up and moving and making choices. If you want groups of four, then students have lined up, the first

---

1. I avoid using some obvious line-up possibilities such as height, shoe size, age, etc. because I find that many people are sensitive to personal characteristics. It's important to be sensitive to our students' feelings. When you consider a grouping strategy consider how your students will feel.

four form team 1, the next four team form 2, and so on.

Line-ups I have used include:

- **Birthdays** - This helps students practice ordinal order. I do this by day and month only, not year. Many students and adults feel uncomfortable sharing just how old they are. It's important to make line-ups as safe for students as possible.

- **Distance Born from Room** - Students must evaluate distance and make choices. This is a great line-up to tie into a math exercise on estimation. It's not necessary that students are exactly correct.

- **Alphabetical** - This could be by first name, middle name, second letter of first name, last letter of first name. I almost never use last name because most students are familiar with last name line-ups. Vary your alphabetical line-ups to keep them interesting to your students.

- **Number of Siblings** - Start at one end with only children and go from there.

- **Number of Letters In First And Last Name Combined** - Have students add up the total number of letters in their first and last names. It's simple math and appropriate for primary as well as older students.

- **Number of Blocks from School to Home** Once again this is a math problem which also gives an indication of just where students live. When they go around they would give their address (unless students are sensitive about living on the "wrong side of the tracks or freeway.")

Line-Ups

Auxiliaries

If you have frequent absences and want to ensure four students on each team you can assign some students to be auxiliary team members. Let's say you have a class of 30 students and you've assigned teams of four to work together for two weeks. This would be seven teams of four with two students left over. These two could be auxiliaries for the week and fill in for whoever is absent. The key is that being an auxiliary should be an honor. Choose only students who have good group skills and can work with a wide variety of team members. Let the students know you are choosing auxiliaries because of these special skills.

Parts of Lessons

Anticipatory Set

Cooperative learning structures help us present information to students in ways which involve them in the learning process. Cooperative learning lessons, are most successful when introduced to students in a manner which catches their attention and relates to their personal interests. To make cooperative learning work well, good lesson design and presentation practices must be followed. The anticipatory set for your lessons may be as simple as telling students a story about your first job, how you felt, how nervous you were, and how it was difficult to keep good eye contact. Then you might explain how this lesson on active listening may give them skills that can help them with their first job interviews.

Using personal stories is a powerful introduction because you are sharing a part of yourself with your students. The more students know who you are, the more they trust you and feel a connection and willingness to share who they are. By sharing personal stories you reveal a part of your personal history. When I talk with high school students about using "I-statements" for developing relationship skills I share examples of how the use of "I-statements" made a difference in a personal relationship I experienced. This models appropriate use of the content I'm introducing and lets students relate to the human side of their teacher.

I also draw from situations in fables, movies, TV shows, books, or wherever a story makes the point I want. If you don't have a story to use, then introduce your lesson in a way you feel will interest students. Don't be afraid to ask for help from your colleagues. They might have some great ideas. Just as your students can learn more through collaboration, so can all of us.

Reflection Questions

At the end of each lesson are reflection questions. These are questions which can be used to help students process and reflect on what occurred during the lesson. Some reflection questions may also involve an extension or application of the content to a new topic. Others questions relate to the process which occurred in learning. Reflection holds up a mirror.

Reflection questions should initially be done in whole class sessions with you modeling how students are to respond to the questions. Once students have demonstrated an understanding of how these reflection questions can be answered appropriately have students answer some of the questions in their teams. Then have the teams share their responses with the class.

Research by Roger and David Johnson has shown the power of using processing. Processing and reflecting on the information presented in any lesson is a powerful way to help students internalize the information and make it relevant. Over the past few years, I have come to believe more and more that having students reflect on their learning activities is one of the most powerful aspects of cooperative learning. When time is tight we tend to skip it and in doing so let the power of cooperative learning slip through our fingers.

Gum and Chew

Suzanne Bailey, of Bailey and Associates, in Vacaville, California, trains people in workshop presentation skills. Suzanne introduced me to the concept of "gum and chew." Gum is the content we deliver. Chew is the time we have to process or interact with the information. Suzanne recommends a 10:2 formula. For every 10 minutes of lecture (gum) there should be 2 minutes of processing (chew). She relates a medical research study of patients at high risk for heart attacks. They were divided into control and experimental group. The control group had experts come in and talk to them every month for sixty minutes about heart disease and how life style changes could improve their chances of successfully dealing with their heart disease. The experimental group had the same experts. However, the experts for the experimental group spoke for only thirty minutes and then the audience spent the next thirty minutes processing in small groups what this information meant to them personally. The results of the research study were that the control group made very few life style changes. The experimental group made significant life style changes. Interacting with the information we present is as important as the information itself.

> *Interacting with the information we present is as important as the information itself.*

Affirmations

I place affirmations at the end of each lesson because it's important for students to acknowledge the efforts of other team members. Using affirmations is also a team maintenance skill. As a classroom teacher, how often are you able to give positive statements to your students? You probably give some every day. Chances are, you are not able to affirm all your students every day because there is only one of you and 30 - 180 students you might teach daily. Teaching students to give appropriate affirmations and giving students the opportunity to practice will help ensure statements of positive regard are received by more of your students.

Affirmations are teambuilders because they help teams maintain a positive working relationship. As your students learn to give affirmations they are learning not to use put-downs. Put-downs destroy working relationships and are counter productive to teambuilding. Using affirmations at the end of each lesson gives students opportunities for the regular practice needed to do affirmations well.

Where Do I Start?

How do you start off that first day you decide to use cooperative learning in your class? Do you jump right into academics or do you start with a classbuilding activity? Generally, I recommend that most teachers start with classbuilding activities before they jump into complex academic cooperative learning lessons. This doesn't mean you can't use simple cooperative structures like Pairs, and Think-Pair-Share. These structures can be used during most lesson formats to actively involve students and I recommend these be used as often as practical. They involve 100% of the class in the topic being taught and are relatively low risk. At the beginning of the year it's important to

remember to keep the pairs work short and to the point. Also, ask pairs randomly for feedback and walk around listening to their conversations to make sure they are on task.

Ideas On Sequencing

Lessons of each type (Classbuilding, Teambuilding, and Relationship Skill Building) are sequenced from primary to secondary and in the order I might use them in my classroom. However, these lessons are not designed to be used one after the other. They are designed to be introduced by you when you feel it is appropriate to do so. Your intuition as a teacher is required so that these lessons are used when they are needed.

At the beginning of the year it is appropriate to start with a few classbuilding activities and cooperative academic tasks which are low risk for students so they can identify cooperative learning with success and fun. Class rules would also be introduced at this time. As you start introducing class rules you will want to lead students through relationship skill building lessons concerning affirmations, put-downs, and active listening. Remember to pace your students so that they understand and are using the first concept before you introduce the next concept. There is usually more than one lesson to introduce a concept. This will allow you to choose the lesson which is appropriate for your students.

On The Sacredness Of These Lessons

None of these lessons are sacred. If you want to modify any of these lessons go ahead and try it out. If it's successful drop me a note and let me know about your version. I might add it to the next revision of this book and give you credit. These lessons have been field tested with students at various grade levels, however there are always other approaches which might work better for your students. Don't be afraid to experiment. Part of the fun of teaching is trying new approaches and finding out what works and what doesn't. Great teachers are great not for the lessons which go well but for the lessons which failed and they and their students learned from.

Establishing Class Rules

All teachers have rules which we expect our students to follow. We create these rules because the classroom is a safer and more considerate place for all students when our class rules are followed. These rules usually reflect societal norms of conduct. Rules commonly found in many classrooms using cooperative learning are: be considerate; take turns; use active listening; ask teammates first; when a team doesn't know, all team members raise their hands; and use affirmations/no put-downs.

Such class rules enhance the success of cooperative learning. They help establish a classroom "mind set" for tolerance and mutual support. Class rules develop a sense of safety when they are consistently enforced and students know they will not be "put-down" for making a mistake. This sense of safety allows students to move beyond where they might in a non-cooperative classroom because they have natural support systems when they are a member of a cooperative team in a cooperative classroom.

Class Rules Lesson	Lesson #
• Developing Class Rules	1

Class Rules

- • Be Considerate
- • Take Turns
- • Use Active Listening
- • Ask Teammates First
- • When a Team Doesn't Know, all Team Members Raise Their Hand
- • Use Affirmations / No Put-Downs

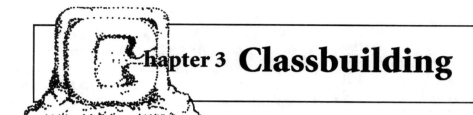

Chapter 3 Classbuilding

Introduction

When we see 30 new faces looking up at us on the first day of school, what goals do we have for our students? One goal, many of us have, is for this class of individuals who do not know one another to end the year with a shared vision and purpose and a sense of community. To further this end, class members need to become acquainted, build class identity, experience mutual support, value individual differences, and develop synergy. This process is called classbuilding.

Classbuilding

Classbuilding occurs whenever the class is involved in a class project where each member is contributing toward its success. This project may be building something such as a class banner or mural to which each student contributes. Another type of class project would be keeping track of team points earned and setting a goal so the class will be rewarded when it earns a certain number of points. The overriding class goal discourages intergroup competition and encourages a sense of positive classroom interdependence. Points earned for the whole class give students a sense of being connected. That's the feeling we want to promote.

Another approach to classbuilding is to lead the class through a sequence of classbuilding lessons. The classbuilding lessons described in this book are designed for you to replicate with your students. Remember to adapt any of the lessons to the needs of your situation.

You make the choices as to which lesson is right for your class, whether it needs to be adapted, and when to do classbuilding.

When to do Classbuilding?

I see classbuilding as something which occurs throughout the year. The classbuilding lessons in this book should be used when you feel your class is becoming too competitive, or students need to feel whole class inclusion. Sometimes students work in teams so much that they need to reconnect to the total class. You may intuitively know it is time for a classbuilding lesson. One aspect of the inclusive classroom is honoring your own intuition. Sometimes we choose lessons because they feel right. This is where the art and science of teaching merge and you can take your lessons and your students to new heights.

Five Aims of Classbuilding

This chapter explores the five elements of classbuilding identified by Spencer Kagan[1]. They are:

1. **Getting Acquainted**

2. **Building Class Identity**

3. **Experiencing Mutual Support**

4. **Valuing Individual Differences**

5. **Synergy**

---

1. *Cooperative Learning* by Spencer Kagan, Ph.D. Published by Kagan's Cooperative Learning Co., 1992.

1. Getting Acquainted

When students enter your room at the beginning of the year, how do you begin to build a sense of inclusion and safety so that students become acquainted and feel comfortable with each other and the teacher? Safety is a necessary component of a class and school if students are to excel. The getting acquainted lessons assist students to to know one another and begin to establish a sense of inclusion and safety within the classroom.

Getting acquainted lessons allow students an opportunity to present themselves to the class in a safe way. One of the students in a workshop I conducted said , "Classbuilding to me means to include me in the class. I'm a person too, with something to contribute. I want to be a part of and want others to be feel like they are a part of this group." Classbuilding lessons make everyone feel comfortable in the classroom environment so that they may share their personal concerns, ideas, or problems with others and trust one another with their thoughts.

Classbuilding lessons are not just for the beginning of the year. Anytime you feel your class is not connected or there's a sense of alienation, it may be time for a "get acquainted" classbuilding lesson.

2. Building Class Identity

One of the identifying factors common to excellent schools is a sense of school identity. Students, parents, and teachers are proud to belong to the school, know the goals of the school, and their purpose for being involved.

This same feeling can be developed and nurtured within the classroom. It's important for students to feel they belong to Room 22 because something special happens there. Their class is unique and important. When your students are proud to be from Room 22, then you know that your class has a class identity.

This class identity can be built in a number of ways. Class projects such as banners, flags, logos, murals, or books can involve all students and let students know they are members of an important class.

William Glasser in his book *Control Theory In The Classroom* discusses how all of us need a sense of belonging. Glasser points out that many students in our schools, particularly at the secondary level, do not feel a sense of connection to the school. These students may try to create their own connection and inclusion by anti-social behavior or they may choose to drop out. We all need to feel that we are OK the way we are and that we belong. Class identity lessons are designed to help students feel they belong to their class by building a feeling of connectedness.

We - Them

As class identity grows, the teacher must re-inforce with students that they are also members of the school. Even as their class is important and they are unique, so all other classes are also unique and important. I've seen teachers attempt to build class identity by creating between-class competition. The secret is to make the class feel special and inclusive, not exclusive. You want to develop the feeling of "We are unique," and not, "We are better than others." That's a difficult distinction to make. Remember, cooperation and interdependence are the goals.

———— **VANSTON SHAW:** *Communitybuilding in the Classroom* ————
Publisher: Kagan Cooperative Learning • 1(800) Wee Co-op

Chapter 3: 2

3. Experiencing Mutual Support

Have you ever felt uncomfortable when you were asked to share something with a group of people you didn't know very well? Was this because you didn't like being "center stage" with all eyes focused on you, or was it the idea of sharing which made you feel uncomfortable? To experience mutual support within a classroom usually requires participants both to share and to receive. Some teachers do not see the need to help their students develop connections and learn how to give and receive support. I stress the concept of giving and receiving because that's the crux of "mutual support." It needs to be a two way street, giving and receiving. Some teachers and students have problems sharing, others have difficulties with receiving. As a result, it's important for the teacher to create structured opportunities through lessons and activities which provide experience in both giving and receiving support.

As a classroom teacher you have a unique opportunity to assist students to find out more about themselves and at the same time to develop positive regard between class members. Once students have gotten acquainted and built class identity, structuring situations for them to "experience mutual support" is the next step in the classbuilding process.

Some Activities

Electricity

This activity can be used as part of a community circle. Tell students you are going to conduct an experiment in "reaction time." Ask them to all hold hands. When they feel a squeeze on their hand students are to pass it along to the person on the other side of them. Squeeze the hand of the person on either side of you. See if you can see the signal travel. Ask students to add a sound when they feel the squeeze. Try having the signal go both directions. You can discuss how energy moves through a group.

Trust Walk

Discuss with students the importance of being able to trust your classmates. Ask students if they have ever seen a person who is blind. Does it look difficult to get around when you are blind? Explain that you would like students to have the opportunity to experience what it is like to be dependent on another person and also have someone dependent on you. Have students pair-up and decide which will be person A and B. Have all the "A's" raise their hand.

"B's" will start by being the "blind" followers. Their job is to keep their eyes closed and allow their partners to lead them around the room. Each "B" needs to pretend they cannot see and to trust their partner.

The "A's" will be the guides and will be responsible for the "B's". They are to carefully take "B" around the room and while doing so, have person "B" touch or smell things which they might find interesting. Remind students that this is a trust building activity and not to lead their partner into uncomfortable situations.

After three to five minutes have students reverse roles. Later, discussion can center on how it felt to be dependent on another and how it felt to be responsible for another? Which was more difficult?

—————**VANSTON SHAW:** *Communitybuilding in the Classroom*—————
Publisher: Kagan Cooperative Learning • 1(800) Wee Co-op

Chapter 3: 3

4. Valuing Individual Differences

In America we live in an ever increasingly diverse cultural milieu. It is projected that by the year 2000, 25% of our population will be made up of "minority" groups. In California schools over 50% of students are from minority backgrounds. Anglos are becoming a minority in other states as well. Differences in ethnicity, language, religion, and culture will continue to abound in our school systems. Currently, we read in the papers about racial incidents at universities across the country and the growth of hate groups. This is another area where cooperative learning can assist schools.

As students do classbuilding activities, they gain an appreciation of individual differences and an awareness of how these differences can strengthen our society. America has always prided itself in being a "melting pot." However, historically the down side of this aspect of America has been intolerance and blatant racism. This is an aspect of our history which we often gloss over. Many people of color today still feel the sting of direct racism or the more subtle forms it takes.

Samuel Oliner, Professor of Sociology at California State University, Humboldt, recently completed a study and wrote a book, *The Compassionate Beast: What Science is Discovering About the Humane Side of Humankind*. In the work Dr. Oliner and a team of researchers looked at the variables involved between those who helped Jews survive Nazi Germany's Holocaust and those who did nothing. He was looking for what led people to be compassionate. He found that those who offered a helping hand, usually at great risk to themselves, were more empathic, more caring and had a much greater sense of responsibility for others. How was this developed? Partially by living among people who were different from themselves and seeing them as human beings.

These lessons on valuing individual differences can assist your students to see one another as creative human beings who laugh, cry, smile, get angry, and express a range of emotions just as they do. The key is for you to provide many opportunities for students to see one another from different perspectives. They must learn that their worth as a person and others' worth is not simply a function of how well they score on a math test or how well they write. It's important for students to appreciate themselves and others for who they are as people. Lessons on valuing individual differences provide an opportunity for your students to get to know one another on a different level. Give yourself and your students this opportunity.

Values Clarification

The Corners structure, used in the classbuilding lessons for valuing individual differences within the class, is an example of helping students clarify their beliefs. It helps students to see how their beliefs relate to what others believe. There has been much concern expressed about children growing up without values. Corners provides students with a mirror for their values and an opportunity to appreciate the values of others. Value clarification activities and lessons are not designed to make children change their values. They are designed to encourage students to face their own values and those of others. Many students today do not have an opportunity to reflect on what is right or wrong and compare their value

──────**VANSTON SHAW:** *Communitybuilding in the Classroom*──────
Publisher: Kagan Cooperative Learning • 1(800) Wee Co-op

Chapter 3: 4

judgments to others. Cooperative learning structures can help students clarify for themselves what is important.

Values Line-ups

When you want to point out to students the need to take a stand and to appreciate the stand of another person you might want to use a values line-up. I saw this structure demonstrated by Spencer Kagan with over 200 secondary teachers. This took place during the "Gulf Crisis" when President Bush was considering using the U.S. military to force the Iraqi's out of Kuwait. Spencer asked teachers who favored U.S. military intervention to stand at the back of their row. Those who did not favor the use of U.S. forces were to stand in the front of the row. Those who were undecided were to move to the middle, closest to the end they favored.

Folded Value Line-up

Spencer then had teachers in the front who felt the strongest about not using force begin moving up the row until the first person in front was face to face with the first person in the back (who felt the strongest in favor of using force). The line was folded so that each person had a partner. This could have been used as a prewriting activity. They discussed why they felt the way they did. One limitation with this approach is that those in the middle when the line folds are talking with others in the middle. To provide those in the middle interaction with others who had a point of view different than their own, a split value line can be used.

Split Value Line-up

Spencer would start off with the same line-up as before with the extremes on each end. The line would count off 1-30 or to the last person. If there were 30 in the line then the middle person #15 would lead the front half of the line toward the back of the room so that #15 was paired with #30 and #1 is paired with #16. This way each person has a partner with a divergent view.

Examples of value issues a classroom teacher could use with split and folded value lives:

- Rap Music is the best music
- The school year should be increased to 240 days per year.
- Free health care should be available to all Americans.
- Students should be graded by other students.

The important consideration to remember when using value line-ups is to give students time to discuss their feelings and include enough time for whole class processing. Talking about what is important to students is valuable to them and to us. It gives us an opportunity to contrast our views and values with others and to reflect on and reaffirm our position. Remember not to pass judgments on the different values expressed. Students will not share their true feelings if they may come under attack. We must trust that students, when they see all the alternatives, will make the choice right for themselves.

Valuing Individual Differences Lessons	Lesson #
• **Animal Corners**	8
• **Sailboat and Rowboat**	9

5. Synergy

When two or more people work together and their efforts create something which is more than any of them could create as individuals, synergy is at work. Most of the lessons presented in this book allow for synergy to occur. It happens especially when brainstorming is used or in creating simple projects where a team in involved. Below are some activities which develop synergy within a classroom.

—————— **VANSTON SHAW:** *Communitybuilding in the Classroom* ——————
Publisher: Kagan Cooperative Learning • 1(800) Wee Co-op

Chapter 3: 5

Living Class Machine

You describe what a machine is. It has various parts and movements. One student start the machine off by moving their right arm back and forth while making a sound. Another student may add on by holding onto the shoulder of the first student and moving his left leg up and down while making a different sound. Students each in turn add their own movements and sounds. Everybody adds on until the entire class is involved and the class has become a living machine.

Class Formations

You can have your class create various formations which involve everyone in the class. For example, as an introduction to studying the continents you could have the class as a whole form the shapes of the different continents. It is easy to start off with geometric shapes: circle, triangle, square, and rectangle. Formations allow all students to create something together.

Synergy Lesson	Lesson #
• Weaving Connections	37

~ ❀ ~

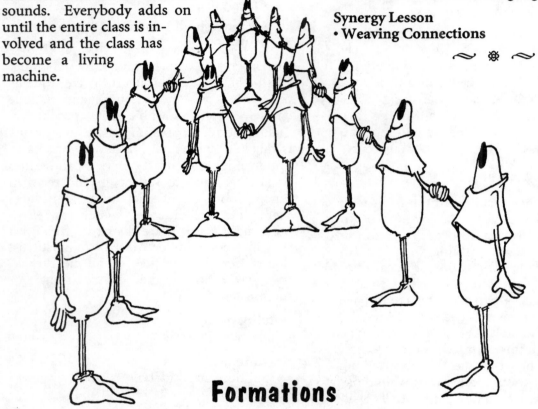

Formations

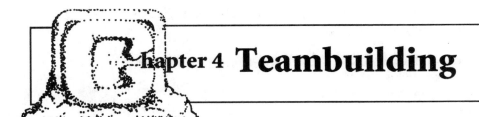

Chapter 4 Teambuilding

We structure lessons and activities to promote classbuilding both as we begin the year and then as appropriate throughout the year. At some point (this could be after four weeks or two months) you will assign your students to teams which will work together for some time; a quarter, semester, or for the year. You'll do this because we know that students function better in long term teams than a continuous string of short term groups. In long term teams students have the opportunity to work intimately with a few other students. In this process they will discover what it means to be positively interdependent. They will discover they must rely on and support one another. They will experience the frustrations and synergy which can occur as teammembers. It is not always easy having students in long term teams. However, this is generally the way the real world works. To continually change teams throughout the school year implies that students do not need to learn positive relationship skills. They can avoid dealing with problems, because if they wait, they'll have a new team.

During this uneasy stage the teacher who doesn't understand group process will sometimes panic and stop using cooperative learning because the teams are not cooperating as they were the first

month. It is also a very dynamic stage. M. Scott Peck in *The Different Drum*, calls this stage "chaos." He expresses that all groups need to go through this stage or they become stuck in "pseudo community," (his term for inclusion).

Teachers can structure tasks which encourage students to express their points of view and can teach conflict resolution skills so students will be able to work through differences without tearing apart their team. This is where problem solving skills need to taught and practiced. Teams will be working through the issues of influence again and again throughout the life of a team.

Struggles for influence are a natural issue of group development and actually a positive sign that your class has passed through initial inclusion. However, this is also the time to recycle back to classbuilding inclusion lessons. Our classroom teams are constantly moving from dealing with inclusion to influence, back to inclusion, on to influence, and so on. As individuals and groups progress up this spiral we may come to that calm water where all of the ducks have learned to swim elegantly.

Teams do not necessarily function well just because you've been careful who you place on each team. It's necessary for team members to learn skills they will need to work well together. The first step in forming teams is to structure activities which allow members to get to know one another. Lessons which promote getting better acquainted are recommended at this time. It's also important to teach students how to relate effectively and to problem solve as the team members experience influence issues. Teambuilding empowers students with the skills to work as an effective team member.

Forming Teams

When I form long-term teams, I usually involve students in the decision by having them write the names of at least six different students they would like on their team. I let students know that I can usually ensure that at least one of the people on their list will be on their team. I then begin forming teams using the cards and assigning each team a mix of academic talent, social skills, and leadership skills.

Other teachers I know have students help form teams. The criteria the students use is that each team have: one student who is academically strong, two students who do not need much help, and one student who needs more help. Give the students your role sheet to use. Let students know that if the teams are not balanced then you reserve the right to make any needed changes.

Refer to Chapter Three, "Getting Started" for strategies to form short-term teams. An in-depth resource on methods for forming long-term teams is Spencer Kagan's *Cooperative Learning*. It describes a number of methods for team formation.

Team Formation

FIVE AIMS OF TEAMBUILDING

1. **Getting Acquainted**
2. **Building Team Identity**
3. **Experiencing Mutual Support**
4. **Valuing Individual Differences**
5. **Synergy**

1. Getting Acquainted

My wife recently took a class in Japanese book binding. The instructor had participants sit four to a table. The first day of the class participants introduced themselves to the total class. That was the only structured getting acquainted activity of the class. Nuria told me how difficult it was for people at the tables to get to know each other. She felt that the class, which met for several days, could have been much more interesting and productive if the instructor would have structured opportunities for the table members to share something about themselves and provided a more inclusive atmosphere.

Some teachers, feel our responsibility is to relay academic content to students, not to structure the social environment of the classroom. But, unless we are cognizant of the social environment of the classroom and take care to design it constructively, our academic instruction will not have as great an impact as possible. Failure to recognize the importance of the social environment occurs because we, as teachers, are not trained to recognize its importance. We also lack models, particularly in universities, which train both teachers and administrators. We need to take responsibility for the social environment, climate, and culture of our classrooms and schools. We are social architects whether we choose to be or not.

Once we have assigned students to teams we can help them become acquainted. We can do this in the same ways we have the class become acquainted, by leading students through lessons which allow them to share themselves. These lessons will help build a sense of trust and safety because students reveal information about themselves and at the same time learn who their teammates are. If we do not take the time to structure these activities it's likely that getting acquainted will happen in a very haphazard way, if at all.

Many of us do not share much about ourselves because we fear others may not accept us or we have been taught not to confide in strangers. This may be good defensive training, however, it stands in the way of productive team work which is the crux of cooperative learning.

Getting Acquainted Lessons   **Lesson #**

2. Building Team Identity

Just as it is important to build class identity, it is also important to build team identity. Building team identity takes place as you form short-term teams and after long-term teams are formed. If, as a child or adolescent, you remember being on a winning baseball, soccer, softball, or basketball team where there was "esprit de corps" then you have an idea of the type of feelings

you are trying to capture for your students. The difference here is that you are attempting to move your students toward this feeling of team cohesion for their skill in working together on academic tasks. At the same time we are developing this team "esprit de corps" we are continuing to nurture classroom interdependence and class "esprit de corps." It is important to intersperse classbuilding lessons and activities throughout the year and while we are doing teambuilding.

Building Team Identity Lessons   Lesson #

3. Experiencing Mutual Support

A few years ago I conducted a five day, forty hour cooperative learning workshop for thirty teachers. Team membership became an issue for one participant. On the second day of the workshop we divided participants into teams of four. One of the participants came up to me at the end of the day to tell me she did not want to be on the team where she was assigned. She confided that she could not stand the personality of one of her team members and couldn't see how she could accomplish anything as a member of that particular team. She requested that she be reassigned to another team.

Adults who pay several hundred dollars to attend a week long workshop can be assertive about the experience they want to have. As the facilitator, I was sensitive to their needs, just as I am to my students' needs. I asked her to give it a "good

Mutual Support

faith" effort for another day and then let me know how it was going. She didn't come back to me the next day. On the last day of the workshop she shared that the most powerful aspect of the workshop had been working though the issues she had with her team mates. She ended the workshop feeling very supportive of her team. In learning to accept differences she developed personal strengths which allowed her to be successful in her team and profit from the experience.

Inevitably, students in various teams will have interpersonal conflicts. Many of these revolve around the issues of "influence". This is where team members want to assert themselves within the team. They want to be heard and have their views accepted by their team.

It's important to recognize this issue of group development and be prepared for its arrival in your classroom. When influence issues arrive, teammates may become unruly, argue with one another, and disagree. Teachers who are unprepared for this stage may become concerned that cooperative learning isn't working and may quit using cooperative learning or reassign team members at the first sign of trouble. Doing so prevents important kinds of learning; it delays learning how to deal with the issues of influence. What are some methods you can use to handle this stage of influence?

Dealing with Influence Issues

I deal with these issues in several ways. One is to teach students decision making and conflict resolution skills which will allow students to deal with conflict in the team in a constructive manner. A second is to assign team roles which will structure the interaction among team members and give members identified assignments. Often this will assist a team by allowing everyone to have "influence" within the team. A third

way is to take teams back through lessons and activities at the inclusion stage of group development. These are generally less threatening and allow students to feel more included and tend to break down negative feelings generated by arguing or disagreeing. Many teachers will try all three. It is important that when students begin dealing with issues of influence, instruction in conflict resolution skills is provided. Otherwise, you have not confronted the issue, only put it off to be dealt with later. A necessary ingredient of this process is trusting that your students can resolve their team problems if you give them the tools and the opportunity to do so.

The mutual support lessons provide some techniques to assign team roles. These lessons also provide skills in non-verbal communication, and gallery brainstorming which allow all team members to participate and be heard in a problem solving process.

4. Valuing Individual Differences

Expressing and accepting individual differences is even more important in the team setting than for the class as a whole. Teams are close knit and may stay together for quarter or semester. It becomes critical for team members to value one another's contributions to a team effort. You can structure lessons in which each team member shares their unique point of view on lesson content, world events, or problem solving.

———————**VANSTON SHAW:** *Communitybuilding in the Classroom*———————
Publisher: Kagan Cooperative Learning • 1(800) Wee Co-op

Chapter 4: 4

5. Team Synergy

When a team is working together on a project there is a high probability of synergy occurring. The synergy lessons presented lead to synergy within a team when the team is successful. Synergy is that feeling of creating something together an individual could not create alone.

Synergy can also occur when students are involved in academic lessons. Several years ago I was working with a 5th grade teacher on implementing cooperative learning. She told me that several of the teams working on a cooperative social studies project became so involved with their project that they didn't want to leave the room for recess. This is an expression of synergy. This example also shows the power of cooperative learning structures to promote intrinsic motivation. Team synergy can occur in lessons designed specifically to create it and in content-based lessons.

$\sim \circledast \sim$

Chapter 5 Relationship Skill Building

Introduction[1]

While you are developing inclusion during the classbuilding lessons, you also need to teach students skills they will need to relate appropriately to one another. Relationship skills help students structure their interactions with each other. They include active listening, the use of affirmations, the use of assertive communication, and cooperative conflict resolution.

Without communication and openness, community cannot occur. Relationship skills are the bricks holding up the building of community. The mortar holding these bricks together is the feeling of inclusion developed using the classbuilding lessons and the feeling of mutual influence developed in the teambuilding lessons. When students feel included and feel they can influence their environment, they are willing to approach openness, and communicate more honestly.

The lessons presented here are intended to give students the skills to relate more effectively with peers and adults. Students will learn how to: 1) actively listen to each other; 2) recognize affirmations, self put-downs, and put-downs of others; 3) give affirmations to fellow students; 4) use "I-Statements" as an assertive communication strategy and a conflict resolution skill when they need to. These skills are not only taught because it would be nice for students to learn them. They are taught because these are critical skills in life; whether in school, at home, or in the world of work. Importantly, they are skills which support cooperative learning structures, and a positive school environment.

One of my motivations for writing this book was because I saw so many colleagues trying to implement cooperative learning who knew they needed something more and didn't know what that something was. One element often left out is teaching relationship skills. If we create a sense of trust without the ability to relate appropriately, we are setting ourselves and our students up for failure. Conflict is a central theme of all communities and living situations. Appropriate relationship skills give students tools to be assertive and confront conflict constructively rather than feeling powerless. When conflict arises in groups or our personal relationships, it is essential to have the ability to relate clearly and honestly.

---

1. Source material for aspects of this chapter came from *Conflict Resolution: A Secondary School Curriculum*, San Francisco Community Boards, and *Tribes: A Process For Social Development and Cooperative Learning* by Jeanne Gibbs, and *STAR: Social Thinking And Responsibility* developed by Irvine Unified School District, Irvine, California.

Relational Skills

Sharing how we feel, even with someone we care about, is a major concern, especially in relationships. Many marriages end because of poor communication. Look at the number of adults in counseling and therapy. They are there to learn "good relationship" skills. It appears to me sometimes that we are waiting for our students to become adults, make their relationship mistakes, and go to therapy to learn these skills. Our students need these relational skills now.

Relational skills:

- **Listen to others attentively and have them know you are listening.**

- **Appreciate the point of view of others.**

- **Be assertive when you need to be.**

- **Affirm others in a genuine way and avoid the use of put-downs.**

- **Accept affirmation from others in an appropriate way.**

- **Use conflict resolution strategies.**

These relational skills will assist our students to be successful in our classroom and beyond the school. This is the content of life.

Active Listening Skills

Unless we have our students' attention and they are able to focus on what we are saying, there is a great possibility that they will not be able to participate at the level we except. As adults, some of us have taken workshops or been involved in counseling sessions where we were taught basic communication skills. Very rarely were we ever directly taught active listening as part of the school curriculum. This section will explain how to teach active listening skills.

Active Listening is the ability of listeners to demonstrate to the speaker that they are "tuned" into what is being said. This is done visually, physically, and verbally and intuitively by the listeners.

The **visual** aspect of this skill is for the listener to maintain eye contact with the speaker. As simple as this statement is, it is a skill that many of our students do not understand and were never taught.

The **physical** aspect of active listening is for the listener to have their body positioned toward the speaker and to give other non-verbal cues such as nodding their head appropriately and leaning forward. These all indicate to the speaker that the listener is attending to what is being said.

The **verbal** aspect is for the listener to check with the speaker to ensure understanding of what the speaker intended to communicate.

Active Listening

- **Eye Contact**
- **Nodding**
- **Leaning Forward**
- **Paraphrasing**
- **Reflective Listening**

This can be accomplished through paraphrasing and/or reflecting. Paraphrasing is the listener repeating in their own words what they believe the speaker said. Reflective listening is the listener sharing with the speaker the perceived feelings that were not said. Both paraphrasing and reflective listening are checks for understanding we would like our students to use. For our students to be successful, however, we must give them many opportunities for practice.

The difference between paraphrasing and reflective listening is that in paraphrasing you are simply restating what you heard the

> ### Paraphrasing and Reflective Listening
> *Susan comes into the classroom after recess and begins talking to her teacher Ms. Brown. "Ms Brown, Johnny is rotten and mean. I don't like him."*
> *Ms Brown (using paraphrasing), "Susan, Johnny was mean to you and you don't like him right now."*
> *Ms. Brown (using reflective listening), "You're really angry and upset with Johnny."*

speaker say. With reflective listening you are sharing the feelings you sense behind the words. This is often more powerful. With students it is best to teach them paraphrasing first and then reflective listening.

Active Listening Lessons   **Lesson #**

Affirmations[2]

How often do you have the opportunity to give praises, statements of positive regard, compliments, validation, or encouragement to each of your students? Whatever term you use, and no matter how hard you try, you are very lucky if you are able to give each of your students statements of positive regard on a daily basis. Most of us end up giving 20% of our students 80% of the affirmations. Usually this is because they are the ones who seek our approval and are most visible. Even if we were able to turn that around and give affirmation to 80% of our students, have we accomplished enough?

One of the advantages of cooperative learning is that you can teach students to affirm one another, and not have students rely only on adults for affirmation. There is generally only one teacher to every thirty students. Even if you are exceptionally diligent at giving affirmations to your students, how many more affirmations would students receive if students were affirming each other?

For a teacher to give each of his thirty students one minute of affirmations would take thirty minutes. For students in pairs to give each other one minute of affirmations takes only two minutes!

Affirmations are not "fluff" in cooperative learning. They are an integral aspect of keeping a group working together in a positive manner. If students support each other with positive regard, groups function better. It is a skill to give affirmations appropriately - a skill which needs to be learned. Initially, students may have difficulty using affirmations appropriately. You will also need to teach students why affirmations are important.

Some of us have difficulty ourselves freely giving out affirmations. We believe that they must be earned and must meet some high criteria to be valid. As mentioned earlier, affirmations can be any statements of positive regard, appreciation, or compliments. If we set our criteria so high that no one can meet it, perhaps we are being "self-defeating." Many of us as adults do not feel comfortable giving affirmations. We were taught that there is a natural scarcity of positive regard. There is no natural scarcity, only the scarcity we create. To teach your students how to affirm, you will need to model it for them. This may push your comfort zone.

---

2. I use the term affirmation to encompass all types of statements of positive regard. It is the opposite of put-downs and understandable to a wide range of people. You can choose whatever word you would like if the term affirmation doesn't meet your needs. other ideas are validation, build-ups, put-ups, etc.

> *There is no natural scarcity of positive regard...*

How do you find out how many affirmations you use? There are several ways to find out how many you use each day. Most schools have a video camera or cassette tape recorder. Video or audio record a thirty minute segment of your class where you are interacting with students. Review the tape segment and count the number of affirmations you used. This could be used as a simple baseline. For a more accurate baseline repeat this procedure two more times and find the average number of affirmations you use per session. This will give you an idea where you are starting. After you count your own use of affirmations, count the number you hear your students giving. This could be used as documentation to show an increase in the affirmations you and your students use after you focus on teaching students to use affirmations.

Affirmations Help Build Community

A colleague and long time friend, Robert Rudholm, taught English classes for 7th and 8th graders who were below the 40th percentile. Robert used cooperative learning structures throughout the year and taught his students how to give affirmations to one another. During the last week of each school year Robert had the students form an "affirmation circle," as their ceremony to end the year. The students sit in a large circle. Each student takes a turn sitting on the "hot seat" (a stool higher than the other chairs). The other students are directed to give as many affirmations as they can to this student in one minute.

Robert shared with me an experience he had with one of his students; let's call him Mark. Mark asked if he could say a few words to the class. Robert told him he could talk to the class after he took his turn on the chair. Mark took the chair. Students started calling out, "Thanks for your help this year" "You're cool" "Mark I really like the way you smile all the time." This went on for one minute. At the end of his turn Mark started talking to the class. He said, "I just want to tell all of you how much this class has meant to me. This class has been more of a family to me than my own family." At this time Mark started crying. A few of the students looked at Robert and said, "Mr. Rudholm, do something, he's crying." Robert responded that Mark would stop crying and finish what he was saying, just give him a few moments. One of the "tough" kids in class went into another classroom, got a box of tissues, brought it back and passed it around. There were several pairs of moist eyes.

Mark finished what he had to say and went over to where Robert was standing, shook his hand and said, "Mr. Rudholm, I love you." No students laughed. Robert shared that this was one was of the most memorable moments in his teaching career. Did this atmosphere of trust between students and teacher happen by accident? I believe that the sense of community which developed in Robert's class was nurtured throughout the year by an excellent teacher who used cooperative learning as a process, not only as a vehicle, to teach academic content. His students improved their writing and they shared a sense of community which they took with them when they entered high school.

Put-downs

The opposite of affirmations are put-downs. Put-downs are words, gestures, or expressions which hurt others' feelings and make them feel bad. When we ask students to do the lesson on brainstorming put-downs and affirmations, students are almost always able to generate many more put-downs than affirmations. Why is this? Are students naturally better at put-downs? Is our society focused more on put-downs than on affirmations?

How many of our students come from homes where they seldom hear an affirmation and often hear put-downs? In some families put-downs are the expected form of interaction. Put-downs may even be considered a sign of affection. "Hey stupid!" is considered by some to be a cute greeting. Many of our students come from families where they face a constant barrage of put-downs and very few affirmations. I have often marveled at how healthy our students are, considering the emotionally abusive situations in which many of them live.

What's the antidote for students who need support and to be affirmed? One support system we can provide is a classroom that is physically and emotionally safe, a place where what they say will be listened to and what they do will be paid attention. This is what most of us want, to be recognized and accepted for who we are. We can give students opportunities to be successful and to be affirmed for who they are not only for what they do.

We can create a sense of community where students know they will be accepted. Perhaps this is the least we can do for our students. We have the power to do this. These affirmation lessons are one step along the road toward building classroom and school communities which affirm students and teach students to affirm each other.

COOPERATIVE CONFLICT RESOLUTION

When conflict occurs within our classroom, our first tendency is often to stop the conflict as quickly as possible. We generally see conflict as a destructive force which we must avoid if at all possible. I propose that conflict creates an opportunity for growth among students and can lead toward a sense of community within the classroom when students learn to cooperatively resolve conflicts. Another reason to teach conflict resolution strategies is that conflict is a certainty in all our lives. Conflict is a natural state and has the potential to occur whenever humans interact. The question is how we approach conflict and whether we see conflict as friend or foe. In the cooperative classroom, conflict is a constant companion. The important issue is how teachers model resolving conflicts and how we teach our students to resolve conflicts.

I use the term "cooperative conflict resolution" because I want to emphasize that conflict resolution works best if a "cooperative" climate is first created in the class, before structured instruction on conflict resolution skills. William Kreidler, author of *Creative Conflict Resolution*[3], said it best when he discussed how he started teaching conflict resolution skills before he used cooperative learning as a classroom structure. He indicated that he was successful before using cooperative learning, but even with some degree of success, there was something missing that led to a feeling of dissatisfaction." After he began using cooperative learning in academic activities, he visibly noticed the trust level in the room rise tangibly and his students integrating cooperative skills with the conflict resolution skills.

---

3. Kreidler, William. *Creative Conflict Resolution.* Scott, Foresman, and Co., Glenview, Illinois, London, 1984.

————————**VANSTON SHAW:** *Communitybuilding in the Classroom*————————
Publisher: Kagan Cooperative Learning • 1(800) Wee Co-op

Chapter 5: 5

I prefer to think of conflict as an opportunity for growth. The Chinese character for the word "crisis" is made up of the characters for "danger" and "opportunity". Conflicts can be dangerous and negative or they can provide an opportunity for growth and positive change. In *The Magic of Conflict* by Thomas Crum, the author discusses conflict as something which should not be avoided and asks the reader to embrace conflict.

"When we [embrace conflict], it becomes one of the greatest gifts we have for positive growth and change, an empowering and energizing opportunity. There is truly a magical quality about conflict which can call out the best in us, that which is not summoned under ordinary circumstances."[4]

Thomas Crum goes on to portray conflict as a catalyst for positive growth when we look at it as an opportunity, not a danger. Teaching students to approach conflicts with a positive attitude and specific cooperative conflict resolution skills is a gift which our students can use far beyond the classroom.

Roger and David Johnson in their book, *Creative Conflict,* propose that teachers should develop lessons which include conflict. We must teach students how to handle conflict appropriately through the curriculum we teach. They also propose that conflicts, "when skillfully managed, can be of great value."[5] They report that conflict can lead to the following potentially constructive outcomes:

- **Higher achievement;**

- **Improved retention;**

- **More higher level reasoning and critical thinking;**

- **Higher quality decision making and problem solving;**

- **Creative thinking;**

- **More on-task time;**

- **Enhanced healthy social development;**

- **Making life more interesting; and fun;**

- **Deepening and enriching a relationships; and**

- **Enhancing students' quality of life, employability, and career success.**

Cooperative conflict resolution is another relationship skill students learn in the same way they learn to actively listen or to use appropriate affirmations. Active listening and the use of affirmations and not using put-downs are good first steps to developing a cooperative, supportive climate in the classroom. This climate makes teaching cooperative conflict resolution a natural extension of the cooperative learning process.

What Conflict Is, And When It Occurs

Kriedler[6] defines conflict as occurring "when two or more people interact and perceive incompatible differences between, or threats to their RESOURCES, NEEDS, OR VALUES. This causes them to behave in response to the interaction and their perception of it." These resources, needs, and values are outlined below.

Conflicts of needs are more difficult to resolve than conflicts over resources because the reasons are not as clear. When an individual or a team is dealing with influence issues, these needs are ripe for conflict to occur. This is why it is so important for students to know methods to resolve conflicts as they work in teams.

4. **Crum, Thomas F.** *The Magic of Conflict.* Simon and Schuster, New York, 1987.

5. **Johnson, Roger and David.** *Creative Conflict.* Interaction Book Company, Edina, MN.

6. **Kreidler, William.** *Creative Conflict Resolution.* Scott, Foresman, and Co., Glenview, Illinois, London, 1984.

> ### *Resources*
> A conflict occurs about resources when two or more people want something which is in short supply.
> - **ATTENTION OF THE TEACHER**
> - **A GIRLFRIEND OR BOYFRIEND**
> - **ART SUPPLIES**
> - **MAKING A SPORTS TEAM**
>
> These conflicts are often the easiest to resolve and they are frequently encountered on the playground.

> ### *Needs*
> Students have the same basic psychological needs as adults.
> - **POWER**
> - **FRIENDSHIP AND BELONGING TO A GROUP**
> - **SELF-ESTEEM**
> - **ACHIEVEMENT**

Our values are those parts of us which are ingrained at the deepest level. Consequently, conflicts dealing with values are the most difficult to resolve. It is important to ground students thoroughly in an appreciation of differences as you do classbuilding and teambuilding. When students appreciate others' differences, they feel safer to express their own differences and feel they will be accepted.

> ### *Values*
> The beliefs we hold most closely to us are our values.
> - **RELIGIOUS**
> - **POLITICAL**
> - **CULTURAL**
> - **FAMILY**
> - **GOALS**

Eight Modes of Conflict Resolution

Spencer Kagan[7] introduces eight modes of conflict resolution which are the heart of the lessons to be presented in this chapter. These eight modes are:

- **S**hare
- **T**ake turns
- **O**utside Help
- **P**ostpone
- **H**umor
- **A**void
- **C**hance
- **C**ompromise

These are basic modes which can be used by teachers and students to resolve many conflicts which occur within the classroom. It's necessary to give students a variety of methods to resolve conflicts because conflicts come in a variety of forms. The first letters of each of these modes forms the acronym **STOPHACC**, which can be used to help students remember them.

1. Share

When a conflict in the classroom or playground results from a limited supply of a resource (ball, paper, paint, playing field), then sharing may be an appropriate response.

---

7. **Kagan, Spencer.** *Cooperative Learning.* Kagan's Cooperative Learning Co., San Juan Capistrano, 1992.

John and his five friends are using the basketball court to play a full court game of basketball. Brad and seven of his classmates want to play also. This could lead to John and his group saying, "We were here first, and we're staying. Go do something else." Obviously, Brad could walk away with some hard feelings and remember this incident or he could refuse to leave and bring about a conflict. John and Brad could also quickly

conclude that sharing the court, with each group using half the court, would resolve the conflict and allow each to get what they want, to play basketball. There are other solutions which could work as well. What could you do to resolve this if you were John?

In the classroom there is frequently conflict over limited equipment or supplies. Sherry and Allen are both doing art projects which require red paint. Sherry started first and is now using the red paint. Allen begins his project and quickly sees he needs the red paint. He approaches Sherry and demands the red paint. Sherry tells him to wait until she's finished. Allen says he can't wait

because he needs to use the red now. Sherry could respond a number of different ways:

- "Wait until I'm finished, then you can use it."

- Use an I-Statement with Allen, "I don't like it when you demand the paint from me, Allen. It makes me mad." And ask for an apology.

> **Note:** A key aspect of looking at conflict is to identify the underlying cause. In the example of John and Brad sharing the basketball court, the underlying issue was both wanting to play basketball. In this case sharing the court made sense to both parties and resolved the conflict quickly. If John is more concerned about projecting a "tough" image than he is about playing basketball, then the potential conflict isn't about basketball, it's about image. Students need to be aware that conflicts are not always as easy to resolve as they appear.

- Suggest Allen move his project closer to where she is, so that he can share the paint.

Conflicts often develop when one person is offended by the other. This may be the way the other person demanded something rather than asking nicely. It could be the tone of voice another perceives as annoying. When an atmosphere of tolerance and trust is developed in the classroom through class-building, teambuilding, and relationship skill building, then it's less likely that destructive conflicts will occur. It's also appropriate to teach the active listening skills before you teach conflict resolution. Active listening is a starting point for cooperative conflict resolution. When students deal effectively with a conflict situation, they feel more empowered to deal with other conflict situations which arise.

2. Take Turns

It seems almost too easy to suggest taking turns as a conflict resolution strategy. However, many of the resource conflicts which arise in a classroom or outside can be handled by taking turns. Taking turns would not have worked well in the case of the basketball court because each could only play for a short period of time and sharing made more sense in that situation. In the example of Allen and Sherry using the paint, taking turns would have been another viable option.

Taking turns is a lesson reinforced regularly within our schools, from the line for lunch to raising your hand for the teacher to call on you. It isn't always seen as a tool for conflict resolution because it's such a common aspect of our everyday existence. However, it needs to be taught as an option for students to refer to when resolving conflicts.

3. Outside Help

When a conflict reaches the point that neither party can see a way to proceed, then, perhaps, it's time to seek outside help. This outside help could be from peers or an adult.

The key is to ask for outside help from another person all people involved in the conflict will respect and listen to. If they are on the same team, then another of their teammates could help. If in the same class, then a classmate could help. The teacher should be seen as a last resort and not the first. If we train students to take care of their own issues, we empower them as problem solvers. If students only know how to get outside help from an adult, then they are not learning to make use of their peers to

problem solve. When those students become adults, does this mean that they may run to the supervisor every time they have a problem on the job. If they learn to rely on peers in school to help resolve conflicts, then they will be more likely to seek the assistance of peers after they graduate.

If you are using students as conflict managers, you can use the eight modes presented here as a beginning point for the managers to you and use.

Note: Many schools have trained students in specific ways to mediate conflicts. Robertson Road School in Modesto, California developed a Student Instructor & Mediator (SIM's) program by training the "toughest" kids on campus as the first mediators. They learned specific ways to handle conflicts between students and how to enforce school rules during recess and lunch. SIM's were recognizable by the red vests they wore. It soon became an "in thing" to be a conflict manager. To become a SIM, students first needed to be successful at being Extra Special Partners (ESP), where they buddied up with a new student or one student who needed extra support during recess and lunch. When the student was successful at ESP, they become eligible to apply for the SIM program. To remain a SIM, students needed to maintain good grades and good behavior. Wouldn't it be exciting if all our students had the skills to be conflict managers? Leslie McPeak, who started this program as principal at Robertson Road School, shared with me that when she started the program at a new school on the other side of town, students were more interested in the Extra Special Partner program and not as interested in the Student Instructor & Mediator program. Different student bodies have different needs.

4. Postpone

How often have you become involved in a conflict and found that you had to leave before you could resolve it. Did you ever suggest to the person you were having the conflict with to get together another time to resolve it? If you're like me, this has happened to you more than once. And, when you finally get together with the other person, the conflict is much easier to resolve because some reflection has taken place since it originally happened.

I find this to be a particularly good strategy when emotions are very tense. William J. Kreidler, author of *Creative Conflict Resolution*, lists reasons conflict will ESCALATE or DE-ESCALATE:

"The conflict will ESCALATE if:

1. There is an increase in exposed emotion, e.g., anger, frustration;

2. There is an increase in perceived threat;

3. More people get involved, choosing up sides;

4. The children were not friends prior to the conflict; and

5. The children have few peacemaking skills at their disposal.

The conflict will DE-ESCALATE if:

1. Attention is focused on the problem, not on the participants;

2. There is a decrease in exposed emotion and perceived threat;

3. The children were friends prior to the conflict; and

4. They know how to make peace, or have someone to help them do so."[8]

Postponing the resolution of the conflict can help de-escalate the conflict in three of the four issues mentioned by Kreidler. It should also be pointed out that postponing a conflict is not always a viable strategy. At some point, conflict needs to be addressed and resolved.

5. Humor

Humor is like the proverbial sword which cuts both directions. It can resolve some conflicts if both participants can see the hilarity of the situation. However, it can also cut the other direction and backfire, if one person refuses to see it seriously while the other person can only see the serious side. In this case, humor can work against resolution of the conflict. I feel humor works

best when one of the parties can step back and ask, "What is funny about this situation?" Not all of us, or our students, have the ability to do this.

---

8. Kreidler, William J. *Creative Conflict Resolution.* Scott, Foresman, and Co., 1984.

6. Avoid

Some things are not important enough for us to become involved in a conflict. At these times, perhaps, it's best to let the other person have their way and avoid a conflict. There are other times when we know that no matter how much we discuss a conflict, we will not come to resolution. This may be the time we say that it's OK to disagree. Both sides may be right. This is particularly true of personal value issues such as politics, religion, etc. which are not easy to change. This is where a consistent effort within the classroom to show appreciation of differences is important. Once students begin to value and respect differences, there will not be the need to change others or to change themselves, to meet others' expectations. In situations such as this, you may choose to avoid a conflict by not approaching a subject or by agreeing to disagree.

7. Chance

There are times when flipping a coin will work as well as anything else to resolve the conflict. Juan and Anita run to get into line for the tetherball, arriving at the same time. An argument erupts over who was first. They ask a classmate to help them resolve who should be first. The mediator quickly concludes they arrived at about the same time and asks if they would both agree to the outcome of a coin flip. They

both agree. The mediator flips the coin with the understanding that if it comes up heads, Juan will be first; if it's tails, Anita will be first.

In this situation using chance was appropriate and easy for both sides to agree on. This only works when neither party has a huge vested interest in the outcome. Chance is not appropriate for conflicts regarding needs or value issues.

8. Compromise

Compromise appears to most of us to be the way the world operates. Certainly, world governments compromise to avoid confrontation and war. Couples in a marriage compromise to avoid a fight. Compromise occurs between two students when they each decide to give up something they want, to resolve the conflict. *Conflict Resolution: A Secondary Curriculum* puts it

succinctly, "In compromise, instead of one person winning and the other losing, each person wins partially and loses partially."[9]

Tanya and Paul were collaborating on a project for the school newspaper. They decided to write something about prayer in school. Paul believed very strongly that the article should come out in favor of school prayer. Tanya felt that prayer in public schools is inappropriate. After lengthy discussion they compromised on another

9. *Conflict Resolution: A Secondary Curriculum*: Community Board Program, Inc., San Francisco, CA., 1987.

topic they could both agree on for their article.

This often works well if what students give up is not important to them, or the choice they make is equally important. The difficulty arises when students must give up something which is important to them. This can lead to resentment and anger and may increase the likelihood of further conflict. When teaching students to use compromise, inform them of both its positive and negative sides.

Teaching Cooperative Conflict Resolution

When teaching students about conflict resolution, I recommend that you first establish a cooperative context in the room. This means that students are using ground rules such as active listening and affirming others. These are taught as the first two aspects of "Relationship Skill Building" because they set a tone of mutual respect and support. The classbuilding, teambuilding, and relationship skill building lessons introduced earlier are essential elements to establishing a cooperative spirit in the classroom.

The cooperative conflict resolution lessons presented here are intended to teach students how to recognize conflict when they see it or are involved in it, recognize the type of conflict (resources, needs, or values), and learn the eight modes of conflict resolution and how to use them.

COMMUNICATING ASSERTIVELY

Sometimes we find ourselves in situa-tions in which we are uncomfortable with what another person is saying or doing. We may know something is not right, yet not quite know what's wrong. It could be that we are sitting in xthe faculty room and feel uncomfortable because of others comments. A teacher may be giving put-downs to other faculty or students, or making ethnic jokes.

Eight Modes	Types of Conflict		
	Resources	Needs	Values
Share	X		
Take Turns	X		
Outside Help	X	X	X
Postpone	X	X	X
Humor	?	?	?
Avoid	X	X	X
Chance	X		
Compromise	X	?	

How do we usually handle this type of a situation? Do we tell the person how we feel, or do we let it go and ignore it? If you are like me, it depends on the situation, how well I know the person, and how much it affects me. I believe most of us would not say anything, even if what the person said was offensive. How can we communicate assertively in situations like this?

1. Passive Communication

A. "Doormat Behavior"

The title of this section is "Communicating Assertively." How are we communicating if we are not communicating assertively? In the above example we chose not to communicate at all. This is an option many of us face when confronted by conflict, especially with a colleague or family member. We believe that by ignoring it, it will go away or possibly solve itself. My experience is that most of these issues do not go away, and that they are still around sometime later. We may be a doormat and let someone walk all over us and show that we do not respect our own rights. However, the feelings generated by their behavior are generally not forgotten. Those of us who are "doormats" often feel guilty that we didn't say the right thing or in many cases anything. I call this attempt to ignore a conflict situation "doormat" behavior. We allow another to walk over our feelings and us. Communicating assertively means not being a doormat.

B. Bagging

Bagging often happens in classrooms. A teacher will let a minor inappropriate behavior slide by with the understanding that it's "no big deal." Then, after a few more episodes with the same student, the teacher over-reacts and the student is offended. The student was doing what they had been doing all along. The student thinks, "Why was it OK then and a capital offense now?" This is called "bagging."

Most of us do this from time to time, if not at school, then with our spouse. How many of us have stuffed resentments into that bag, and then when we have an argument about who's going to do the dishes all the resentments for the past month are taken out of the bag at once and, "Who does the dishes?" becomes grounds for a major explosion. Communicating assertively means dealing with issues as they arise, not "bagging" them.

2. Aggressive Communication

Aggressive communication is different from assertive communication because generally someone who is being aggressive is trying to intimidate the other person. Aggressive communication may be intended to hurt the other person's feelings. With aggressive communication we do not respect others rights. I often ask participants in my workshops to remember their best experience with a teacher in school and their worst. Invariably their worst was when they felt they were treated unfairly by a teacher, often publicly. We are the caretakers of the social environment of our classroom. We need to model for students how to handle conflict in an assertive way, neither passive nor aggressive. When we do not take our responsibility seriously, it's our students who bear the burden. That's not to say we won't blow it from time to time. Part of the wonder of being human is our propensity to make mistakes, or, as we often tell our students, to create "learning opportunities." Our humanness also allows us to realize we made a mistake and to be brave enough to apologize and or do better next time. How often have we regretted not apologizing to a student or our spouse for whatever reason, even though we knew it felt like the right thing to do.

3. Assertive Communication

A third option is to share your feelings about the other person's comments in a way in which you take ownership of your feelings and do not "blame" the other person for being who they are. In Assertive Communication you respect your rights and the rights of the person you are talking with.

I-Statements

Most of us have heard the phrase "I-statements". This refers to sharing how you feel about a particular situation. This situation could be something another said, did, or did not say or do. The key point is that "I-statements" reflect back to the person how some behavior of theirs has effected you.

Components of I-statements[1]
- "**I feel** _____" (State the emotion you have)
- "**when you** _____" (State the behavior - be SPECIFIC)
- "**because** _____" (State the effect the behavior has on YOUR life).
- "**and what I want is** _____" (State what would make the situation better for you).

_____

1. *Conflict Resolution: A Secondary School Curriculum,* The Community Board, Inc., San Francisco, CA.

An "I-statement" can be put into a general formula. Almost always "I-statements" begin with "I feel" followed by a description of what behavior makes you feel this way. For example, " I feel hurt when you put Patty down."

Next, you tell what effect the behavior has on your life.

"Patty is my friend and I want her to feel good about herself."

Finally, you state what you would like, as in,

"What I want is for you not to put Patty down.

The idea of giving "I-statements" is to share honestly about yourself without blaming the other person or making them feel guilty.

The purpose is to open communication and to express your feelings to the other person.

As with all communication it's important to know what you want to communicate. If you are angry it will come through, which may be all right if the situation warrants it. Often when we are angry an "I-statement" can turn into a "YOU statement" in which you blame the other person for how you feel, rather than only sharing an emotion.

Inappropriate Use of "I-Statements"

"I-statements" can be used inappropriately. For example, they can be used to put someone on the spot in front of others. If you choose to do this, I recommend you use something other than an "I-statement." You'll not usually obtain a positive response from someone you've put on the spot. The best guide is to think about how you would like people to approach you if you were doing something that might annoy them. Would you want the person to point it out to everyone in listening distance or would you like them to talk to you individually? Many teachers I have worked with have found that it works best to approach most communication issues with a private talk, particularly when sharing personal feelings via "I-statements."

Using "I-Statements"

Colleagues often ask, "How can I use an 'I-statement' when a student is 'out of control." In that case don't use an "I-statement," use a command. When you begin to practice "I-statements" use them sparingly. Practice with family and friends, and remember to be kind to yourself. Using a new skill takes practice and time to master. It's all right to make mistakes. "I-statements" are not only intended to convey negative feelings or concerns. Use "I-statements" to share appreciation towards a colleague, friend, student, or family member. You may find "I-statements" more comfortable when sharing feelings of positive regard. Ease into it if you are not used to using them. "I-statements" will help you take care of your needs and express your feelings more openly.

Teaching "I-Statements"

When you first help students to use "I-statements" you can begin by teaching them the first two parts of an "I-statement" the "I feel..." and the "when you..." In teaching

---

Sample "I-Statements"

"I feel <u>great</u>
when you <u>smile at me in the morning</u>
because <u>it starts my day off right</u>
and <u>keep it up</u>."

"I feel <u>sad</u>
when you <u>yell at me</u>
because <u>it hurts my feelings</u>.
I would like you to not <u>yell at me</u>.

---

primary students, I might use only these first two parts of an "I-statement." This is reflected in the first "I-statement," activity in the lessons. Have students practice using these before you introduce the other two components. Some groups may have difficulty mastering this concept. As the teacher, you should model using "I-statements." If you are not using "I-statements," it is much less likely that your students will.

Assertive Communication Lessons

~ ✳ ~

"I" vs. "You" Statements[1]

I-Statements	You-Statements
Feelings	
• Speaker owns their own feelings.	• Speaker blames another for feelings.
Objectivity	
• Speaker describes behavior.	• Speaker judges behavior.
Control	
• Speaker does not want to control others.	• Speaker does want to control others.
Attitude	
• Respect toward others.	• Possible disrespect
Example	
• "Johnny, I'm angry you spilled milk on my drawing. I would appreciate your being more careful next time."	• "I'm angry. You idiot, you spilled milk all over my drawing."

1. *Conflict Resolution: A Secondary School Curriculum.* The Community Board, Inc., San Francisco, CA.

Chapter 6

Structures

Structures

Introduction

To make sense of the world, we each need to establish a framework or schema as to how the world operates. By identifying and summarizing the different cooperative structures here, I'm attempting to give you a framework which is more understandable. Several approaches to cooperative learning give the reader the components included in each lesson without giving the reader enough clear examples. The structures included here are designed to assist you in developing a schema in which the cooperative learning structures make sense to you and you will be able to apply them to your classroom situation.

What Are Structures?*

Structures are a way of organizing the interaction of individuals in a classroom. Structures are generally content free and can be used across a variety of grade levels. As an example, Brainstorming is a structure where teams (as opposed to the whole class) quickly share ideas about a subject as directed by the teacher. There are specific guidelines for the brainstorming you will be introduced to. It is used in teams rather than as a whole class so that more students can participate at the same time. Brainstorming can be used in English, science, or math. It can be used in kindergarten, sixth grade, or university level. The structure remains relatively the same, what changes is the content which the teacher provides. This is true of the other structures introduced here.

The definition and analysis of structures allows systematic design of cooperative learning lessons; the structures have predictable outcomes in the academic, linguistic, cognitive, and social domains. Structures are building blocks of a lesson; they may be combined to form multi-structural lesson with predictable results.

* Much of the information in this section is taken from *Cooperative Learning* by Spencer Kagan.

Why Cooperative Structures?

Cooperative structures allow the teacher to practice one approach to organizing cooperative learning a number of different times across different settings. Some approaches to cooperative learning give you a broad framework, including several components, of how lessons should be designed. Some teachers feel overwhelmed by the responsibility of totally designing every lesson from scratch. The different cooperative structures shared here allow you to already have a framework of structure. You provide the content, the teacher, and facilitation necessary for the students to be successful.

These cooperative learning structures are content free. Once you learn how the structure works you will be able to apply it in other situations from teaching math to science to literature. The essence of these structures is that they assist you in using cooperative learning teams successfully. The structures facilitate your entry into using cooperative learning groups and may give you a new view of cooperative learning if you've felt less than successful using other approaches.

> *Note: For more information on these and other structures, consult a recent catalogue of materials from Kagan's Cooperative Learning Co. There are books, videos, posters, and workshops which provide assistance with learning to use the structural approach.*

Cooperative Learning is a Process

To be successful using cooperative learning structures over an extended period of years you will become aware that just as it takes time for your students to become comfortable using cooperative learning, it will take time for you to feel and think "cooperative learning." Using cooperative learning structures is not easy. It takes practice, practice and more practice. Too often teachers give up on using cooperative learning because they've tried a few lessons and were not successful. To use cooperative learning well may take months or years of practice.

These structures will give you a framework you can use as you become familiar with cooperative learning. As you become more comfortable with the structures you will begin to see where different structures might work in different learning situations to help your students to be more successful. Some structures will lend themselves more to practice situation while others are better for concept development. As you become familiar with the different uses of these structures you will begin to naturally link them together into multi-structural lessons. This takes commitment, effort, and ability to trust your instructional intuition. You don't become a great cooperative learning teacher overnight or in a few months. It's a lifelong process and it's fun and challenging.

Arrangement of Structures

The structures appear in alphabetical order. This section gives you an overview of each structure. The following sections will give you sample lessons. Each lesson is composed of a number of structures. The multi-structural lessons are designed for your use and as a model of how to develop multi-structural lessons.

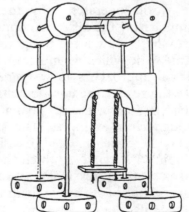

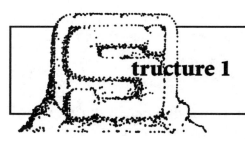

Structure 1

Brainstorming

See Lessons
6, 18, 19, 20, 23, 24, 25, 26, 277, 28, 31, 36

Steps of Brainstorming

1. Place Students in Teams.
2. Topic Selection.
3. Assign Roles.
4. Teams Begin Brainstorming.
5. Share Results and Record.

Brainstorming is a powerful structure for opening the doors to creativity for a group. This structure demonstrates the power of synergy faster than any other structure.

It's great for problem identification and problem solving.

Steps of Brainstorming

1. Place Students in Teams

At the beginning of the year you may choose to create random teams. Later, you may assign students to long term teams. Team size for brainstorming is best at four or five students. Fewer than four limits the flow of ideas. More than five limits the amount of interaction on a team.

2. Topic Selection

The first thing you will need to do is select a topic for the class to brainstorm. This might be solutions to a behavior problem a student experiences during lunch. It could be possible outcomes for a problem in a book

the class is reading. You could have groups brainstorm what the ending might be. A brainstorming topic can be anything involving creative thinking and multiple alternatives.

3. Roles and Four S's

Assigned roles ensure full participation as each student has a task during brainstorming. The roles are:

- **SYNERGY GURU/SCRIBE** - Helps combine all ideas and records all ideas generated by the team.

- **SPEED CAPTAIN** - Encourages the team to go faster to create more ideas.

- **SULTAN OF SILLY** - Comes up with and encourages off-the-wall, silly ideas.

- **SUPER SUPPORTER** - Accepts and encourages all ideas.

The roles can be selected by the team or you may assign particular students. I often have the teams count off 1-4, if I have teams of four, and assign all #1's the task of synergy guru/scribe, #2's to be speed captain and so forth. All students should have the opportunity to try each role. If a student doesn't have the skill to perform a specific role, then allow teams to switch roles with your permission.

Four S's of Brainstorming[1]

These guidelines provide a necessary structure for students to learn how to brainstorm successfully. The four rules are:

Speed

Students should share ideas as quickly as the scribe can write them down. Remind students that they have a limited time (usually 2-3 minutes) to brainstorm.

Suspend Judgment

It's important that students understand why we suspend judgment when brainstorming. If we compliment a student for one idea and don't compliment an idea offered by another student, it's likely that students will be discouraged from sharing for fear that their ideas won't be "good enough." Either positive or negative comments can stifle creativity and spontaneity in brainstorming. All ideas are OK.

Silly

Off-the-wall ideas are encouraged and all ideas are accepted because these ideas are the seeds for truly creative solutions. Many great ideas have been proposed which initially seemed silly. Many people used to laugh when others suggested that the earth was a sphere or that man would be able to fly. In brainstorming there is no such thing as an idea which is too silly.

Synergy

The synergy which happens during brainstorming is the power behind the brainstorming process. It involves combining ideas to create even better ones than one person might come up with on their own.

4. Teams Begin Brainstorming[2]

Allow teams only 2-5 minutes to brainstorm. Too much time allows them to go off task. When you're ready to stop, give students a signal that time is up.

5. Share Results and Record

This is the time for teams to share their ideas with the class. You can structure it so teams share their total list or one response at a time, permitting each group to be involved. You or a student can record a summary of the lists as they are shared. Items which are repeats or very similar can be checked rather than written out. Having teams share

Speed Captain "Let's Hurry"

Super Supporter "All ideas are great."

Synergy Guru "Let's combine those two."

Chief of Silly "Let's have a crazy idea."

---

1. The Four S's are from *Cooperative Learning*, Spencer Kagan, 1991.

2. Listen to the noise level in the room. When the noise level drops it means that students are finishing up the task. This is the time to stop students before the noise level goes back up on an off task topic.

one idea at a time, Roundrobin style, allows equal opportunity to share and ensures that no one team will dominate . It's also a good method if your time frame is short. If you need to stop before all ideas are shared, make sure each group has had at least an opportunity to share their favorites.

Note:

Brainstorming is one way for you to draw forth ideas for solving not only academic problems, but also behavioral issues which come up during the year. When students are having persistent behavioral concerns involving the class, it may be appropriate to ask the class to brainstorm solutions to the problem. You make the final decision, but include your students in the decision making process.

Comments on your use of Brainstorming:

—————— **VANSTON SHAW:** *Communitybuilding in the Classroom* ——————
Publisher: Kagan Cooperative Learning • 1 (800) Wee Co-op

Structure 1   Chapter 6: 5

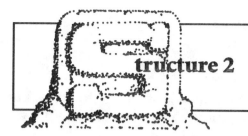

Structure 2 — Choral Response

See Lessons
21, 22, 32, 35

Steps of Choral Response

1. Teacher selects appropriate material.
2. Class practices choral response.
3. Teacher uses correction procedure for 100% participation.
4. Teacher rewards/affirms the class or team.

With Choral Response the total class (or selected group or certain groups) respond verbally to a question you ask, when you give a signal.[1] This is a way to actively involve 100% of your students in responding. It can be used to check for understanding and to review information already presented. The information students are to remember is usually one or two words or a short phrase. This technique has been used for centuries as a way to help the entire class remember information. Also, by responding in unison, this structure can be used as a classbuilding tool. Students are all responding in unison and can take pride in how well they do. It becomes a teambuilding activity when teams respond well together.

There is a tremendous amount of information that we want students to memorize and to be able to retrieve quickly. This is a way to assist your students in learning and prac-

---

1. I first began to see Choral Response as a cooperative structure after working with Dr. Anita Archer of San Diego, California. Dr. Archer is a master at using Choral Response.

ticing information in a quick and fun manner. When material must be memorized, we need as many quick and enjoyable ways to practice recalling information as possible.

The Multisensory Nature Of Choral Response

I've seen this approach used successfully in a number of settings. I believe one of the reasons it is so successful is that it engages different senses. It's verbal because the students are responding verbally. It's visual if students are responding to a visible signal given by the teacher. It's auditory because students are hearing the correct response from their classmates as they give their response. It becomes kinesthetic (rhythmic) when the class becomes good at responding in unison. These aspects of this structure make it appealing for students with various learning styles.

Steps of Choral Response

1. The Teacher Selects Material which is Appropriate to this Structure

Choral Response can most easily be used with a content of a single word or a short phrase. It can be a sentence or longer if exact word order is essential. I've used this structure successfully in math, science, history, literature, reading skills, spelling, and geography. In math, use it to review number facts, information about geometry, or time differences around the globe. In literature, we review main characters, place names, plot information. As I describe the next few steps you'll begin to feel how this content can be used with Choral Response.

2. Students Learn to Respond to given Signal (demonstrate and evaluate practice)

I tell students that we are going to learn how to give Choral Responses. I explain this is a way students have learned for hundreds of years. It's a method for the total class to respond together. The visual signal I use is my right hand held up in front of me so that all students can see it. I might tell the class that our school name is Davis High. Then put my hand up. I direct all students to tell me our school name when I drop my hand. I give students a few seconds of think time and then drop my hand. Usually the responses are somewhat ragged the first time. I immediately repeat the question and hand signal with think time. The response will be a little better. I keep doing it until nearly all students respond in unison. I praise the

students for doing a good job as they improve in responding together.

Lead and Pace
It's important to help students be successful when you first use this approach and when studying new information. I lead the students by giving clues I feel they need. If we were studying the Four S's of Brainstorming I might ask students for the name of the first "S" which had to do with being fast in Brainstorming. If it was our first round I might give them a clue. "The second letter is a 'p.'" I would then give students the signal with a few seconds of think time, drop my hand, and observe and listen as the class responds.

Developing Rhythm
Use the same rhythm and timing every time you use this structure. That is, use the same amount of wait time before dropping your hand each time. This way students can anticipate and their choral response will be in unison. The rhythm for a Choral Response develops as you use it several times consecutively.

3. Correction Procedure
It's important with this structure to work with your class so that they are all involved. As students are responding you monitor by watching for

Choral Response

their responses. If you notice a student is not responding, ask for the response again and see if the student will respond. When you watch, continue having the class repeat the Choral Response as you make eye contact with the student who is not responding. You must let students know that you expect 100% participation. The correction procedure is to have the class or team repeat the choral response until you have a correct response with 100% participation or as close to 100% as you feel is appropriate.

4. Affirm Class and Team Participation

Let students know how you appreciate their participation and ability to respond in unison. I usually give only verbal affirmation as a show of appreciation. I give an affirmation when the class is making a good faith effort toward mastery. If all but one or two members are participating, you can have the class respond when sitting with their team. You can then praise those teams which have 100% participation. You'd be surprised at how quickly a student will respond without your saying a word to them when their team members ask them to "get with the agenda." Choral Response is enjoyable itself; extrinsic rewards are not usually needed.

What About Students Who Do Not Want To Participate

If a student isn't responding, repeat the question and signal. Move closer to the student and maintain eye contact. If, after several attempts you still haven't gotten the student to respond, then go on. Have the student stay after class and let him or her know you expect their response with the class the next time you do Choral Response. This will usually get them involved.

Another strategy is to award class or team points for total participation. If one person doesn't respond then the team or class is not rewarded. Students understand they have some responsibility to their team or to the class. Keep trying. Most students want to participate when given an opportunity and encouragement. If the student still chooses not to respond, take a deep breath, relax and go on. The student will still be getting the practice by hearing the class practice. Do not turn it into a power struggle, it doesn't need to be a win/lose situation.

Sample Use of Choral Response with Brainstorming

You are teaching students the "Four S's" of Brainstorming. You review the "Four S's" and have students explain the different roles. For review, you decide to use Choral Response. You might ask students to name the "Four S's" of Brainstorming when you give the signal of dropping your hand. You could give the students a clue for the first one. "The first S of Brainstorming ends with the letter D." Give the signal, hand raised, allow students three-five seconds of think time. Drop your hand. About seventy five percent of students respond with "SPEED," the correct response. Immediately, use the correction procedure. Say, "Again on the signal." Hand raised, think time, drop your hand. Ninety percent of students respond with the correct response. Repeat the correction procedure until you have 95 to 100% correct responses. You would then go on to the second "S" and follow a similar pattern. Choral response is a method for students to practice giving the correct response.

Team Responses

If you want to encourage team support for Choral Response, then use this structure when students are in their teams. You can have some questions answered by certain teams. You can ask the question. "What is the capital of Texas?" [Hand signal] .... Pause...... "Teams One and Two." [Drop hand] "AUSTIN." You can then repeat this process with various teams responding. You can vary this approach with whole class responding. It's a way to lighten it up and make it more enjoyable. It is also easier for the teacher to monitor the responses of one or two groups for correctness.

Limitations

This structure, like other cooperative learning structures, is not designed to take the place of testing for knowledge. These structures are designed to actively involve students and make the process of learning more fun and inclusive.

Comments on your use of Choral Response:

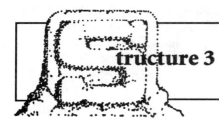

Structure 3 Community Circle

See Lessons
2, 4, 10, 11, 30, 37

Steps of Community Circle

1. Students form large class circle.
2. Teacher discusses rules.
3. Teacher writes starter sentence on board.
4. Teacher models response and passes feather to next student.

This is an excellent structure to begin or end each day. A large feather (or other object) is held by the person speaking. When introducing this activity you might explain some Native American tribes had similar traditions of passing a feather or talking stick. All attention is given to the person with the feather.[1]

Steps of Community Circle

1. Students Form a Class Circle

Have students sit in a large circle facing the middle. In elementary settings it works best to have students sit on the floor. In secondary settings this activity is often done in advisement period or home room with desks or chairs in a circle.

---

1. I was reminded of passing the feather by Jeanne Gibbs, author of *Tribes,* the setting in which I first used Community Circle. *Tribes: A Process for Social Development and Cooperative Learning.* Center Source Publications, Santa Rosa, 1987.

2. Teacher Explains Rules

Begin by explaining the rules for this structure. These would include:

- Take Turns, talking only when you have the feather
- Use Only Affirmations; No Put-Downs
- Right to Pass
- Active Listening

The teacher sets the tone for this structure by sharing first. This models for students what they are to do. It also allows students an opportunity to know you better. Taking turns in order allows every student an opportunity to share. Community Circle provides an excellent opportunity to monitor the ground rule of "no put-downs" and the use of affirmations. It's critical for students to know that put-downs are not accepted in your class and that affirmations are actively encouraged.

Students always have the right to pass if they do not wish to share personal feelings. This allows the student who doesn't feel safe sharing personal feelings an opportunity not to participate. It also increases the safety of the classroom as students see that they all have a choice. It's likely that some students will test you to see if you are serious about this. Generally, this lasts only a couple of times before they want to participate. The right to pass honors students' right to confidentiality, and gives them practice in making choices.

3. Starter Sentence Posted for Students to See

Post a starter sentence on the board or overhead. You might want to have it prepared before you begin this lesson. The starter sentence should be something appropriate to the age and interest level of your students. Examples of various starter sentences or phrases are listed on the next page.

4. Teacher Models and Passes the Feather

Once the preliminaries are taken care of, the teacher starts off the circle by completing the starter sentence or phrase which will be completed by each person in the circle as they receive the feather. This is an opportunity to work on classbuilding and active listening skills. Students have an opportunity to share something about themselves in a supportive environment.

Active listening is one ground rule which you will more than likely use for all activities in your classroom. Community Circle is an excellent opportunity to monitor its use. Careful monitoring here will provide students with models for small group use.

You can model for students how to handle a person who is not using active listening. How you handle these situations will also give your students an indication if you are serious about the ground rules.

Variations

After students know the ground rules of Community Circle you may introduce the use of two, then three, and later even four simultaneous Community Circles. The disadvantages are that only one circle at a time gets the teacher's direction and input. The advantage is that with four circles you can have four times as much sharing at the same time and there can be greater intimacy. In a full class community circle where each student speaks for one minute it takes thirty minutes for 30 students to share. The same process takes eight minutes with four simultaneous circles.

Pass-The-Sentence-Strip

Mary Torrens Parker of Turlock, California, found that having students pass the "starter sentence strip" worked best for her first grade class. I also found the sentence strip worked well with my fourth grade class.

Community Circle

Starter Sentences for Community Circles

Today I feel _____ .

Yesterday I felt _____ , today I feel _____ .

I like to _____ .

I like to _____ because _____ .

My favorite toy (movie, T.V. program, candy bar, book, football player, baseball player, basketball player) is _____ .

My last dream was about _____ .

Last weekend I_____ and _____ .

Last night I _____ .

My best vacation would be _____ .

My best meal was _____ .

My favorite holiday is _____ because _____ .

Yesterday I _____ Today I _____ Tomorrow I _____ .

My goal for today (this week, year, ten years) is to _____ .

I want to know more about _____ .

My favorite book is _____ .

My favorite character in _____(name of book, etc.)

   was _____ because _____ .

I'm good at _____ .

Sentence Starter Strip:

Today I Feel_____ .

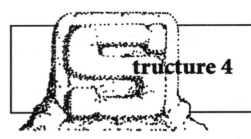

Structure 4

Corners

See Lessons
1, 8, 28

Steps of Corners

1. Choose three, four, or five alternatives, post them in different parts of room.
2. Introduce Corners to students, give them think time, and have them record their choice.
3. Students go to corners and share in pairs or triads.
4. Spokespersons from each corner share with the class, after which students in other corners paraphrase.

Corners has a wide range of uses. It is particularly good for promoting an appreciation of individual differences. Students realize that they can be accepted while making choices which are different from their friends. Corners can be used as an ice breaker/inclusion activity, or to introduce material at the beginning of a lesson. It can help students feel more comfortable with one another and gives students an opportunity for decision making.

Steps of Corners

1. Choose and Post Four Alternatives

To start Corners, you must choose three, four, or five dimensions which will allow students to make individual choices. The alternatives could be different animals, cars, famous people, or anything which can provide students an opportunity to express their individual preferences. See the suggestions at the end of this structure. Next, the four alternatives are written or drawn or both and are posted in the four corners of the room.

2. Students Look, Think, Write

Introduce the Corners activity to the students by telling them to look around the room at the different signs posted. Ask students to choose the sign with which they most identify at the present moment. Give them 30-60 seconds to decide. Then have students write their choice on a small slip of paper. For nonreaders the signs are color coded or numbered; they put the appropriate color or number on their paper.

Corners

3. Students Move, Pair, and Share

Direct students to go to the corner with the sign they selected. Once by the sign, students form pairs or triads and discuss the reasons they chose as they did.

4. Students Discuss in Corners, Share with Class, then Paraphrase

Have pairs and triads meet with all others in their corner and share their reasons for choosing the corner. Once students have heard several reasons for choosing their corner a spokesperson from the corner shares the reasons with the class. Students in the other corners are then asked to pair up with someone in their corner to paraphrase what was just said. This process is repeated for each corner.

Comments on your use of Corners:

Corners Suggestions

1. Animals
Mountain Lion, Bear, Deer, Fox, Sheep, Horse, Goat, Bull, Elephant, Giraffe, Zebra, Gazelle

2. Sea Life
Whale, Shark, Dolphin, Swordfish, Trout, Salmon, Bass, Catfish, Squid, Octopus, Eel

3. Birds
Canary, Cockatoo, Parrot, Finch, Chicken, Duck, Turkey, Goose, Dove, Eagle, Robin, Crow

4. Trees
Oak, Willow, Mountain Pine, Sycamore, Apple, Orange, Plum, Apricot

5. Flowers
Orchid, Daisy, Rose, Lily, Tulip, Mum

6. Buildings
Skyscraper, Cottage, Palace, Restaurant, Cabin, Tent, Castle

7. Fast Food
McDonald's, Carl's Jr., Burger King, Wendy's, Taco Bell

8. Colors
Red, Blue, Green, Yellow, Forest Green, Lime, Turquoise, Light Green

9. Vehicles
Porsche, GTO, Mercedes, Maserati, Pick-up, Limousine, Sports Car, Sedan, Bicycle, Roller Skates, Skis, Skateboard

10. Boats
Row boat, Power boat, Sail boat, Canoe, Steam ship

11. Famous People
George Bush, Joe Montana, Rock Star, Movie Star, Sports Star, Statesman, Writer, Poet, Inventor, Scientist

12. Jobs
State Governor, State Senator, Congress Person, Mayor, Doctor, Lawyer, Teacher, Policeman

13. Seasons
Spring, Summer, Winter, Fall

14. Places
Big City, Country, Small Town, Suburb, School, Home, Friend's Home, Neighbor's, Moon, Jupiter, Neptune, The Sun, River, Mountain, Valley, Ocean

15. Siblings
None, One, Two, Three or More

16. Birth Order
Only Child, youngest, Middle, Oldest

17. Favorite Number
One, Seven, Ten, Five, Two, Three, Four

18. Metaphors
Flowing River, Babbling Brook, Calm Lake, Rough Seas, Mountain Top, Meadow, Dark Cave

19. Literature
Four Endings To A Story, Characters In A Story, Vocabulary Words, Favorite Books, Stories, Authors

Note: Alternatives do not have to be just one word, consider these: Four definitions of a friend, four topic sentences, four alternative art pieces, four geometry proofs, and four science hypotheses.

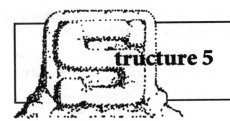

Structure 5 # Formations

See Lessons
10, 11, 14, 15, 19

Steps of Formations

1. Direct students to create a shape.
2. Have students change the shape as directed.
3. Discuss improvement and leadership.

Students form shapes or figures, "Formations," with their bodies as a team or as an entire class. An example might be having each of the four represent a different number 1-4. The first team becomes the numeral 1, the second team a 2, and so forth. Formations is excellent for initiating lessons or as an energizer in the middle of a lesson when you want students up and moving.

Another example: while discussing happy and sad feelings, you might direct the students to form two groups. One group forms a sad face while the other group forms a happy face. You might then have students use Three-Step Interview to discuss the last time they felt very happy or very sad.

if the class is studying an upcoming presidential election.

2. Ask Students to Change Shape

If they form the donkey first, then ask them to form the elephant. Once you have the first shape the second one usually comes quicker. This gives you an opportunity to affirm the class for learning quickly. It's an opportunity for the entire class to be successful. See the box for suggested topics for formations.

3. Discuss Improvement and Leadership

Ask some reflection questions to the teams about how students might improve next time. This gives students a goal for improvement. Formations is an excellent starting point to discuss leadership skills. Who were the students who took charge? Who agreed to change position for the good of the team or class? How does it feel to work together?

Steps of Formations

1. Ask Students to Form a Shape

Students work in teams to form the word you assign. This might be the shape of a donkey or an elephant

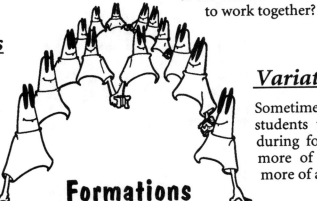

Formations

Variation

Sometimes you might tell students they cannot talk during formations -- it is more of a challenge and more of an equalizer.

Ideas For Formations

Whole, Half The Class, Or Teams:

Feelings - Happy or sad face, excited, or depressed face

Positions - A person sitting, standing, standing with arms up

Body Parts - Hand, hand outstretched, foot with toes, side view of a face

Science - Body systems (circulatory, respiratory), inventions

Geography - Map of your state, map of the USA, map of the world, continents

Math - Math equation (4 + 5 = 9), Shapes (circle, triangle, equilateral triangle, square, rectangle, parallelogram, etc.)

Spelling - Spell words. Start with easy words like Cat and Dog and Wake Up.

Comments on your use of Formations:

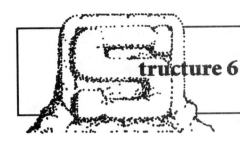

Structure 6 Inside-Outside Circle

See Lessons
2, 26, 28, 34

Steps of Inside-Outside Circle

1. Students form two concentric circles.
2. Circles face each other to share or quiz.
3. Students rotate to share or quiz with a new partner.

Inside-Outside Circle is a great structure for students to share personal information about themselves or review and practice academic and relationship skills in a short period of time. It's also energizing because students are moving.

Steps of Inside-Outside Circle

1. Concentric Circles

Have your students form two concentric circles, one inside the other. The outside circle faces in, the inside circle faces out. Each student faces a partner. If you have an even number of students, let's say thirty, then you'll have fifteen facing in and fifteen facing out. If you have thirty-one students, place the thirty-first student in either circle and have them become a "twin" with one student. They will share and rotate together with their twin.

2. Students Face Each Other and Share

Now that each student is facing another student, they share information about themselves such as their best ever summer vacation, or favorite TV program. Students can quiz the student across from them on information presented by the teacher or with flash cards.

3. Students Rotate

Have the the outside circle move one person to the right to a new partner, while the inside circle is stationary. In this way you can have students share personal information or quiz each other very quickly with everybody involved. If they are quizzing each other, students have different flash cards, and may trade cards before they rotate to double the practice.

Variation

Another way to make the rotation less predictable and more exciting is to have the students make a "right face" or a "left face" and then tell students how many to rotate while both circles move. If you tell students to rotate three then each student passes two students and stops at the third. You may have the class count together in a choral response. This adds spice to the structure and makes it more lively.

Inside-Outside Circle

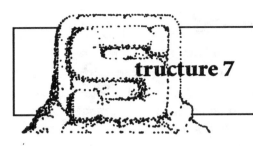

Structure 7

Line-Ups

See Lessons
4, 10, 24

Steps of Line-Ups

1. **Provide the poles of the line-up and directions.**
2. **Model for students.**
3. **Students line-up.**
4. **Students discuss why they chose where they stand.**
5. **Students report to the class.**

Line-ups is a multifunctional structure. I've used Line-ups as the basis for forming short term groups, to develop relationship skills, and to teach simple concepts.

Characteristic Line-Up

Students line-up by a characteristic such as; number of blocks they live from school, time they go to bed, number of items they had for breakfast, number of times they have moved, alphabetically by first name.

Value Line-Up

You can have students line-up by the extent to which they agree or disagree with a certain statement such as, "It's all right to hit another person if they give you a bad look," or "The most important word in the poem was 'love'." Those who strongly agree with the

statement stand at one end of a line, and those who disagree stand at the other. Students who agree only somewhat stand somewhere between the middle and the "agree" end of the line. Each takes a stance. Later they talk to those who took a similar stance and to those who took a different stance to discuss, for example, how to handle conflict, or the meaning of the poem.

Steps Of Line-Ups:
1. State Poles of Line-Ups

Tell students what it is you want them to line up for. Tell them where the two ends of the line will be and what each end represents.

2. Model for Students

Once you've given students the dimension they are lining up for, show them how to line-up. Actually move to the different places on the line, to model different responses.

3. Students Line-Up

Have students line up. Assist classmates who need help. If they are lining up according to this statement: "America should never have gotten involved in the Gulf War," have students line up by how strongly they

Line-Ups

agree or disagree with the statement. Students who believe strongly in this position will line-up at one end of the room; those who strongly oppose this position will line-up towards the other end of the room.

4. Students Discuss Why They Chose Where They Stand

This step is only for value discussions. They may meet in pairs or groups of four and discuss their reasons for their choice. Give students three to four minutes for discussion.

5. Students Report to Class

Have students report back to the class. If this is a factual line-up, such as birthdays, have each student state their birthday in order by month and day. If it's a values line-up, have several students state the reason they chose to stand where they did.

Line-Ups: Characteristics
- The number of blocks students live from school.
- The month and day they were born.
- The number of letters in their first name.
- Alphabetically by first or last name.
- Number of siblings.

Value:
- Kids should be allowed to drive at 14.
- Students should have homework Monday through Thursday only.
- School should be four days per week not five.

Variations
Folded Value Line-Ups

After students have talked with someone near them in the line-up, fold the line-up so they can interact with someone at an opposite end. This is done by having the student who agrees the strongest walk to the other end of the line, while each person behind the agree person follows. When the student who agrees the strongest is across from the strongest disagree student, become partners. Students continue to pair up as the line folds. Students discuss and paraphrase their partners point of view.

Split Value Line-Ups

In a split value line-up, the person in the middle walks to the end while each person behind the person in the middle follows. In this way, at one end the student with the strongest views interacts with a person who is undecided, while at the other end the person who disagrees the most interacts with a different person from the middle.

Note: See Chapter 3:5 for an example of a folded and split value line-up.

Comments on your use of Line-Ups:

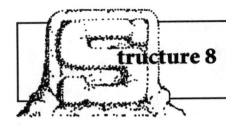

Structure 8 Numbered Heads Together

See Lessons
16, 20, 21, 22, 23, 24,
26, 27, 32, 33, 34, 36

Steps of Numbered Heads Together

1. Students number off in teams one through four.
2. Teacher asks question.
3. Students discuss possible answers.
4. Teacher calls number and students with that number raise their hand, ready to respond.

Numbered Heads Together is a simple four-step structure primarily used to review information previously taught. This structure is designed for teams of four. It is successfully used with kindergarten through adult levels. Numbered Heads Together is an excellent teambuilding structure because students must exhibit positive interdependence.

Steps of Numbered Heads Together

1. Students in Each Team Number Off

If you have an odd number of students or students are missing from a group and you have a team of three, then person number three is also number four. If you have one group with five members then persons four and five both respond when four is called out by the teacher. Once students have numbered off, check by asking all the number one's to raise their hand, etc.

2. Teacher Asks Question

A high consensus question for math might be, "How many degrees are there in a right angle?" It should be easy for students to come up with the answer with a minimum of discussion. You can use a low consensus question if you want to give a number of teams an opportunity to answer.

3. Heads Together: Students Discuss Possible Answers

For high consensus questions this step usually only takes a few seconds or so. If you ask a more difficult question, it will take a bit longer. Visually monitoring the groups is usually most effective because the groups come up with an answer quickly. You can have students indicate they are ready with a hand signal such as all hands in their laps or all students giving you eye contact.

4. Teacher Calls Number; Students with that Number Raise their Hand, Ready to Respond

This is an exciting review format for students, and when done well, increases students' alertness because they do not know which number you will call. Some teachers use a spinner with all the numbers represented so that the choice of who will be called on will be random. Spinners can make it even more exciting and fun for students.

If you ask a question with several parts to the answer, have each team answer only a part of the question and then move on to another team. In this manner you can have several answers for one question and a number of students respond in a short period of time.

If a team is not ready, you can have them sit out that round. If a student gives a wrong answer, impress on the class that it's the team's responsibility to come up with the correct answer.

Remember to call equally on all teams. If you have students raise their hand when you ask for a response and only a couple of students raise their hand, ask the teams to put their heads back together and try again. The next time around you should have more participation.

Variations

"Stand & Deliver"

A variation which was first introduced to me by Russ Frank from Saddleback School District was a variation of numbered heads called Peer Response Groups. It involves having students stand when their number is called. Usually the first student to stand answers first and receives team points for the answer which is recorded on an overhead projector. My colleague Robert Rudholm, now an instructor at California State University, Turlock, California, became a master at this approach when teaching middle school. Robert uses it as a major structure to review information.

"Stand and Deliver" and "Pop Corn"

Other colleagues, Gordon Chan and Tom Myers of Modesto City Schools, coined the terms "Pop Corn" for primary grade children and "Stand and Deliver" for fourth through twelfth grade for the same response mode described above - having students stand up to respond. This response mode actively involves students by having them commit their bodies by standing up. It also uses appropriate competition if the first student up is recognized, which can be monitored and directed by the teacher. Points for correct responses are recorded on the overhead. The key to this approach is to insure all teams have an equal opportunity for success.

Numbered Heads Together

1. Students Number Off

2. Teacher Presents Question

3. Heads Together

4. A Number is Called

Available as a poster from Kagan Cooperative Learning

Simultaneous Numbered Heads

Simultaneous Numbered Heads Together can be accomplished several ways. One way is to have all number ones give a choral response on the count of three. Another approach is for each student with the number called to write the answer on a piece of scratch paper or slate and then hold it up when directed to do so. A third approach is to have all number threes go to the board to designated team spots and write the answer.

The advantage here is that everybody is involved at the same time and different answers can be contrasted and/or corrected. With Simultaneous Numbered Heads Together there is far more active participation and you know what each team has done.

Comments on your use of Numbered Heads Together:

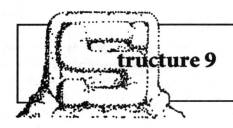

Structure 9 **Pairs**

See Lessons
1, 5, 6, 7, 8, 9, 10, 13,
21, 22, 23, 26, 35, 36

Steps of Pairs

1. Forming pairs.
2. Teacher provides task.
3. Pairs work; teacher monitors.
4. Teacher asks for response.

Pairs is one of the most versatile structures you can use. It is simply having students pair up to work as directed. It might be used to discuss information from a lecture. You might direct the students to pair-up and work on an assignment just given. You may have formal pairs outside of the teams, as in selected pairs who will regularly meet for pair reading, or informal pairs who may only work together once, or in Corners when you say, "Talk to the person next to you about...." The difference between Pairs and Think-Pair-Share is that Pairs does not always follow a think time or precede a share time, and Pairs can involve a wider range of activities.

pairs and begin working quickly. If you are pairing students for the first time, either pair up students sitting next to one another or have them move to assigned study-buddies. If you already have your class divided into teams of four, who sit together, you can have the the four divide into two pairs.

2. Directions For Task

You might be lecturing; stop, and ask Pairs to discuss that last point you made. Pairs could be directed to work out a math problem which uses the process you have been describing. If you are reading to the class, you could ask Pairs to write five descriptive adjectives which would be appropriate to describe a character, place, or object in the story.

3. Pairs Work; Teacher Monitors

Steps of Pairs

1. Forming Pairs

It's usually best to prearrange the pairs if you want the students to move into

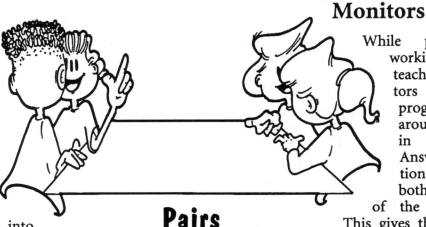

Pairs

While pairs are working, the teacher monitors their progress. Walk around, listen in on pairs. Answer questions only if both members of the pair ask. This gives the message that pairs must work together and cooperate. Your moni-toring will give you an opportunity to acknowledge appropriate on task behavior. You can affirm various pairs for their work together and point out the use of social skills you are trying to reinforce.[1]

4. Teacher Asks For Feedback

Feedback is important because it holds the pairs accountable for being on task. If pairs know that you are going to be asking for individual responses, then they are much more likely to be on task. This feedback could be asking randomly selected pairs to respond to a question. If it calls for a short response, have pairs write the answer down on a slate. Pairs could be numbered off one and two. "All number ones write the answer," [writing time], "Now hold it up so I can see it." This allows individual accountability and a method to check for understanding.

Comments on your use of Pairs:

---

1. Have a norm in the classroom: when in Pairs, if you don't understand, ask your partner. If you both give up, then two hands go up to show it is a "Pair Question." Similarly, four hands up during teamwork means the students have a "Team Question."

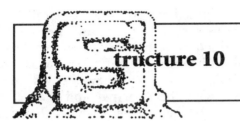

See Lessons
15, 17, 36

Structure 10 **Pairs Compare**

Steps of Pairs Compare

1. Teacher assigns pairs and teams of two pairs each.
2. Teacher asks pairs to discuss a question or issue.
3. Pairs discuss question or issue.
4. Pairs compare what they discussed with another team pair.

When you want to increase interaction between students, Pairs Compare is one way to do this within your current team structures. I usually have students in teams of four students, and within the teams they are in working pairs. One advantage to this structure is the high degree of simultaneity present here. When pairs are involved fifty percent of your class is talking, while the other fifty percent is listening.

Steps of Pairs Compare

1. Teacher assigns pairs and teams of two pairs each

I usually assign students to pairs who are different in some way, but can work together. With my class of 5/6th grade students,

Pairs Compare

I have pairs of boys and girls. Since I have an equal proportion of boys and girls it works out that each team has one pair of boys and one pair of girls. How you develop pairs will depend on the variables associated with your class.

2. Teacher asks pairs to discuss a question or issue

Questions or issues can relate to a subject you are presenting in class or have already covered. Let's say you are teaching a unit on the Aztec, Maya, and Inca cultures. You might ask your pairs to discuss the differences in farming practices among these three cultures. The complexity of your question will determine the amount of time you will need to allow each pair to discuss the question.

3. Pairs discuss question or issue

During this step I ask pairs to discuss the question only with their partner. Let the pairs know the time limit so each person will have an opportunity to share. Generally, I begin this structure allowing only two-three minutes. As they become familiar with the structure, I lengthen the time frame as the question warrants. It is better to begin with too little time than too much time. You can always allow more time if you see that it is needed.

4. Pairs reform with other team pair and compare

Each pair now has an opportunity to summarize what they discussed with their teammates. I usually ask that each pair share what they discussed and look for similarities and differences. You might ask afterwards if they learned more by working together than if they had been on their own. Most students will admit that they learned more working with their partner and then comparing with their team than if they had worked alone.

Comments on your use of Pairs Compare:

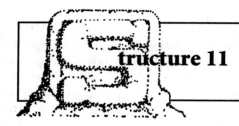

Structure 11

Roundrobin/ Roundtable

See Lessons
1, 2, 3, 7, 8, 9, 10, 11,
12, 13, 14, 15, 16, 17,
18, 21, 24, 25, 26, 27,
29, 30, 31, 32, 33, 36

Steps of Roundrobin

1. Directions by the teacher.
2. Students share or read in turn.

Steps of Roundtable

1. Directions by the teacher.
2. Students take turns in order, writing on a paper.

These are two of the most frequently used structures. Roundrobin and Roundtable both involve students in teams taking turns in order. The difference between the two is that Roundrobin is verbal and Roundtable is written. These are great practice structures and teambuilders.

Roundrobin

Roundrobin can be used in any situation where you want a team to verbally share information of one form or another or to take turns reading. You want to ensure that the information they are to share is general knowledge and not information they have not mastered. Roundrobin is designed to go quickly, it isn't designed for the study of difficult concepts. If you are using it for reading, make sure students have had an opportunity to preread the information, or already know it.

An Example of Roundrobin

Your class has been discussing the differences between affirmations and put-downs. Perhaps they have already done a brainstorming session on this topic. For further review you ask teams to Roundrobin affirmations. This means that they each take turns giving one affirmation that they have heard or used. This task is easy enough that the vast majority of students will be able to do it without any assistance. If a student is stumped then their teammate can provide them with assistance. The important point here is that everyone is sharing in order. An extremely verbal student cannot monopolize. Team accountability can be added by having one student on the team act as a recorder. Often that isn't necessary if you are using Roundrobin for a quick review leading into something else.

Roundtable

Steps of Roundtable

When I want each team member to contribute something in writing, I will often use Roundtable. In Roundtable teams are sitting together with all materials, pencils, books, paper on the floor or under their desks. One sheet of paper and one pencil are on the desk for each team. The students are given a problem or questions to answer. Students take turns writing their answer as the sheet of paper and the pencil are passed around the team. Generally, Roundtable is designed to be quick and is for information which is easily recalled. Sometimes it can be used for a simple project, such as when each student adds an item to a Venn diagram.

Roundtable Examples

Take the example of the group using Roundrobin to share affirmations they had used or heard. The Roundtable extension to this would be to have the students each write down an affirmation they have heard before. This gives you instant individual accountability with contributions of each student in writing. Roundtable writing is simple, but powerful. The teacher provides teams a starter sentence and then each student writes a word or sentence, as the paper is passed around, with the intent to create a story. Students find this enjoyable and everyone is included.

Variation

In Simultaneous Roundtable more than one paper is passed at a time. Example: four papers are labeled, each with the name of a food group. As the students pass the papers they look at the label and add an appropriate food to the paper they receive.

Comments

Both these structures are great for beginning cooperative learning. They are done quickly and have a high success rate. They involve teambuilding by their nature because of the turn taking, helping, and high success rate. Incorporate these structures into your lessons when the opportunity presents itself. Discover where Roundrobin and Roundtable can work for you.

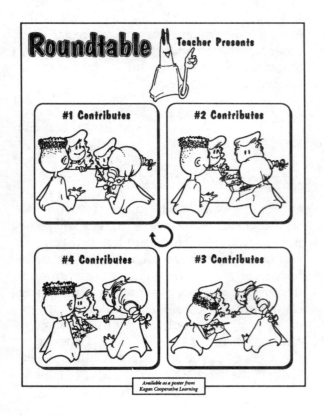

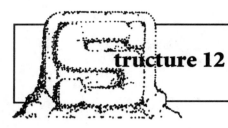

Structure 12 Similarity Grouping

See Lessons
5, 14, 15

Steps of Similarity Grouping

1. Teacher presents a characteristic or preference.
2. Students group with others having a similar response.
3. Students discuss in groups.

Similarity Groups are an energizing way to to have all your students moving quickly while learning more about each other. Their use for classbuilding provides immediately a strong sense of inclusion.

Steps of Similarity Grouping

1. Teacher Presents Dimension

Begin Similarity Grouping by announcing to the class a personal characteristic (number of siblings, number of times you have moved), preference (favorite color, pet, ice cream flavor) or other topic (ending to a story, a reason for getting out of school early).

2. Students With Similar Characteristics Form Groups

Students are to find other students with similar responses and form a group. Similarity Grouping differs from Corners in that the students in Similarity Groups determine how many groups there will be. There is far more discussion and students make their own decisions about where to go.

3. Students Discuss

When students have formed groups, have them discuss their response or use these groups to discuss another related topic.

An Example Of Similarity Groups

I've used Similarity Groups to introduce the concept of conflict in families. I have students form groups by the number of siblings they have. I split groups of more than eight; and when there is one person on their own, I merge this person with another group. I ask those in the groups to pair and discuss if they ever had disagreements with their siblings. For children I might ask about disagreements they might have with their parents. What were the disagreements about? How were they resolved? After pairs discuss these questions in their Similarity Groups, I ask the Similarity Groups to share with the total class. This evolves into an art project (drawing of the family relationships) or an essay on the same topic. I usually use Similarity Groups as an introduction to a unit and as classbuilding.

Similarity Grouping

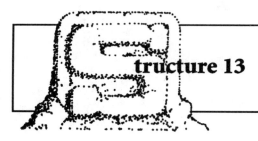

Structure 13 — Talking Chips

See Lessons
13, 16, 33

Steps of Talking Chips

1. Explain rules to students.
2. As each student talks, s/he places his/her "chip" in the center.
3. No chip, no talking.
4. When all chips are down, students retrieve their chips and start over.

We have all seen situations where one student dominates the discussion in their team. You may have wondered about how to equalize the opportunity for participation. One way to do this is through Talking Chips. This structure ensures each student has an opportunity to participate. It also helps you monitor individual accountability.

Steps of Talking Chips
1. Explain rules to students

When students are asked to discuss a topic, ask them to place their chip (pen or pencil will do) into the middle of their desk when they begin to talk. When they finish talking, they are not allowed to contribute again until everyone else has had a turn and placed their "chip" on the desk. When everyone has had an opportunity to speak, everyone picks up their chip (pen or pencil) and the sequence starts again.

2. As each student talks, they place their "chip" in the center

Before a student begins to share they place their "chip", this could be their pen or pencil, in the center of the group. This structure doesn't necessarily control the length of time of what each student has to say. You can place a time limit on individual contributions if it's a problem.

3. No chip, no talking

Once they finish talking they cannot talk until every other "chip" has been tossed into the center. If a student doesn't have anything to share on this particular topic, they can place their chip in the center at the end. If this is a continuous response with one student, then it would be appropriate to discuss this lack of participation with the student.

Talking Chips

4. When all chips are down, students retrieve their chips and start over.

Generally, this structure is used to ensure that each student has an opportunity to participate. It doesn't ensure that all students will participate equally. Once students use this structure you will often see more equal participation, even when not using Talking Chips.

Comments on your use of Talking Chips:

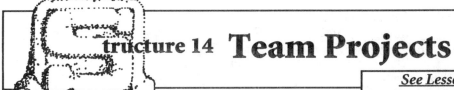

Structure 14 **Team Projects**

See Lessons
7, 12, 16, 17, 19, 26, 34, 35

Steps of Team Projects

1. Teacher assigns topics.
2. Students may have specific roles.
3. Teams complete their project.
4. Teams present the project to class.

There are an infinite number of projects for teams to work on. Team Projects are usually short and easy for the team to accomplish, taking from a few minutes to a class period. This structure promotes teambuilding, decision making and problem solving among team members.

Steps of Team Projects

1. Teacher Assigns Topic

The project assigned to teams can vary from group finger painting for Kindergartners, to a collage of "striving for democracy in the 1990's" for high school students. There are no limits on content except that it be appropriate for the abilities of your students. Clearly define the task for students so that they know what to do and what the time line for doing it is.

Team Projects

2. Students May Have Specific Roles

One way to insure interdependence and individual accountability is to assign roles to team members. Roles depend on the project. For a painting, each student may be responsible for a different color. For a collage, each student might be responsible for a different material (scissors, magazines, newspapers, glue, or markers). Students must understand from the beginning that they each have a role and must participate in developing the project and presenting it to the class.

Sample Roles

Sample roles which might exist throughout the project would be:

- **Gatekeeper** - ensures everyone participates.

- **Timekeeper** - monitors time and lets team know how they are doing.

- **Encourager** - keeps team going with encouraging comments.

- **Affirmer** - affirms teammates for their efforts.

- **Taskmaster** - keeps team on task and brings team back on task if it strays.

- **Materials Monitor** - manages all the materials a team needs for the project.

3. Teams Complete Project

Give teams a specific time to complete the project. Completing Team Projects on time means managing time. You might need to adjust the time if you see that you were unrealistic in your expectations. Hold students accountable for monitoring their own time as they become more experienced in working in teams.

4. Teams Present Project to Class

Set aside a specific time for teams to present their project. It's important for teams to receive recognition for a job well done. It also gives the message that the projects you assign are important. Members of some teams may not be happy with their team project. Have teams process how they could improve on their project if they were to do it again.

Examples Of Simple Projects

Mood Collages - happiness, sadness, depression, love, anger

Team Scrapbook - current events, families, pets, America, South America, cultures

Dioramas - dinosaurs, early New Mexico, ancient Egypt

Holiday Banners

Complicated Projects

If the project is more complex, it is recommended that you use the steps of "Co-op Co-op" rather than Team Projects. Information about "Co-op Co-op" can be found in Cooperative Learning by Spencer Kagan.

Comments on your use of Team Projects:

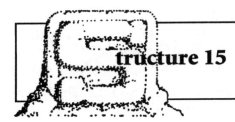

Structure 15   Team Discussion

See Lessons
2, 4, 6, 8, 18, 19,
21, 24, 25, 27, 29

Steps of Team Discussion

1. Teacher asks teams a low consensus question.
2. Teams discuss the question.
3. Students share their ideas with the class or another team.

Team Discussion is a very simple structure: teams discuss an issue or question presented by the teacher. This is an excellent structure to have your students "chew" on information presented during a lecture or video. It is a versatile structure which is used frequently because it allows students to interact with the information. For variety and to increase participation, you can sometimes direct the students into a pair rather than team discussion.

Steps of Team Discussion

1. Teacher Asks Low Consensus Question

If you were studying the westward movement during American History an example of a low consensus question might be, "How did native Americans feel about the coming of the white man?" or "What were the effects on Native American culture resulting from the mass slaughter of the

buffalo?" Team discussion works well with higher level thinking questions which call for analysis and synthesis. Students have the support of teammates to look at different perspectives.

2. Teams Discuss

Students discuss the question within their team. During the first Team Discussion you may have one team model the type of discussion you are looking for. A good way to do this is to ask a question and walk around the room to monitor teams. When you find a team having the type of discussion you would like, ask the team if they are willing to demonstrate what they were discussing for the class.

While all teams are discussing, walk around the room monitoring the teams to ensure they are on task and to listen for the level of thinking occurring. Ensure that the students have the necessary background information to answer the question before the discussion begins.

3. Sharing Ideas

Following the Team Discussion students may share their ideas with the whole class or

Team Discussion

─────**VANSTON SHAW:** *Communitybuilding in the Classroom*─────
Publisher: Kagan Cooperative Learning • 1(800) Wee Co-op
Structure 15   Chapter 6: 41

another team. Because Team Discussions are often followed by sharing, students learn they will be accountable for discussing the question.

Pairs Discussion

Students can be directed to discuss things in pairs rather than teams. Pair discussions have several advantages over team discussions. During the same amount of time, students have more opportunity to speak. Following a pair discussion, pairs, within a team can compare and contrast as they talk as a team.

Variations on Sharing[1]

- **Simultaneous Share** - One member of each team goes to the chalkboard or a chart paper to record their response.

- **Team Notebooks** - Each team records their ideas in a team notebook to be read later by the teacher and/or other teams.

- **Team Share** - Each team exchanges views with the team next to it.

- **Stand Up and Share** - All students discuss an issue until each member of the team has an idea to share. Everyone stands up. Quickly the students begin to tell their ideas around the classroom. After a student speaks, they sit down as well as anyone else in the class that had the same idea or one similar to it.

- **Light bulb!** - The teacher asks students who feel that they have something insightful or important to share.

---

1. From *Cooperative Learning & Language Arts,* 1991 by Jeanne Stone. Published by Resources for Teachers, Inc.

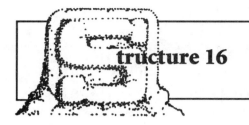

Structure 16　Three-Step-Interview

See Lessons

2, 3, 5, 6, 7, 9, 12, 13, 14, 19, 27, 28, 31, 33

Steps of Three-Step Interview

1. In pairs, one interviews their partner.
2. Students reverse roles.
3. Student pairs meet in teams of four and paraphrase what they heard in the interview in Roundrobin.

Three-Step Interview allows students to interview one another in pairs on a topic, and then paraphrase the results of the interview to their teammates. It involves all students in discussing a question and then using their paraphrasing skills. This is an excellent structure to use to have students relate their personal experience to a topic you are discussing with the class. This structure is designed to be used with teams of four, but can be adapted to teams of three.

Steps of Three-Step Interview

1. Students Interview a Partner

Students begin this structure in pairs, usually as part of a team of four. In each pair one student is an interviewer and the other is an interviewee. Students two and four will be the interviewees. It's a good idea to model it the first time you use this structure so students understand their roles. Discuss and model what happens in a good interview (asking open-ended questions, showing you are listening, asking for details).

2. Students Reverse Roles

In each pair the person who was the interviewer next becomes the interviewee. By the end of this round, both students have been the interviewer and the interviewee.

3. Students Paraphrase in Roundrobin

In a group of four, each take a turn (Roundrobin) paraphrasing what their partner said during the interview.

Variation for Groups of Three

With a group of three, at each step in the process, two team members interview the third member. This allows you to have groups of four with some groups of three. What is missed in the group of three is the paraphrasing aspect.

Example Of Three-Step Interview

If you are starting a unit on attentive listening, you might begin by having the students use the Three-Step Interview structure to find out what they know about attentive listening. They would interview each other in pairs and then Roundrobin share in their team. Listen in to discover how much they already knew about attentive listening. Then begin your unit on attentive listening. You could have students repeat this Three-Step Interview at the end of your unit to evaluate the amount of improvement.

Structure 17 — Think-Pair-Share

See Lessons

1, 2, 4, 5, 6, 7, 11, 12, 14, 16, 17, 18, 20, 22, 23, 25, 26, 27, 29, 30, 31, 32, 33, 34, 35, 36

Steps of Think-Pair-Share

1. Teacher presents a question and asks students to think about a response.
2. Students pair and discuss with a partner.
3. Students share their answers.

Think-Pair-Share is one of the most widely used structures. During a lecture format stop after no more than ten minutes, ask a question about the information presented, and ask the students to Think-Pair-Share. This is a quick way to actively involve all students in the lecture material and assist students to "chew" on the information presented so they can make it their own. This structure is used most often for concept development.

Steps of Think-Pair-Share

1. Think: Teacher Presents a Question/Students Think

Ask a question and give students some time to think about the answer. The amount of think time depends on the difficulty of the question.

2. Pair: Students Discuss the Question in Pairs

After think time, direct students to pair with another student and discuss the question.

It's quicker and provides students with a sense of safety to know who their partner will be. It's certainly all right to mix partners up from time to time, just not on a daily basis. The time you allow students to discuss in pairs will depend on their age, the difficulty of the question, and what you feel is appropriate. If you have an odd number, or one partner is absent, have the extra person meet with one of the pairs to form a triad. A good way to know when students have finished answering the question is to listen to the noise level within the room. Soon after you direct students to answer the question, students will, for the most part, be on task. As they finish, the noise level will drop slightly, and then start moving back up, usually louder than before. This "second talk" is usually about topics other than the question you asked. The time to ask students to stop is when the noise level drops off, and before it climbs.

3. Share: Students Share Their Answer

Once students have finished discussing the question in pairs, it's time to have them share their answers with others in the class. This can be accomplished several ways. You can ask the pairs to share with another pair.[1] If they are in teams of four, then pairs already have a natural pair to share with. Another option is for you to call on individual students. I never ask who would

---

1. If pairs share with another pair the structure is called Think-Pair-Share-Square.

like to answer. By randomly calling on individual students you are creating a sense of individual accountability. Students need to know you expect them to seriously discuss the question and that they will be held accountable.

An Example Of Think-Pair-Share

I was discussing with my class the benefits of using affirmations as opposed to put-downs. I asked students to think of the last time they remember giving an affirmation to someone. Then I asked students to pair with a partner and share that experience. The result was total involvement. How often have you asked questions and had only two to four students raise their hand to answer? Think-Pair-Share involves the whole class in answering your question and interacting with the information presented. It's difficult not to participate in a pair.

Available as a poster from
Kagan Cooperative Learning Co.

Chapter 7 | # Lessons

Introduction

It isn't enough to know why classbuilding, teambuilding, and relationships skill building are important. It isn't enough to only know the different cooperative learning structures. This part provides you with the meat and the potatoes. Here are actual lessons you can use with your students. These lessons have been field tested by educators of different grade levels and socioeconomic areas. The key will be for you to choose the lessons which are appropriate for you and your students.

Sequence of Lessons

These lessons are designed for you to use as you begin the school year and choose to intentionally build a sense of class and to develop the relationship skills of your students. They are sequenced in the order I might use them at the beginning of the year towards the end of the year. They begin with several classbuilding lessons. Next will come relationship skill building lessons, followed by teambuilding. I start with classbuilding because I feel it's important to develop class identity and relationship skills before I form permanent teams. If you choose to form teams earlier, and that works for you, then do it. Realize as you do these lessons, you are the person who decides when and which lessons to use.

Lesson Format

Each lesson is written in a similar format with Lesson-At-A-Glance, Structures, Lesson Overview, and Lesson Sequence as the main headings. This consistent format will make it easier for you to know what to expect as you move from lesson to lesson.

Concrete or Jello

As you use these lessons realize that they are yours. If you come up with a structure which works better for you in a particular lesson, then use it. These lessons were not made in concrete and are to be revised as you need to. As you find approaches which work for you, please contact me and let me know how you have modified it to meet your needs.

Process vs. Content

What I have tried to present in this book is as much a process for approaching Communitybuilding as it is lesson content. It's more important to establish a supportive, trusting climate within your classroom than to worry about sticking closely to the content presented in these lessons. One goal I have is for you to integrate the concepts behind Communitybuilding into how you approach teaching. As you develop academic content, you will also develop an awareness of how students relate to one another as they study and learn this content. The processes we use to teach our content are as important as the content itself. Cooperative learning is a process. It is a process which evolves as a teaching skill over time. The lessons presented here can provide you a vehicle to present this process to your class and develop a class climate conducive to greater academic and social achievement.

Simultaneous Interaction

One goal of using these cooperative structures is to involve students actively with the information they are learning as often as possible. Spencer Kagan introduced this concept to me a few years ago as simultaneous interaction. Simultaneous interaction is one of the principles of cooperative learning Spencer teaches in the workshops he conducts for teachers throughout North America.

For an example of the difference between traditional and simultaneous interaction, let's look at a high school history class. At the end of a lecture session, the teacher might ask students to respond to the lecture. Invariably, the same few hands will shoot up into the air. He/she will call on one of the students. All the other students who had their hands up will be disappointed that they weren't called on. If it looks like the student might give the wrong response, these same hands go back up with glee, hoping they still have a chance. It actually sets up a situation of negative interdependence, where students are hoping the student called on will fail so they will have another opportunity to respond.

If this same teacher were using cooperative structures, he/she might choose to use Think-Pair-Share. At the conclusion of the lecture, the teacher would ask students to **Think** of what was just presented. After a minute or two, he/she would ask students to turn to their partner (**Pair**) and discuss what was presented for a minute or two. Then the teacher would ask a few students to **Share** their experiences with the class.

In the Think-Pair-Share scenario, rather than only one or two students having an opportunity to share their views on the topic, all students have an opportunity to share with a partner. Thus at any one time, 50% of students are talking, on topic. How much more powerful this is for retention of the information and keeping student interest.

The lessons presented here are designed to encourage simultaneous interaction among students. It is also a concept to consider including into your daily lesson planning where ever possible.

Lesson 1 Developing Class Rules

Lesson-At-A-Glance

Goal: Classbuilding (Building Class Identity)
Grades: 4-Adult
Time: 30-40 Minutes

Outcomes — Students Will:
* Collaboratively develop a list of class rules.
* Write and share their list.
* Identify the need for class rules.

Materials:
* Signs to post around room that say Parents, Principal, Teacher, Students
* Pencils and paper for students to develop lists
* Chart paper or butcher paper and colored markers to record student responses

Structures:
* **Corners**
* **Think-Pair-Share**
* **Pairs**
* **Roundrobin**

Lesson Overview

This lesson is designed to include students in the process of developing class rules. Students are more likely to identify with and abide by rules which they helped develop. The teacher gives final approval to the rules. Students are directed to select between corners as to who should make class rules. Students will then Think-Pair-Share class rules.

Lesson Sequence

Corners: Class Rules

(1) Have the four signs in different corners of the room (Principal, Parents, Teachers, Students).

(2) Tell students to look around at the four signs and decide who they feel should make the classroom rules for the year. Tell students to write down their choice on a piece of paper.

(3) Now direct students to go to the corner they have chosen and pair with another student to discuss why they think their choice should design class rules.

(4) Ask for feedback from pairs. Discuss with students your own experience with class rules and how you want the class to be involved in making its own rules. Make it clear that you must feel comfortable with the rules which "we as a class create."

Think-Pair-Share: Class Rules

Think Time

Assign students to pairs and ask students to think of a classroom in w hich the class rules were fair. Give them a minute to think about it without talking.

Pairs Discuss

Ask pairs to list at least three class rules they remember which were fair and they would like to have in their classroom.

Pairs Share

Ask each pair to share one rule they came up with from their list which they feel is extremely important. The person who shares is the person who did not write the list.

As students share lists, you (or a student you select) list them on chart or butcher paper so students can see a record of their responses.

Post & Discuss List

Explain to students that the rules on the list will be used to develop class rules for the year. The list is used for discussion of class rules, the reason for rules, and to make sure we haven't forgotten any important rules. If a rule was not listed which you believe should be there, now is the time to add it to the list.

Teacher Talk

Now you must develop the class rules from the list generated. You have several options. Choose the option which works best for your situation.

1. Choose the rules you want. You could take what students and you have developed and bring the completed "Class Rules" back to class.

2. Have students sign up to stay after school to help you develop the "Class Rule." Those students who choose to help you will meet with you and together you decide on the rules. The students can record the rules developed in their printing on butcher paper. The next day, they can present the rules to the class.

3. Let student teams select one rule they especially want to have. Let students know there are a few rules which you will want also. You could show the students how to use "Spend-A-Buck" to select their choices. Each student would have an imaginary dollar (four quarters) to spend on the rules of their choice. They then spend their buck on the rule or rules they prefer the most.

Note: Refer to Spencer Kagan's book, *Cooperative Learning,* for more ideas about presenting class rules.

Reflections & Affirmations
Pairs: Reflections

Choose questions from those you would like your students to answer below. Assign pairs to discuss how they might answer. Give them a few minutes. Then match pairs to another pair. Now have students in pairs compare their answers.

- How have your feelings about class rules changed?
- How was everyone involved in this process?
- What would you think of this list if it was developed by a teacher without your input?
- Were some of these rules stricter than most teachers would suggest?
- Why might you like to be included in making rules in your home?
- How are citizens involved in making rules for society?
- Why are rules or laws necessary in society?

Roundrobin: Affirmations

Ask students in their teams to take turns giving affirmations. Give students the option of using the openers below, which you can write on the board or an overhead, or coming up with their own. The student whose first name starts closest to the beginning of the alphabet can start. This student will give an appropriate affirmation to the student on their right. The only response a student is to give to an affirmation is, "Thank you." The last student in the team affirms the person who started.

Affirmation Starters:

I liked your idea about.......
I enjoyed working with you because......
You made an important contribution with.......

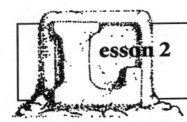

Lesson 2   Alliterative Names

Lesson-At-A-Glance

Goal: Classbuilding (Getting Acquainted)

Grades: 3-Adult

Time: 30-45 Minutes for a class of 32

Outcomes—Students Will:

· Learn class members' names.
· Share personal information.
· Use the cooperative class rule.
· Practice Active Listening in a large group setting.

Materials:

· Posted affirmation starters

Structures:

• **Three-Step Interview**
• **Community Circle**
• **Team Discussions**
• **Think-Pair-Share**

Lesson Overview[1]

Students will have fun while quickly and effectively learning the names of classmates. I've seen adults become very anxious when they were about to do this activity. I find it amazing how well children and adults, who don't think they can remember so many names, do so well.

Lesson Sequence

Teacher Talk: Explain Task

Students Think

Explain to students that they will be coming up with alliterative adjectives to go with their first names. Alliterative means words that

---

1. Adapted from *Tribes: A Process For Social Development And Cooperative Learning* by Jeanne Gibbs.

---

start with the same sound as their first name. Adjective means a word which describes something. Another rule is that the alliterative adjective must be positive (no put-downs). Give students an example using your own name. My name is Vanston. My alliterative adjective is Valiant so my alliterative adjective and first name is Valiant Vanston. Give other examples students might choose: **Bold Billy, Kind Karen**, etc. Now ask students to think of a positive alliterative adjective they could use. Give students a full minute of think time. If they need help, they may consult with a person next to them.

Three-Step Interview:

Share Alliterative Adjective with Partner

Step 1: Students stand is pairs. Person "one" interviews person "two" about what their alliterative adjective and name is and why they chose their alliterative adjective.

Step 2: Person "two" interviews person "one" about what their alliterative adjective and name is and why they chose it.

Step 3: Arrange pairs into teams of four. Each person takes a turn and Roundrobin shares their partner's alliterative adjective, first name, and why they chose their alliterative adjective.

Community Circle: Share Rules

While students sit in the whole class circle discuss the need to know one another's first names and something about each other, tell students that they are going to be playing a game with an alliterative name; the purpose

---

VANSTON SHAW: *Communitybuilding in the Classroom*
Publisher: Kagan Cooperative Learning · 1(800) Wee Co-op
Lesson 2   Chapter 7: 5

of the game is to learn everyone's first name and something about one another.

The rules for this game are that each person will share their alliterative adjective and their first name with the class. However, before they give their adjective and first name they need to repeat all the adjectives and names that have gone before them. The ground rule for this activity is positive statements only ; no put-downs of self or others.

Give students a model by starting first. When I lead this activity I might start off with "I'm Valiant Vanston." Then direct the student on your right or left to be second. They should begin with your adjective and first name. In my class, the person to my right would start with "Valiant Vanston" and then add their adjective and name: "I'm Super Sue." Person three would say, "Valiant Vanston, Super Sue, and I'm Enlightened Elena."

Helpful Hints

Helping is OK

Mention to the class that if they get stuck they can ask for help from someone near them. Most students will be surprised by how well they remember the names as they go around. When the last student finishes, it's time for you to try to remember the entire class. Don't worry if you make mistakes. That's part of the fun of this activity and shows your students that you are human too.

Intervene if Necessary

Occasionally, students will offer put-downs of classmates for the names they choose or students will choose adjectives which are self put-downs. You may choose to intervene immediately and gently remind the class of the "no put-downs" rule and that the adjectives must be "positive." If an adjective

is borderline I usually let it pass. Often it's a good lesson for the person who chooses a less than positive adjective to live with the adjective for awhile.

Second Chance

After everyone has taken a turn and chosen their positive alliterative adjectives, encourage students to change their adjective if they wish. Often these adjectives will stay with students for some time to come and it is important to give them a second chance to feel more comfortable with their choice.

Variations

If you are doing this activity with younger students you can use such adjectives as: colors, number, ice cream flavors, or any positive adjective (i.e. "I'm Red Ronnie").

Reflections & Affirmations

Team Discussion: Reflections

- What was it like coming up with a positive alliterative adjective?

- How have your feelings changed since you entered the room this morning?

- What was the advantage of being at the beginning of the circle?

- What was the advantage of being at the end of the circle?

- Was it sometimes easier to think of something not so positive as an adjective?

- Would it be fun for you and your family to come up with positive alliterative adjectives for your parents, brothers and sisters?

- Could you select a second, equally acceptable, positive alliterative adjective?

- Why do you think it's easy to think of something negative?

Think-Pair-Share: Affirmations

Explain the importance of affirmations. Post the incomplete statements below so everyone can see them. Have students in pairs give each other an appropriate affirmation.

Affirmation Starters:

_____, thanks for your alliterative adjective. I liked it.

Good job remembering, _____.

_____, you're great!

~ ❁ ~

───────**VANSTON SHAW:** *Communitybuilding in the Classroom*───────
Publisher: Kagan Cooperative Learning • 1(800) Wee Co-op

Lesson 2   Chapter 7: 7

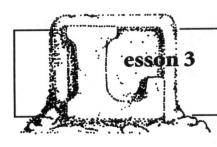

Sharing Shields

Lesson-At-A-Glance

Goal: Classbuilding (Getting Acquainted)

Grades: 3-Adult

Time: 15-30 Minutes

Outcomes — Students Will:
- Share information about themselves.
- Become better acquainted.
- Share feelings.
- Actively listen in small and large group settings

Materials:
- Copy of the Shield on 8 1/2" by 11" paper or blank 5" x 7" card for each student and a pencil
- Reflection questions on board, overhead, or ditto
- Posted affirmation starters
- Shield Handout
- Pencils or colored crayons or markers

Structures:
- **Roundrobin**
- **Three-Step Interview**

Lesson Overview

This is an opportunity for individuals within the classroom to share information about themselves in a safe manner. They will write and share personal information they are willing to reveal to others.

Lesson Sequence
Teacher Talk:

Explain the Task

Hand out either the 8 1/2" X 11" shield, or 5 x 7 card. Check to be sure all students have pencils, colored crayons or markers.

Directions for What to Write, Demonstration

Middle: In the middle band of the shield students are to write a positive adjective in front of their first name. Give an example. I use Valiant Vanston. Tell students "If you get stuck, ask a neighbor for help."

Upper Left Corner: Write or draw your favorite TV program.

Upper Right Corner: Write the name or draw a picture of your favorite sport or game.

Lower Left Corner: Write or draw what you enjoy doing the most in the summer.

Lower Right Corner: Write or draw what you would like most to learn in school this year.

Random Team Formation or Mix-Freeze-Group:

Share Cards

Tell students they will use Roundrobin to share different parts of their shields as you give them directions. They are to stay with their partners, until you give them the signal to switch.

a. Pairs: Find a partner in the room you haven't talked with today and share your alliterative adjective and favorite TV program (upper left corner). Students move, locate a partner, and share. (Give them two minutes to share.)

b. Triads: Find two new partners and tell your name and favorite sport or game (upper right corner).

c. Groups: Find three new partners (group of four), and tell your name and what you enjoy doing most in the summer (the lower left corner).

d. Groups: Find three new partners (another group of four). Share what you would like most to do in school this year (the lower right corner).

Variations

Other ideas for shields: favorite colors, numbers, car, movie, sports team, movie star, teacher, subject, vacation; or their goal for the week, month, semester, career.

Reflections & Affirmations
Three-Step Interview:
Reflections

Have the reflection questions on the board, overhead, or ditto. Direct students to answer the questions within the last group of four. They are to answer the questions using a Three-Step Interviewing procedure.

Step 1. Person one in each pair asks their partner one of the questions; partner answers.
Step 2. Partners reverse roles.

Step 3. Pairs team up in another pair to form groups of four. They then take turns paraphrasing what their partners said.

∾ What kinds of new information did you find out about each other?

∾ Was this lesson fun? If so, what made it enjoyable?

∾ Was it more difficult to share in your first group or last? Why?

∾ How could you have changed anything you've written on your card?

∾ What would it be like to make a family shield at home?

Roundrobin: Affirmations
(Done with last group)

Ask students in the last group to think about affirmations they might give the members in this group. Have students Roundrobin to share appropriate affirmations. Remind students they can refer to the posted affirmation starters if they need to. In the group of four, have partners paraphrase the affirmation starters to the other members of their group. Remind those who receive affirmations that their only response can be "Thank you."

Wonder Years

Skiing Tennis

Valiant Vanston

Hiking Relaxing

How to teach 5/6 combination class

Affirmation Starters:

Thank you for sharing about.......

I enjoyed when you shared.......

I liked it when..........

You are a good............

∾ ❊ ∾

*(Permission to reproduce for
classroom use.)*

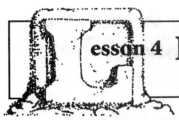

esson 4 Pass the Feather Sharing

Lesson-At-A-Glance

Goal: Classbuilding (Getting Acquainted)
Grades: K-Adult
Time: 20-40 Minutes
Outcomes — Students Will:
• Share information about themselves.
• Line up.
• Actively Listen in a large group setting.
Materials:
• Teacher generates a question
• A starter sentence on the board
• A feather or another object to pass
• Affirmation starters posted
Structures:
• **Line-Ups**
• **Community Circle**
• **Team Discussion**
• **Think-Pair-Share**

Lesson Overview[1]

This is an excellent way to start or end of the day. "Pass The Feather" allows all students an opportunity to share in a whole class setting. While students are in a Community Circle remind them of class rules such as using affirmations and appropriate relationship skills. The more often you do this type of lesson, the more comfortable students will be. The person holding the feather is the person who shares. The feather[2] is then passed to the next student.

---

1. This lesson was adapted from *Tribes: A Process For Social Development And Cooperative Learning* by Jeanne Gibbs.

2. Don't get stumped if you can't come up with a feather. Bill Richards, 5th grade teacher at Waterford Elemen-

Lesson Sequence

Line-Up: Alphabetical by Last Letter in First Name

Have students line-up by the last letter of their first name. For example the last letter of my first name (Vanston) is "N," so I might be towards the middle. Ask another student to tell the last letter of their first name. Have this student state where they might line-up. Let students know they can help each other. This should be a different order then they are used to. After they line up, have students turn their line into a circle. When they are finished, start with the first student in the line. Ask the student to say the last letter of their first name and then their name, e.g. "N, Vanston." Go around the circle and give each student a turn.

Note: For K-1, you might have them line up alphabetically by first letter of their first name.

Community Circle:

Students Share Favorite Food

Now the students are in a large circle facing in. Primary students can sit on the floor, older students or adults can sit in their chairs or on the floor.

Introduction and Class Rules

Explain to students that this is a community or class circle and that the goal of this lesson

---

tary School in Waterford, California reported that, since he didn't have a feather to start with he substituted a red wooden block. From then on that red block became the "feather" for his class.

is to share information about ourselves and have fun. Review the class rules for this structure:

- Taking Turns
- Affirmations only - no put-downs
- Right to Pass[3]
- Active Listening
- Only the person with the feather speaks

Teacher Models: Starter Sentence for the Class

You need to go first in this activity. Have class starter sentences on the board with blanks (see next page for examples) while holding the feather. Another option for younger children is to have them pass a starter sentence strip rather than the feather[4], or use a Think Pad to write down their answer.

"My favorite food is _____ because _____"

"My favorite food is mashed potatoes because I always think of my grandmother when I eat them."

Students Pass the Feather

Explain to students that you would like them to name their favorite food and why they like it. Start with the student sitting next to you. It helps the first few times you use this lesson format to have a willing student start off. Hand the student the feather. If a student wants to pass, go to the next student. After everyone has had a turn, ask this student a second time if they would like to share their sentence yet. If they still choose to pass tell them "thank you" and move on to the next student.

---

3. Right to pass is used when students are sharing personal information. It allows students to trust their feelings of safety and to make a decision to share or not to share. Trust the process. It's all right if a few students pass. Always give students who chose to pass another opportunity to share before you finish.

4. This suggestion came from Mary Torrens Parker of Cunningham School in Turlock, California.

Reflections & Affirmations

Team Discussion: Reflections

- What did you feel was difficult about this lesson?
- How did it feel to share something about yourself with the class?
- What did you find out that you didn't know about one another?
- How did this activity help you to know one another better?
- If you could share a second answer with the class, what would it be?

Think-Pair-Share: Affirmations

This is an excellent time to practice affirmations. Model affirmations by giving one to a specific student about what they said. An example might be: "Sheryl, I enjoyed your telling us about your new sister. Thank you." Place students in pairs. Ask them to think of an appropriate affirmation to give their partner. Have students refer to the posted affirmation starters if they get stuck.

Affirmation Starters:

Starter gambits are helpful:

"I enjoyed your sharing..........."

"I felt good when you shared.........."

"Thank you for sharing about........."

"You are good at........."

～ ✿ ～

Starter Sentences for Community Circle

(*Note:* Modify sentences and words to fit
your grade and students.)

1. My favorite _____ is _____ because
   _____ .

   Possibilities:
   toy, color, car, friend, book, movie, TV program, food, restaurant,
   shirt/dress, candy, fruit, vegetable, animal, pet, tree, vehicle for
   transportation, singer, movie star, friend, athlete _____ .

2. I have fun when I go _____ because _____ .

   Possibilities:
   to the movies, to the store, shopping, to town, to grandmother's,
   to the country, to the mountains, out to eat, to recess, running, to play.

3. I feel (happy, sad, lovable, angry, upset, scared) when ....

4. The funniest (scariest, biggest, saddest) thing is ....

5. When I think of (orange, blue, black, red) I think of ....

6. Today I feel ......

7. If I were an (animal, color, building, car, TV character) I would be
   _____ .

8. When I grow up, I want to be _____ .

9. (Sunshine, wind, rain, clouds, thunder) make me feel ....

   [*Could be content oriented:*
   My favorite scene was _____ because _____.
   The greatest President was _____ because _____.
   The strongest character in the novel was _____ because _____.
   The experiment proves _____ because _____.
   The hardest part of the project was _____ because _____.]

—————— **VANSTON SHAW:** *Communitybuilding in the Classroom* ——————
Publisher: Kagan Cooperative Learning • 1(800) Wee Co-op

Lesson 4   Chapter 7: 15

esson 5 Student Search

Lesson-At-A-Glance

Goal: Classbuilding (Getting Acquainted)

Grades: 3-Adult

Time: 25-45 Minutes

Outcomes — Students Will:
- Talk with one another and ask questions.
- Sign their names in appropriate places on others' Student Search handout.
- Share personal information.
- Exhibit ability to ask others' questions.

Materials:
- Student Search Handout for each student
- Timer and way to let class know when 30 seconds is up. This could be a bell, whistle, or switching the lights off/on.
- Post reflection questions and affirmation Starters

Structures:
- **Pairs**
- **Three-Step Interview**
- **Think-Pair-Share**

Lesson Overview

This lesson is designed so students make Similarity Groups and then have others in the room sign their Student Search handouts if they meet the criterion described. Three sample Student Searches are attached. Others can be developed with your own students in mind. This is an excellent lesson to develop inclusion very quickly.

Lesson Sequence

Teacher Talk:

Introducing the Lesson

Discuss with students that we all have differences and that sometimes students don't know very much about the other students in class. This will be an opportunity to find out more about fellow students.

Teacher Talk:

Explain Student Search

(Variation of instructions for Student Search #3 are at the bottom of that handout.) Tell students that they will be given a handout that has descriptions written on it. Their job is to gather signatures of as many different students as possible on their Student Search Handout. During the first five minutes, they will form pairs and alternate with their partner asking questions from their search sheet until they each can sign only one place on their partner's sheet or they are given the thirty second signal, whichever comes first. They will continue exchanging with different partners every 30 seconds till the 5 minutes is up.

Pairs:

Distribute Student Search Handout

Distribute Student Search Handout. Before students start, explain that they are to get as many different students to sign their Student Search Handout as they can in the next five minutes. Remind them that they will only have 30 seconds in each pair to get a signature. <u>Students should sign in only one space on any one handout</u>. Ask students to repeat the rules. Answer any questions. Tell students you will let them know when to switch pairs.

Students Find Others On Their Own

When five minutes are up, tell students they are on their own in filling out the rest. They must interview students with whom they haven't yet talked. Let this go on until it looks like most have filled up their student search handout. When you are ready to quit, then have students stop.

Reflections & Affirmations

Three-Step Interview: Reflections

Give one of the questions below. Ask students to think of their answer. Have students pair with a teammate or have prearranged pairs. They discuss their answer to the questions below in their pair. Then have two pairs spin together for a team of four.

Step 1: One student in the pair asks the other the question. The student answers.

Step 2: The students change roles.

Step 3: Two pairs form a team and students each take a turn paraphrasing their partners response to the question.

- What kinds of new information did you find out about classmates?
- What did you find out that surprised you?
- How did the Similarity Groups help in the student search questionnaire?
- Which was easier, the thirty seconds and switch, or on your own? Why?
- How was the Similarity Groups <u>different</u> from the student search?
- How was the Similarity groups <u>similar</u> to the student search?
- How might you use this type of a student search sheet in your home?

Think-Pair-Share: Affirmations

Quickly review the use of appropriate affirmations if necessary. Have students work in the pairs they have been in. Ask students to think of an appropriate affirmation for their partner. Refer to the affirmation starters which you will have posted. Students can use these if needed.

Affirmation Starters:

_____, thanks for signing my sheet.

I liked the way you laughed.

I appreciate your help.

STUDENT SEARCH #1

FIND A STUDENT WHO:

1. Has four or more pets at home. _____

2. Doesn't like chocolate cake. _____

3. You don't know very well. _____

4. Has more than one TV at home. _____

5. Went to a park within the last month. _____

6. Likes to eat the skin on oranges. _____

7. Can roll tongue into a U. _____

8. Likes scary movies. _____

9. Went to a scary movie within the last three months. _____

10. Knows who _____ is. _____

11. Likes to go swimming in the summer. _____

12. Has played in the snow. _____

13. Is good at math. _____

14. Has taken a ride in a boat. _____

15. Laughs a lot. _____

16. Hasn't signed this sheet yet. _____

_____

_____

(Permission to reproduce for classroom use)

STUDENT SEARCH #2

FIND A STUDENT WHO:

1.   Plays sports on the weekend._____

2.   Has gone to a museum in the past year._____

3.   Enjoys listening to music._____

4.   Likes chocolate cake._____

5.   Is new to this school._____

6.   You would like to get to know better._____

7.   Has a sister and brother._____

8.   Has a pet bird or fish at home._____

9.   Watches sports on TV._____

10. Has the same number of brothers and sisters as you do. _____

11. Likes the color blue._____

12. Wore the color red yesterday._____

13. Likes to read at home_____

14. Has gone to the library in the past month._____

15. Hasn't signed this sheet._____, _____

(Permission to reproduce for classroom use)

STUDENT SEARCH #3

Self / Friends

1. Favorite Color _____/_____

2. Favorite Movie Star _____/_____

3. Month You Were Born In _____/_____

4. I Am The (Only, Youngest, Middle, Oldest) Child _____/_____

5. Favorite Sport _____/_____

6. TV Show You Like The Most _____/_____

7. Favorite Pet _____/_____

8. Blocks You Live From School _____/_____

9. Astrological Sign _____/_____

10. Favorite Food For Dinner _____/_____

11. Hair Color _____/_____

12. Last Affirmation You Gave Someone _____/_____

Instructions: Fill in the answers for <u>yourself.</u> Then find another student and ask him/her for a match. If you get a yes, sign each other's Student Search Sheet. If you get a no, that person asks you a question looking for a match. Continue alternating asking questions until you find a match, then form new pairs. Try to get all your boxes filled in <u>by different students.</u>

(Adapted from a people hunt from *Cooperative Learning* by Spencer Kagan who adapted it from Laurel Robertson.)

(Permission to reproduce for classroom use)

Lesson 6 Developing a Class Name

Lesson-At-A-Glance

Goal: Classbuilding (Building Class Identity)
Grades: 2-Adult
Time: 45-60 Minutes
Outcomes — Students Will:
• Choose a class name by voting.
• Collaborate in making the choice of the class name.
• Participate in group discussion.
• Practice using a prioritizing system.

Materials:
• One sheet of butcher paper for each group
• Enough blue, yellow, and red stickers so each student has several or one set of blue, yellow, and red felt tip pens per team.
• Affirmation starters posted

Structures:
• **Think-Pair-Share**
• **Brainstorming**
• **Team Discussion**
• **Three-Step Interview**
• **Pairs**

Lesson Overview

This is an opportunity for the class to participate in a decision making process as the class chooses a name for itself. Teams first brainstorm possible names. Teams then discuss the merits of each name and use a prioritizing system to select their top two choices. Next, all teams write their choices on the same piece of butcher paper. This is posted. Individuals then use a color coded prioritizing system to select the class name. The name with the most points becomes the class name.

Lesson Sequence

Think-Pair-Share:

Why Names are Important

1. Ask students to think about why names are important. Why is their name important? Why is a school or city name important?
2. Students pair with another student and discuss why names are important. Give students only a few minutes to do this.
3. Ask several students to share with the class the reasons they came up with for names being important.

Teacher Talk:

Discuss the Procedure

Explain to the class that they are going to choose a class name. First, teams will brainstorm the names their team might want. Then their team will choose the two possibilities they like the best. Next, each individual class member will pick the names they like the best. The name with the most points will become the class name.

Brainstorming:

Teams Brainstorm Class Names

Ask students to form their teams and prepare to brainstorm. They need to select a scribe/recorder, speed captain, sultan of silly, and a superintendent of suspended judgment[1]. Review the role responsibilities. Review the four S's of brainstorming with the

1. Review Brainstorming in Part II: Structures.

class. Direct teams to brainstorm as many possible names for the class as they can. Teams brainstorm names. Teams discuss which names they prefer and why. When teams are finished discussing names explain the point system for selecting their teams top choices.

Color-Coded Prioritizing[2]:
Teams Select Favorite Class Name

Show an overhead or have a poster with the point system indicated as follows:

BLUE   = 25 Points
RED   = 15 Points
YELLOW = 5 Points

Explain that each student will have one of each colored sticker and will use each sticker to select their top three choices for names (or students will be able to make one mark with each colored pen for their top three choices). Students should use the blue sticker for the one they like the best. Red for their second choice and yellow for their third choice. Remember students only use each sticker once. Pass out one set of colored stickers for each student. Check for understanding by having students explain what they are to do with the stickers (or pens). When you are satisfied that they understand have them proceed.

Note: You can use the Spend-A-Buck structure for the prioritizing. In this case, each student would have four quarters to spend however they choose to select their favorite name.

Students Select Top Choices and Add up Points

Students place their stickers next to their top three choices on their list. Let students know that they must choose a different name for each sticker. Each student takes a turn. When they have all placed their stickers have students add up the points received for each name on their list. Have teams identify their top two choices (those with the most points) by circling them or placing a star next to them.

Teams Record Choices on Class List

Have the recorder from each team list their team's two top choices for the class name on a class list. Post this list so that all teams can see it.

Team Discussion:
Teams Discuss Pro's and Con's

Ask teams to look at all the names listed and discuss in their teams the pro's and con's of the various names. Give the students several minutes to discuss the names. Now ask for teams to share their conclusions. Why do they prefer one name over another? What should a class name convey to others?

Color-Coded Prioritizing:
Class Selects Class Name

Now review the prioritizing point system used earlier. Remind students that each of the colors represent a different number of points:

BLUE = 25, RED = 15, & YELLOW = 5

When their team is called each student is to individually select their top three choices from the chart. Have teams take turns during the day selecting their top choices.

Another option would be to do this step the next day after the class has had time to think it over. Whenever you have students come up to make their choices, monitor to make sure they are doing it correctly.

2. I first heard about this in *"Tribe's: A Process for Social Development & Cooperative Learning"* by Jeanne Gibbs

Representative from Each Team Adds up Points

Have a representative from each team add up the points for each name. They need to identify the top three vote winners. The top vote winner becomes the class name.

Reflections & Affirmations

Three-Step Interview: Reflections

Students will do their reflection questions in their teams using the Three-Step Interview structure. In pairs they will interview each other on the questions and then Roundrobin paraphrase what the person they interviewed said. Review the steps for Three-Step Interview as detailed in Chapter Two.

- What was the most difficult part of this lesson for your team?

- What could your team do to improve your decision making process?

Pairs: Affirmations

Divide teams into pairs. Have pairs discuss what affirmations would be appropriate for their teammates. Next pairs return to their teams and share affirmations. Have affirmation starters posted.

—————**VANSTON SHAW:** *Communitybuilding in the Classroom*—————
Publisher: Kagan Cooperative Learning • 1(800) Wee Co-op

Lesson 6   Chapter 7: 25

esson 7 Class Banner

Lesson-At-A-Glance

Goals: Classbuilding (Building Class Identity)

Grades: 2-Adult

Time: One to two class periods

Outcomes — Students Will:

- Create a class banner.
- Cooperate as they create this banner.
- Participate in group discussion and planning.
- Work together on a simple project.

Materials:

- One sheet of butcher paper large enough for a class banner (8' X 2')
- One smaller piece of butcher paper for each team which can be attached to the larger class banner
- Felt pens, glue, paste, scissors, construction paper, and other items as needed by the teams
- Think Pads

Structures:

- **Pairs**
- **Roundrobin**
- **Team Project**
- **Three-Step Interview**
- **Think-Pair-Write-Share**

Lesson Overview

This will be an opportunity to create a class banner which can represent your class. <u>Prerequisites to this lesson are choosing a class name and team name.</u> The teacher will introduce the idea of a class banner. In pairs, students will try to recall banners they have seen and tell the class about them. Then in pairs, they will explore what the class banner might look like while consulting with other pairs in the room. Next, they will get back together in their teams to discuss their portion of the class banner so that it will fit the overall theme. The Team Project will be for team members to design and create their part of the class banner.

Lesson Sequence

Pairs:

Discuss Why a Class Banner is Important

Explain to students that each team will contribute to a class banner which will have the class name on it and other art work to represent each of the teams within the class. In pairs (within teams), students are to discuss why it might be valuable to have a class banner. Pairs discuss and share with the class when called by the teacher.

Roundrobin:

Team Members Share and List Ideas

Pairs are to regroup with their team and take turns explaining ideas they have for a class banner. A recorder on each team will list the team's ideas on a piece of butcher paper. It can then be posted for the class to see.

Team Project:

Team Creates A Part of the Class Banner

Tell the teams that their part of the class banner needs to be a particular size. If the banner is 8' X 2' and you have eight teams in your room then each team could have two square feet of space. Make templates for the teams to use so they know exactly how much space they have. The templates might be 2' X 1' or 1' X 2'. Let students know which edge is the top, so the team doesn't make something that must be turned on its side to fit into the banner.

Roles

Assign each student a different role. Most of the teams will be doing something with art materials. The roles might be:

#1 - Materials Monitor - passes out materials and turns them in.

#2 - Taskmaster - Helps team members get the job done.

#3 - Encourager - Gets everyone to participate

#4 - Time Captain - Watches the time on task, and hurries team alone.

Answer any questions students have and turn them loose to create. Give the teams a time limit to finish their portion of the banner.

Present Their Portion of the Banner to the Class

Have each team present their portion of the banner and then they will attach it to the banner. Your class name could go above the class banner or be superimposed over it. Let the class decide. This is a very powerful time for the class and the teams. They are creating something which each team has ownership for and at the same time represents the entire class.

Reflections & Affirmations

Three-Step Interview: Reflections

Select questions you want students to answer. Show it on an overhead or on the board.

Step One: One student in the pair asks the other the question. The student answers.

Step Two: The students change roles.

Step Three: The team reforms and students each take a turn paraphrasing their partners response to the question.

- How did your group go about deciding what to do?

- Why was this easy or difficult for your team?

- What does a class banner represent?

- What could you do differently to help your team be more successful?

- If you made a banner for your family, what might it look like?

Think-Pair-Write-Share: Affirmations

Have students think about what kinds of affirmations they could give other teams. Pair with your partner and discuss what kinds of affirmations you would give to another team. Pairs form teams of four, write their affirmations on think pads and give to another team.

esson 8 Animal Corners

Classbuilding
• *Valuing Individual Differences*

Lesson-At-A-Glance

Goals: Classbuilding (Valuing Individual Differences)

Grades: 2-Adult

Time: 30-45 Min. (depending on the sophistication of the students and the depth of the questions)

Outcomes — Students Will:

- Appreciate individual differences.
- Make individual choices and enumerate reasons for their choices.
- Reflect on individual differences.
- Share feelings.
- Listen and paraphrase.

Materials:

- Signs with animals, names or drawings (Deer, Bear, Dove, Lion)
- Paper and pencil for each team
- Reflection question and affirmation starters posted.
- Think Pad for each student

Structures:

- **Corners**
- **Pairs**
- **Roundrobin**
- **Paraphrase Passport**
- **Team Discussion**
- **Round Table**

Lesson Overview

It's important for students to value individual differences. Students will have an opportunity to make choices which differ from other students'. This lesson allows students the opportunity to make an individual choice in selecting which animal they like or identify with. Then they write

their choice down and go to the sign representing the animal they chose. In the group they pair-up and share the reasons they chose the animal. Students then share in their group and with the whole class.

Lesson Sequence

Post Signs: In Four Corners

Post the four signs (Deer, Bear, Dove, Lion) in four different corners of the room. They can be covered or uncovered depending on your preference. If this is the first time you've used corners, they can be uncovered because students will not be familiar with the procedure. If you use corners with more than one set of signs you might want to cover the signs from view and uncover them when you are ready to proceed.

Teacher Talk: Introduction

Introduce Corners to the class by asking students to look at the signs around the room of the different animals they might find in the wild.

Corners: Students Think and Write

Direct students to think of the animal they identify with: the animal students might want to see, or the animal who is the fiercest, or for any other reason. Tell students to silently make their choice and to write that choice down on their think pad (or on a piece of paper). If they cannot read, then you can number the animals 1-4, and they can write the number of the animal they chose. You can also color code the signs. Give students 30-60 seconds of think time to decide which animal to choose.

Pairs: Go to the Sign and Discuss

Direct students to go to the sign of the animal they chose. Now students form pairs or triads to discuss why they chose the animal they did. Pairs are what I use most often. This discussion time needs to be only long enough for everyone to share, usually one to four minutes depending on the age and communication skills of your students.

Note: I use triads for a change of pace. Also, I find that for short tasks it's not as easy to get off task in triads. The third person keeps the group discussing the subject. Experiment and find out what works for you.

Roundrobin: Group Sharing

Ask students to thank their partners and direct them to each take a turn and give their reasons for coming to this animal with the others in their corner. This will take from two to four minutes.

Paraphrase Passport:
Spokesperson Summarizes

Ask for a spokesperson from each corner to summarize some of the reasons their group members gave for choosing the animal they did. Before the next group summarizes their chose, they must paraphrase what the group before them shared. This continues with each group. The group which went first paraphrases what the last group said.

Additional Corners Variables: See Corners (structure 4) for more ideas. Some quick suggestions include: barnyard animals[1], endangered species, birds, etc.

Teacher's Note:

The reflection questions are essential elements to this lesson because they allow students to reflect on the lesson and hear from others how they felt it. Too often our students think of themselves as different or weird when they don't go along with everybody else. One of the goals for this lesson is an appreciation of individual differences. This can only be accomplished by sharing and reflecting on their feelings. Remember, we are trying to allow students to safely share how they feel. No put-downs should be tolerated. For information about dealing with put-downs see Part I, Chapter 5:4.

Reflections & Affirmations
Team Discussion: Reflections

Post the following questions or have them on an overhead. Let teams know they only have five minutes to discuss the questions. You can also post only one or two questions for teams to discuss. Once the time is up, ask for individual teams to share what was discussed.

- Did you find out something new about other members of the class?

- Was it all right for your friends to make different choices? Why?

- How is the world more interesting when we make different choices?

---

1. I was first introduced to the barnyard animals in *Tribes: A Process for Social Development & Cooperative Learning* by Jeanne Gibbs

- Was it difficult to make a decision about the corner you went to? Why?

- Did you want to be with your friends? Why?

- Did you feel uncomfortable at first sharing your reasons? Why?

Simultaneous Roundtable:

Affirmations

Students write their name at the top of the paper. They begin by putting that person's name at the top of the paper. After they write their affirmation, they pass the paper to their teammate to the left. Students then write one affirmation for the student whose name is at the top of the paper. Students then pass the paper again to the student to their right. This process is repeated until each team member gives a written affirmation to each teammate. Then papers are given to their "owner." The only response to affirmations is "Thank you."

Affirmation Starters:

I like what you shared..

Good job.

You're great.

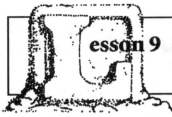

esson 9 Sailboat and Rowboat

Lesson-At-A-Glance

Goals: Classbuilding (Valuing Individual Differences)

Grades: 3-Adult

Time: 20-30 Minutes

Outcomes — Students Will:

• Develop their appreciation of differences.
• Share feelings with another student.
• Experience making choices.

Materials:

• Small piece of paper and pencil or pen for each student
• Selected reflection questions and affirmations posted.
• Think Pads for each student

Structures:

• **Corners**
• **Three-Step Interview**
• **Roundrobin**

Lesson Overview

This will be an opportunity for students to experience individual similarities and differences. Students will choose either a sailboat or a rowboat to identify with. Students will then meet with a student who has made a similar choice and share their reasons for the choice. Students will then meet with students who made a different choice and share their reasons for the choice.

Lesson Sequence

Corners:

Contrast Sailboats vs. Rowboats

A. Ask students if they have ever been in a boat before and what types of boats they've been in.

B. Ask younger students if they know what a sailboat is and to describe a sailboat.

C. Ask younger students if they know what a rowboat is and ask them to describe a rowboat.

D. Ask students to think about the differences between a rowboat and a sailboat. Ask students to choose one or the other they can identify with. They don't need to clarify their reasons right now. They need to make a quick choice. Have each student mark their think pad with the letter S if they chose a sailboat or the letter R if they chose a rowboat. Now direct all the "sailboat" people to move to one side of the room and "rowboat" people to move to the other.

Have all those who chose sailboats form pairs to discuss why they did. Ask all students who chose rowboats to do the same. Give students two minutes to share what is unique about their choice.

Have each sailboat pair find a rowboat pair and form a team of four. If the sides are unequal, have same boat teams form.

Three Step Interview: Differences

Within the team, have those who are "sail-boats" pair with a "rowboat." If there are more of one than another, group students accordingly so each boat is represented in each small group. They will interview one another about how rowboats are different from sailboats and visa-versa and why they chose the boat they did.(One to two minutes for each interview.)

Step One: Sailboats interview rowboats.

Step Two: Reverse the process. Rowboats interview sailboats.

Step Three: With teams of four, individuals take turns paraphrasing what their partner shared in their interview. (Allow 30 seconds per person to paraphrase).

Note: If you want to adapt this to younger students then you might want to use a metaphor other than a sailboat and rowboat. You could use train / truck (one can only go where the track goes, the truck has more flexibility but carries less) or a hang glider / parachute (one you can control much more than the other). Come up with your own.

Reflections & Affirmations
Teacher Led Questions:
Reflections

- What are some of the important differences between rowboats and sailboats?
- How are these characteristics metaphors for us as people?
- Why might it be important to have different types of boats in the world?
- Why is it important to have different types of people?
- Why is it important to appreciate differences which people bring to relationships?

Roundrobin: Affirmations

Have students stay within their Three-Step Interview teams. Ask students to think of one affirmation they could share with each person within their team. Ask students to number off 1 to 4. Person number one will be on the affirmation seat first. Each other team member gives this person an affirmation. Person two is next and so on. Allow three minutes for this activity. Monitor groups' participation.

Affirmation Starters:
Thanks for sharing about...........

I appreciated it when you said................

You are...........

~ ❀ ~

esson 10 Shoulder Rub & Lap Sit

Classbuilding
• *Valuing Individual Differences*

Lesson-At-A-Glance

Goal: Classbuilding (Mutual Support)
Grades: 2-Adult
Time: 15-30 Minutes
Outcomes — Students Will:
  • Give and receive support.
  • Look at how it felt to give and receive.
Materials:
  • Reflection questions and affirmation starters posted on wall
Structures:
  • **Line-Up**
  • **Community Circle**
  • **Class Challenge**
  • **Roundrobin**
  • **Pairs**

Lesson Overview

This is an opportunity for students to physically support each other in a game format. Students will line up by birthday, and then form a community circle. Next, students will be directed to tighten up the circle, turn to their right, place their hands on the shoulders of the person in front of them and give them a comfortable shoulder massage and a lap sit. Students will then share how this felt in a Three-Step Interview process.

Lesson Sequence

Line-Up: By Birthday

Have students line up in a circle by birthday (month and day, not year). Have students born in January start lining at one spot with students born in December finishing up at another. Encourage students to assist one another. For younger students you might model for them where you would go.

When the line-up is complete, have the join the ends of the line to form a circle.

Community Circle:

Birthday Check

Now that they are in a circle, have students tell their birthdays to check if they lined up correctly. Let students know that there will probably be at least one set of birthdays which are the same in class. If it happens to be someone's birthday or close to a birthday, it might be appropriate for a round of applause. Make sure you place yourself in the circle so that students know when your birthday is.

Class Challenge:

Class Circle and Shoulder Rub

Now ask students to form a tight shoulder-to-shoulder circle. Ask students to turn to the right 1/4 turn. Everybody should be facing counter clockwise. Direct students to place their hands on the shoulders of the student in front of them. Then, they are to give a <u>gentle</u> shoulder rub to the person in front of them while receiving one from the person behind. Put the emphasis on "gentle." Have students do this for thirty seconds.

Class Challenge: Lap Sit

Have students end the shoulder rub. While students still have their hands on the shoulders of the person in front of them have students tighten up the circle again by taking one step toward the middle of the circle. Ask them to imagine what might happen when everyone sits down slowly at the same time on the lap of the person behind them. Now, count to three and everybody sits down. Ask students to look around and see their class mates. After 15 seconds ask students to stand up exactly on the count of three. One-two-three; everybody is standing. If students are not successful, try the whole exercise again.

Note: It is a good idea before you do shoulder rub and lap sit to ask if anyone has any knee or leg problems. Give students who do not feel comfortable participating the option of passing and watching from outside the circle. This much physical contact can be uncomfortable for some and the lap sit can be physically threatening for others. Honor their feelings and physical needs.

Reflections & Affirmations

Roundrobin: Reflections

Break students into groups of four based on their position in the circle. If any students chose not to participate in the circle bring them in now. Have the following questions posted on the board or overhead. Student #1 asks their team the 1st question, #2, the second question, etc. All four students respond.

- What was difficult or easy about the shoulder rub and the lap sit?
- What kind of support did you feel?
- How did it feel to see the whole class participating in the same activity?
- Why is it valuable to be a member of a class which supports one another?
- What other class activities could demonstrate class support?

Pairs: Affirmations

Students are to form pairs by closest birthdays (March 22 & 28 would be a pair, April 1 and April 30 would be another pair). In those pairs, they are to develop one affirmation for each of the other two members of their group. They will only have two minutes. They may use the affirmation starters which you have posted. At the end of two minutes ask the pairs to go back to their group and give the affirmations directly to the person for whom they were developed.

Affirmation Starters:

I appreciated your support in the lap sit.
Thanks for the shoulder rub.
I liked it when you ....

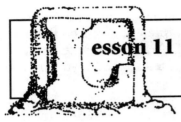

esson 11 Pass-A-Classmate

Lesson-At-A-Glance

Goal: Classbuilding (Mutual Support)
Grades: 3-Adult
Time: 40-50 Minutes

Outcomes — Students Will:
• Experience giving and receiving support.
• Share feelings about this with another student.

Materials:
• Reflection questions and affirmation starters posted on wall or overhead

Structures:
• **Formations**
• **Think-Pair-Share**
• **Think-Fastwrite-Pair**
• **Community Circle**

Lesson Overview

This lesson builds trust between students and develops a sense of mutual support. Students form groups of eight (this could be two teams together or eight students selected by you). They will start by doing formations of numerals as you direct. Explain how they are to do Pass-A-Student. One student is in the center while the other seven students form a close circle around the one student. The student in the center has his/her eyes closed and hands folded over his/her chest and stands rigid. The student in the center leans against the palms of his group-mates. The other students are directed to gently pass the student around the circle with their hands at chest level. Each student takes a turn in the center. The class answers discussion questions and the groups do affirmations.

Lesson Sequence

Formations:
Students form numbers and Pass-A-Student

Have students form groups of eight.[1] All teams should have at least eight members. Divide extra students among teams so no team is larger than twelve. Once students are in teams, have the groups form the shapes of numerals as directed. Have each of the groups form the number 8, then 4, then 5, 6, and others if you choose to. Compliment the groups for doing a good job as they begin to work together more efficiently. This is done to involve them in a successful experience before advancing to a more difficult activity.

Demonstration: Pass a Student[2]

Have one group demonstrate how to do it correctly while other groups watch. Have the demonstration group form a circle with a volunteer in the center. Have students on the outside of the circle take one or more steps in to make a tight circle with the student on the inside. The students will put both hands toward the person in the center at chest/shoulder level, positioning their feet so the forward foot points toward the stu-

---

1. This could be two already existing teams of four or a random grouping of eight students. If some students are left over after forming teams, place them in teams of eight, divide them equally among the teams.

2. Students in the center are volunteers. Do not force anyone to be in the center if they are uncomfortable doing this.

dent and the other foot is about two feet behind, perpendicular to the forward foot. Students should have their knees and elbows bent a little and hands facing in. The student in the center has eyes closed, arms folded across their chest, and body rigid, feet together. The other students in a tight circle gently pass this student around the circle with the hands at chest level. Caution students not to touch other students inappropriately and to pass the student slowly. Explain that the idea for this lesson is to experience mutual support. Students need to feel comfortable as they take this risk.

Group Challenge: Pass-A-Student

After the students have seen a successful demonstration, have them reform their groups and get ready to begin. Before groups begin, monitor the groups for proper body positions and that the student being passed is rigid and has their arms folded across their chest. Each student in the center will be passed for 30 seconds. Remind students in the center to keep their eyes closed as they are being passed around. Remind those doing the passing to be gentle and slow. This isn't meant to be fast.

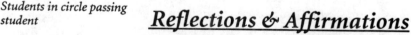

Students in circle passing student

Let students know when the 30 seconds is up and it's time to change.

You can use a signal which will get their attention. Don't use the signal where everyone raises their hand. This could lead to the student in the center taking a tumble and we don't want that.

Note: If you have older high school students or adults, then you can be the person who goes first. It's always best to be the first person to try something when you are introducing it.

Think-Pair-Share:
Discussion Questions

Have the students stay with their groups for discussion questions. Ask the questions below, have the students Think-Pair (with one of their group mates). Randomly call on one or two to share for each question.

Discussion Questions (have these on an overhead projector or written on the board)

What made this activity enjoyable or uncomfortable for you?

How did it feel to be passed around in your group?

How did it feel to be passing around one of your group members?

Note: If for some reason a student doesn't want to participate, have them help in the circle. They may change their minds when they see the other students' success. However, do not force a student to do this activity. Some students are very sensitive to touch and uncomfortable with their bodies. Allow them the option of participating without getting in the center.

Reflections & Affirmations
Think-Fastwrite-Pair:
Reflections

This is a variation of Think-Pair-Share where students write a short answer to the question, then pair and share that answer with their partner.

- What was your greatest fear as this lesson began?

- Were you able to overcome this fear and do the activity? Why?

- Did you feel support from your classmates?

- How might you make this lesson more successful for you and your classmates?

Community Circle: Affirmations

Have the students each take a turn sharing any affirmation they have for another member of the class relating to this lesson. Have the following affirmation starters posted or use your own list.

Affirmation Starters:

I appreciate_____for_____ .

_____ , thanks for_____ .

I like the way _____ helped me _____ .

Thank you for _____

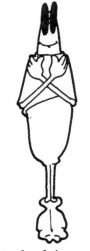

Student being passed

Student in circle

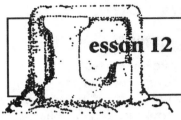

esson 12 Personal Life Map

Lesson-At-A-Glance

Goals: Teambuilding (Getting Acquainted)

Grades: 3-Adult

Time: 45 Minutes

Outcomes — Students Will:
• Draw a personal lifeline of their life to date.
• Share this lifeline with others in a Three-Step Interview.

Materials:
• Pencils, colored pencils or crayons, and large paper for students to create lifeline
• Posted affirmation starters
• Reflection questions on overhead or posted

Structures:
• **Think-Pair-Share**
• **Three-Step Interview**
• **Team Discussion**
• **Roundrobin**

Lesson Overview

Students will have an opportunity to share personal information in a fun and non-threatening way. Students are asked to create a life map of the significant events of their life to date which they will share with one other student in their team. They will then join the other two members of their team to form a group of four where they paraphrase what each student said about their lifeline.

Lesson Sequence

Think-Pair-Share:

Set the Stage

Ask students to <u>think</u> of times in their life which were important, such as where they were born, when and where they first went to school, the first friend they can remember, family events (vacations, birthdays, happy moments, sad moments), and other significant events. As you ask students to remember, pause so they will have enough time. Have students <u>pair</u> with another student and share some of the things they remember. After a few minutes, ask a few students to <u>share</u> with the class what they remember. Explain to students that they are to draw a representation of their life with all the important details which occurred. This could be a road map, a time line, a spiral, a trail map, or however they would like to represent their life.

Note: It's important to show students a model of what you want them to do, preferably a model of your own life map. Explain the other ways they could create on: map, spiral, timeline, trail map, wordwebbing, etc.

Teacher Reading: Share the Poem

(Optional Step for 10th Grade - Adult) Read the poem "The Road Not Taken" by Robert Frost (attached) to your class. Ask students to think of those important decision points which made a significant difference in where they are today. Ask students to include these in their life map.

Students Draw:

Personal Life Map

Hand out the paper and pencils, pens, or crayons to students. Tell students they have ten-fifteen minutes to complete their life map. As students are drawing their life maps monitor their progress. If students need a few more minutes, decide if you can give them the time. Let students know two minutes before you stop them that time is nearly up. Caution that they should not include anything they do not want to share as they will show their life map to their team.

Three-Step Interview:
Students Share Their Life Maps
Step One
Pair students who are members of the same team of four. When they are in pairs they are to take turns sharing their life maps. Remind students that they need to use their active listening skills because they will be paraphrasing what they hear their partner say. Students are to explain the significance of what they have drawn to their partner. Give students one-three minutes each to share. Give students a reminder before time is up.

Step Two:
Now students reverse the role of speaker and interviewer from step one above.

Step Three: Roundrobin Sharing
Students are to move to their group of four and share. If persons A & B were a pair then person A will share person B's life map. Person B will share person A's life map. Person C will share person D's life map and D will share C's. Students are to share the drawing with the team as they explain it. Once students have completed sharing, they could start on the reflection questions which you can have on the overhead.

Reflections & Affirmations
Team Discussion: Reflections
Ask students one or two of the following questions. Give students a couple of minutes to discuss the question and then ask for feedback randomly from various teams.

- Was it difficult to draw your lifeline? Why was it difficult?

- How could you tell your partner was using good active listening skills?

- What made you aware that your team members were good listeners?

- What important details did you leave out of your life map?

- Why do you feel you left out what you did?

- How might an activity like this be important to you personally?

Roundrobin: Affirmations
Ask students to Roundrobin, giving each person in the group affirmations. Let students know they can refer to the posted affirmations list.

I appreciated ...

Thank you for sharing...

I especially liked it when...

(Adapted From *Tribes: A Process For Social Development And Cooperative Learning*, by Jeanne Gibbs)

~ ❀ ~ ֍

The Road Not Taken

Two roads diverged in a yellow wood,
And sorry I could not travel both
And be one traveler, long I stood
And looked down one as far as I could
To where it bent in the undergrowth;

Then took the other, as just as fair,
And having perhaps the better claim,
Because it was grassy and wanted wear;
Though as for that, the passing there
Had worn them really about the same

And both that morning equally lay
In leaves no step had trodden black.
Oh, I kept the first for another day!
Yet knowing how way leads on to way,
I doubted if I should ever come back.

I shall be telling this with a sigh
Somewhere ages and ages hence:
Two roads diverged in a wood, and I-

I took the one less traveled by,
And that has made all the difference.

by Robert Frost

Examples: Life Maps

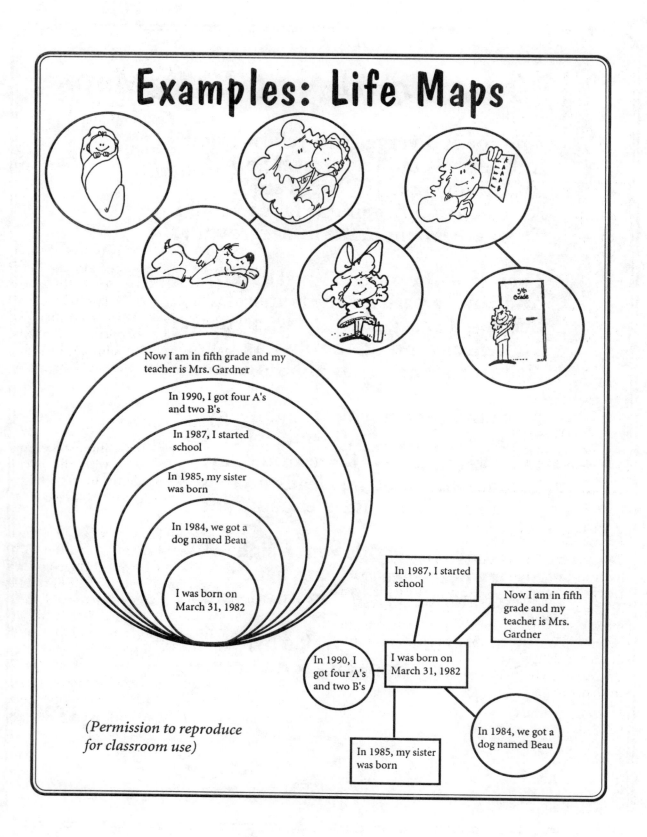

Now I am in fifth grade and my teacher is Mrs. Gardner

In 1990, I got four A's and two B's

In 1987, I started school

In 1985, my sister was born

In 1984, we got a dog named Beau

I was born on March 31, 1982

In 1987, I started school

Now I am in fifth grade and my teacher is Mrs. Gardner

In 1990, I got four A's and two B's

I was born on March 31, 1982

In 1984, we got a dog named Beau

In 1985, my sister was born

(Permission to reproduce for classroom use)

 **esson 13 Collaborative Life Maps**

Lesson-At-A-Glance

Goal: Teambuilding (Getting Acquainted)

Grades: 3-Adult

Time: 45-75 Minutes

Materials:
- Pencils, colored pencils, crayons, and paper for students to create Life Map
- Reflection questions

Outcomes — Students will:
- Draw their partner's personal Life Map as their partner describes it.
- Share their Life Map with their team.

Structures:
- **Pairs**
- **Roundrobin**
- **Talking Chips**
- **Three-Step Interview**

Lesson Overview

This lesson allows students to practice active listening and translate it into a drawing activity. Students are asked to create a life map of the significant events in their partner's life. One student in the pair will explain his/her life while the other draws it. Students then share the life map with their other two team members using a Roundrobin structure.

Note: use either Lesson 12 or Lesson 13 with your class, but not both.

Lesson Sequence

Teacher Talk:

A. Guided Imagery

Ask students to think of events and times in their lives which were important to them. Ask students to remember such things as: where they were born, when and where they first went to school, the first friend they remember, events which happened with their family (vacations, birth of siblings, birthday parties), and times they were very happy or very sad.

B. Directions

Explain that they will be sharing these events only with their team, not with the entire class. As you ask students to remember, pause between topics to give students time to remember.

Assign students to pairs in existing teams. Explain to students they will be doing a partner drawing. Students will tell their partner about the significant events in their life while the partner draws a representation of their life with all the important details which occurred. This could be a road map, a time line, a spiral, a trail map, or however they would like to represent their partner's life. The person doing the drawing chooses how to represent what the person sharing says. Remind students that this is not an art contest.

Student/Teacher Model:
Partner Drawing

Ask another student to volunteer to help you model partner drawing. Sit at a table or do it on the overhead so that all the students can see. Ask your partner to do the drawing while you tell them about your life. Tell them where you were born. Your partner starts to draw. If they ask what to draw, emphasize it's up to the partner who is drawing to draw it their way. There are no right or wrong answers. **The purpose of this activity is not art but rather communication and collaboration.** Show students some other examples of timelines, spirals, and trail maps if they need visual models.

Teacher Talk:
Share the Poem "The Road Not Taken" (Optional Step for 10th Grade - Adult)

Read the poem "The Road Not Taken" by Robert Frost (preceding this lesson) to your class. Ask students to reflect on important decision points that they have made. Suggest students include these decision points in their lifeline.

Pairs:
Create Partner's Life Map

Hand out the paper and pencils, pens, or crayons to those who need them. Tell pairs they have 10-15 minutes to complete each of their life maps. Let students know you will tell them when they are at the halfway point so that each partner has an equal amount of time. As students draw their partner's life map monitor their progress. Decide if they need more or less time. Let students know a minute before half time that they need to be ready to switch.

When time is up (10-15 minutes) for the first partner have them switch and repeat the process with the other partner speaking while their partner draws their life map.

Roundrobin:
Share with Teammates

Pairs are to move to their team of four and share using Roundrobin. Students will share their own map and receive any help they need from their partner.

Note: Refer to Page 12:4 for sample life maps to share with students.

[This is adapted from a similar activity conducted by David Sibbet of Sibbet and Associates of San Francisco.]

Reflections & Affirmations
Team Discussion with Talking Chips:
Reflection Questions

As each person answers the question, they place their pencil or pen in the center of the table. Once everybody has answered and placed their pen in the middle, everyone picks up theirs and starts on the next question.

Have teams begin answering the questions below as they finish the partner drawing and sharing. These can be written on the board or on an overhead. (Adapt for younger children)

- Was it difficult to draw your partner's life map? Why?

- How could you tell your partner was trying to draw what you said?

- How could sharing your life map be difficult for some of us?

- Did you realize afterwards that you left out important details on your life map?

- Why do you think that was so?

- If you were to do this lesson again, what changes would you make in your personal life map?

- How might this activity help you personally?

Three-Step Interview:
Affirmations

Direct students to stay within the same team in pairs. Ask students to interview their partner as to: "What affirmations would be appropriate for the other pair in their team?"

Step 1: Interview one way.

Step 2: Interview the other way.

Step 3: Share affirmations with the other pair in a Roundrobin format and give those affirmations.

~ ❁ ~

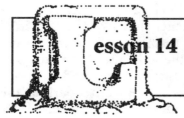

esson 14 Zoo Sounds

Lesson-At-A-Glance

Goal: Teambuilding (Team Identity)

Grades: K-Adult

Time: 30-45 Minutes

Materials:
• Slips of paper with animal names
• Posted discussion and reflection questions

Outcomes — Students will:
• Participate in using their imagination.
• Locate their team members.

Structures:
• **Formations**
• **Similarity Grouping**
• **Three-Step Interview**
• **Think-Pair-Square**

Lesson Overview

This lesson allows students to form groups by sharing a common experience and having fun.

Students will form similarity groups and be handed a slip of paper with an animal written on it. They are to find their teammates who have the same animal. Next, they will listen to "The Zoo Story." Students will Think-Roundrobin about the ending of the story and share their own ending with their teammates.

Note: This lesson is for forming teams which will stay together for a length of time. You can also use it other times. It should be done after students are following the class rules and after sense of inclusion has developed.

Getting Ready

Preselect Teams and Write Names on Paper

Divide students into teams which will stay together for a length of time. Prepare small slips of paper with each student's name on one side. Label papers for students in the same group with a zoo animal name (zebra, elephant, lion, cobra, chimp, owl, wolf, gorilla, etc.). Remember not to give a group an animal name which would offend them; be sensitive.

Lesson Sequence

Formations: Things in a Zoo

Have the class in a space with plenty of room and no obstacles. This could be in the cafeteria, on the yard, in the gym, or in your room with all the desks moved to the wall. You would be amazed at how quickly students can move furniture when they are motivated. Now tell the class you would like them to form a large circle as quickly as they can. Explain that the topic for today's lesson will be zoos. Have them, as a class, do formations of: (a) a cage with bars; (b) add wheels to the cage; (c) an elephant's head with big ears and a long nose; (d) whole elephant. Step back and watch how they proceed. Watch for the natural leaders. Let the class figure out how to do it. Do not direct it: allow your students the opportunity to try it on their own.

Similarity Grouping:

A. Favorite Animal

Ask students to think about all the different animals there are in the zoo. Ask students to name a few and write these on the board. Now ask students to recall what their favorite zoo animal is. Give students a full minute to think about this. Ask students to find other students in the room who have this same animal as their favorite. Students are to find other students who chose the same animal. They can do this by walking around and saying the animal name or making the animal sound. There will be clusters around the room of similar animals. When students find others who chose the same (or a similar animal), ask students to form pairs in their clusters and discuss what is special about the animal they chose. Give students two minutes to discuss, and then randomly choose several students to share.

Guided Imagery: Zoo Story

You are going to read a story to them. Students are to try to imagine they are actually in the story and in the world you create for them. Students are to imagine the colors, the smells, the sounds, everything they can about the place you describe. Suggest they may want to close their eyes so they can better imagine everything they will see in the story. Read "The Zoo Story" which follows this activity.

B. Zoo Team Animals

Have the students meet as a class where there is plenty of room and enough space clear of furniture or obstruction to walk around. This is the time for forming teams. Hand out the slips of paper with each student's name on one side and the zoo animal which represents their team written on the other side. Ask students to look at what is written on the slip of paper and not to say anything. With younger children or non

readers use animal stamps instead of names. Now tell students that like the zoo in the story they are to pretend for a few seconds that they are the animals. It's midnight at the zoo and they are to find the other animals like them. Since it's dark at midnight, ask students to close their eyes. Students are to make the sounds that their animal makes and keep making that sound until they find all their team. When students find their other teammates, they are to sit in a circle at the edge of the room (desks, chairs or on the floor, whatever is appropriate).

Reflections & Affirmations

Think-Roundrobin:

Sharing Their Wish

Let each student think for one minute. Roundrobin with your group what you would wish for if you were in the zoo story.

Three-Step Interview:

Reflection Questions

Have students pair up in their new teams and do a Three-Step Interview with the following questions. They take turns within their pair answering the questions. See Structure 16:1 for directions for Three-Step Interview.

- Why did or didn't you enjoy this way of forming groups?
- Could you think of a another interesting way to form groups? Share it.
- Why is it enjoyable to have everyone laughing during this activity?
- How could you relate to the children in the Zoo Story?
- How might you make your wish come true?

↜ How might your team help you grow as a person?

Think-Pair-Square: Affirmations

Think: Have students **think** about their new team members. What affirmations could they give their new team members which would be supportive and honest? If they need affirmation starters have some posted.

Pair: They then **pair** with a fellow teammate and discuss which affirmations they might give.

Square: Students then share with the team.

Affirmation starters:

Thank you for _____.

I liked when you_____.

_____, you're great!

~ ❀ ~

The Zoo Story

Once four children lived in a large city which had the most wonderful zoo. These four children often walked by the zoo on their way to school. On weekends they would go to the zoo to explore. They would run through the primate exhibit and laugh at the chimps and monkeys. They enjoyed the trumpeting of the elephants and the howl of the howler monkeys. One of their favorite spots was the lawn across from the elephant area. Here they would stretch out on the grass to watch the elephant keeper feed the elephants. The elephants sometimes squirted the keeper with water.

Something else they enjoyed about the zoo was watching people. Sometimes they would pretend what it would be like to be an animal in one of the cages. From an animal's perspective humans seemed very strange. They would watch families as parents and children laughed at and talked to the animals. They saw old people with sad eyes and others with twinkling eyes who came to the zoo alone or with their grandchildren. The grandparents seemed to enjoy the zoo. They seldom, if ever, were harsh with their grandchildren and genuinely enjoyed the wonder in their grandchildren's eyes.

They would watch young human lovers who came to the zoo holding hands and kissed when they thought no one would notice. They walked close to one another and looked at each other funny with big eyes. These humans were indeed strange. Then there were the humans who ate too much and those who fed all the animals even though the sign said not to feed the animals.

Occasionally, they would see groups of school children or Sunday school classes come to the zoo. The children ran around looking at everything at the same time. The adults tried to keep them together. They decided that mother ducks had an easier time keeping all their ducklings together than human adults did.

Then the sun would begin to go down and the kids would lie on the grass and wish.................

--Vanston Shaw

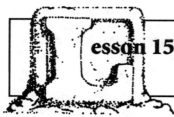

esson 15 Geography Teams

Lesson-At-A-Glance

Goal: Teambuilding (Team Identity)

Grades: 4-Adult

Time: 30-40 minutes

Outcomes — Students will:
• Locate their team members using a world map and share.

Materials:
• Slips of paper for each student's name matched with a geographic place name
• Appropriate maps (globes if you are using the world)
• Team Reflection questions written on board, overhead, or ditto

Structures:
• **Formations**
• **Similarity Groups**
• **Pairs Compare**
• **Roundrobin**

Lesson Overview

This lesson gives you another way to place students into teams through a common experience. Finding their new teammates is fun and incorporates learning geography. My friend, Robert Rudholm, of California State University in Turlock, California, shared this idea with me.

Getting Ready

Preselect Teams and Write Names on Paper

Choose long term teams by whichever method you select. Most teachers have students work in a variety of short term teams during the first several weeks of the school year to evaluate who might work well with whom. Once teams are decided have a list of the students grouped by team.

Select Place Names from a World Map or Globe

Using a world map or globe in the classroom choose place names such as countries or capitals. Don't use those that are too obscure. It's frustrating and may not allow your students to be successful without your help. Ideas following the lesson.

Write Student Name and Place Name on Paper

Using slips of paper folded in half, write the student's name on the outside and a place name on the inside. You will match all the students in team One with place names in Europe, team Two - Asia, team Three - Africa, Four - South America, Five - North America, Six - Australia, and Seven - Antarctica. (Remember, students should have already studied these place names. If not, change the geography to something students are familiar with.)

Prepare the Room: Place Names

Have the class in a large area with no obstructions. You could have the students move the furniture in your room to the sides and use the middle, go outside, use the gym, or the multi-purpose room.

Note: I recommend you tie this in with a geography unit you've been studying, if possible. If you've been studying North America then choose place names from North America. If you've been studying a specific state, then use place names from various states for each team (or regions of the country, Southeast, Northeast, etc.). To make it fun you must make it at a level appropriate to your students. **Whatever you do, don't make it frustrating for the students. If anything, it would be better to make it easier than harder.**

Lesson Sequence

Formations:

Explaining Task and Forming Shapes

When your students are in this large open area begin your explanation. Explain to students that they will be doing a lesson on continents (or states, or regions) and that to start with you would like to test their knowledge as a class.

- Have them form the outline of North America
- South America
- Africa, Asia, Europe
- Their state

Similarity Groups:

Same Geography Location

Pass out the slips of paper to each student. Ask students not to look until you give the directions. Once all the slips have been passed out ask the students to look at the place name on their slip of paper and direct them to try to find the other students in the room who have place names on the same continent, country, state, etc. They can use the maps on the wall or the globe if you are using continents. Be available to help students if they are having problems finding their team.

Note: Other Subjects -- If you are a science or math teacher you could form teams dealing with your subject matter, rather than geography.

Science: geology, biology, etc.

Math: addition, subtraction, multiplication, division, fractions, decimals, etc.

Reflections & Affirmations

Pairs Compare

Reflection Questions

Assign each team the reflection questions to answer. Have **pairs** within each team discuss the same reflection questions. Give pairs a few minutes to discuss the questions. Have pairs come back together with their teammates. Now each pair **compares** their answers to the reflection questions.

- What they were feeling when they first got their slip of paper before they knew who would be on their team? What was going through their mind?

- How did their feelings change when they found their team and sat down?

The above questions can be written on the board or on chart paper so that students can see them. Monitor student sharing by walking around and listening in on teams.

Roundrobin: Affirmation

Have the teams use the Roundrobin format, each taking a turn receiving affirmations from their team members. Affirmation starters should be posted so students can refer to them if needed.

Affirmation Starters:

_____, I glad you're on my team.

Thanks for finding me.

You're a fantastic team member.

Ideas for Geography Teams

Continents, Countries, and Cities, Geographic Features[1]

CONTINENTS

Asia
Africa
Antarctica
Australia
Europe
North America

AFRICA

Sahara Desert, Nile River
Algeria
Angola
Egypt: Cairo
Ethiopia: Addis Ababa
Ivory Coast
Kenya: Nairobi, *Mount Kilamanjaro*
Liberia
Libya
Mali: Timbuktu
Morocco
Mozambique
South Africa
Tunisia
Uganda
Zimbabwe

ASIA

Afghanistan
Armenia; Yeravan
Azerbijan; Baku
Bangladesh
Burma; Rangoon
Cambodia
China: Beijing, Canton, *Yellow River, Gobi Desert,* Hong Kong
India: New Delhi, Calcutta, Madras , *Ganges River*
Israel: Tel Aviv, Jerusalem, Bethlehem
Korea: Seoul
Laos
Mongolia
North Korea
Pakistan: Indus River
Russia: Moscow, *Volga River, Ural Mountains*
Saudi Arabia: Mecca, Jedha
South Korea
Thailand
Vietnam
Yemen

ANTARCTICA

Queen Maud Land
Byrd Station
Ross Ice Shelf
Wilkes Land
Amery Ice Shelf

AUSTRALIA

Great Barrier Reef
Melbourne
Sydney
Tasmania
Adelaide
Darwin
Perth

---

1. Geography features are in *Italic*.

NORTH AMERICA
Belize; Belmopan
Canada; Montreal, Quebec, Vancouver
Costa Rica
El Salvador
Guatemala: Guatemala City
Nicaragua: Tagucigalpa
Panama: Panama City
USA: Washington D.C., New York, Los Angeles,
San Francisco, Chicago, All the states, *Sierra
Nevada, Mississippi River, Colorado River, Mo-
jave Desert*
Mexico; Mexico City, Guadalajara, Veracruz,
Monterey, *Sonoran Desert, Yucatan Peninsula,
Baja California*

EUROPE
Alps Mountains
Pyrenees Mountains
Danube River
Albania
Austria: Vienna
Belgium: Brussels
Bulgaria: Sofia
Czechoslovakia: Prague
Holland: Amsterdam
France: Paris, Lyon, *Pyrenees Moun-
tains*
Great Britain: London, Edinburgh,
Manchester, Liverpool, Birmingham
  England
  Scotland
  Wales
  Northern Ireland
Greece: Athens
Germany: Berlin, Bonn, *Black Forrest*
Hungary: Budapest, *Danube River*
Italy: Rome, Polarmo, Venice
Poland: Warsaw
Rumania: Bucharest
Serbia
Turkey: Istanbul
Ukraine: Kiev

SOUTH AMERICA
Andes Mountains
Amazon River
Oricioro River
Tierra del Fuego
Argentina: Buenos Aires
Bolivia: La Paz
Brazil: Brazilia, Rio de Janeiro
Chile: Santiago
Colombia
Ecuador: Quito
Paraguay
Peru: Lima
Uruguay
Venezuela

VANSTON SHAW: *Communitybuilding in the Classroom*
Publisher: Kagan Cooperative Learning • 1(800) Wee Co-op
Chapter 7: 56   Lesson 15

 **esson 16 Presenting Your Team**

Lesson-At-A-Glance

Goal: Teambuilding (Team Identity, Mutual Support & Synergy)

Grades: 2-Adult

Time: One to two class periods (this could be spread over a few weeks)

Materials:
- One sheet of scratch paper per team for Roundtable
- One sheet of butcher paper large enough for a shield (8' X 2').
- Felt pens (a different color for each team member), glue, paste, scissors, construction paper, and other items as needed by the teams.

Outcomes — Students will:
- Cooperate as they create their team name and project.
- Create a team name and present their team to the class.

Structures:
- Numbered Heads Together
- Roundtable
- Spend-A-Buck
- Team Project
- Talking Chips
- Think-Pair-Square

Lesson Overview

Prerequisites to this lesson should be lesson 6: Class Name. This will be an opportunity for each team to develop a team name and present their team to the class. You need to discuss with students how names tell who we are. Use the class name or school name as an example. Teams will then develop their own team name and develop a presentation and present their team to the class. This is a lesson which might be accomplished in two periods.

Lesson Sequence

Numbered Heads Together:
Developing Guidelines

Discuss with the class the concept of your name defining who you are. Each of us as individuals have a name, first and last. Our school has a name. Our class has a name. It is time for each team to come up with their name. Ask students in teams to come up with one or two guidelines or rules which it might be good to have when developing team names. Randomly call on teams* and record some of their ideas to consider. Once you have a list of 10 or so items, pick out the ones you believe are most important and ask the class if this is reasonable. These usually have to do with names being in good taste and positive.

* Using the Numbered Heads format (see Structure 8:1 for more information.)

Roundtable:
Students List Different Possibilities for Names

Ask each team to get out one piece of scratch paper and one pencil. Everything should be off students' desks, knees, etc. except for one piece of paper and one pencil per team. When directed to start, the team member with the piece of paper will write his idea for a team name, and pass the paper to the right. The next person will write down another idea. Students continue until you call time. If students cannot think of a name to write, they write "PASS" on the paper before they pass it to the next person. Give teams three minutes to write down as many ideas as they can. Stress that they should come up with as many ideas as possible. As teams are writing names down, circulate around the room to monitor the team's progress.

Spend-A-Buck:
Choose a Team Name

Each team will have several possible choices for team names. Explain to students that they will be using a structure called "Spend-A-Buck" to make a choice of their team name. Each team member will have one dollar (consisting of four quarters or four marks of their colored pen) to spend on the names they like the most. They take turns spending a quarter at a time. They can spend their money on one or more names. When the students have spent their money, add the total value for each team name. The team name with highest value is the new team name. *Announce that those teams which have selected their team name within the five minute period will be eligible for a drawing for free team time.* This is a management technique which will encourage teams to complete the task on time.

Team Project:
Presenting Your Team

Now that teams have their names, let them know they have twenty minutes (or more if you want this to be a two-period project) to develop a way to present their team to the class. Assign each team roles to use as they do this task:

- **Gatekeeper** (see that everyone on the team participates)
- **Taskmaster** (watch time, keep everyone on task)
- **Cheerleader** (have teams celebrate good ideas)

- **Encourager** (keep the team going)

They can use a skit, song, poster, poem, or other way to introduce their team and its new name. The only rules are that all team members participate in the presentation and the presentation can last two minutes at the most. Field any questions which might arise from your directions. Have teams start.

Note: As teams work, walk around the room listening the conversations teams are having. I usually find that some teams come up with a presentation quickly and others will be struggling right down to the deadline. It is possible to have the presentations presented the same day. I usually prefer to have the presentations developed one day and presented the next day. That allows teams to have more after-class time to prepare, if they choose.

Team Project:
Team Presentations

Let teams know when the presentation will take place. Have teams take turns presenting their team to the class. After each presentation, have the class give a round of applause.

Reflections & Affirmations
Team Discussion with Talking Chips:
Reflection Questions

As each student on the team answers the question, they place their pencils or pens on the table in the center of the team. They may not talk again until everyone has placed their pencil in the center. Once everyone had a turn, they pick up their pencils and begin the next question.

- How did your team do during the Roundtable portion of the task?

- Why was this easy or difficult for your team?

- How did each member of the team participate in developing the team presentation?

- What was the most difficult part of presenting your team?

- What might you do differently to help your team be more successful?

Think-Pair-Square: Affirmations

Think: Have students think about what kinds of affirmations they could give the other members of their team.

Pair: Pair with your partner and share what kinds of affirmations you would give your other teammates.

Square: Pairs form teams of four and share their affirmations.

Affirmation Starters:

I liked your suggestion of ...

You were great when...

Thank you for ...

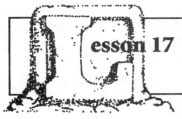

esson 17 Team Handshake

Teambuilding
• Team Identity • Mutual Support • Synergy

Lesson-At-A-Glance

Goal: Teambuilding (Team Identity, Mutual Support & Synergy)

Grades: 2-Adult

Time: 30-45 Minutes

Materials:
- Reflection question written on the board, overhead or ditto

Outcomes — Students will:
- Cooperate to create their team handshake.

Structures:
- **Think-Square-Share**
- **Team Project**
- **Pairs Compare**
- **Roundrobin**

Lesson Overview

Prerequisites to this lesson should be the developing of a class and team names. This will be an opportunity for each team to develop a team handshake. Discuss with students the concept of symbols. Use the class name or banner as an example. The school mascot might be another example. Teams will then develop their own team handshake.

Lesson Sequence

Teacher Talk: Symbols

Discuss with the class the concept of having a symbol to help represent who you are. Each team has developed a team name. Basketball teams have team handshakes. Now it's time to develop a team handshake.

Think for a moment of the types of handshakes there are. Ask for a few students to demonstrate some examples of handshakes.

Think-Square-Share:

Teams Think of Handshake

Ask students to **think** for a minute of a handshake which their team might use to identify themselves as a learning team. Give students a good minute or two of think time. Ask students to **square** and meet with their team and to take turns **sharing** their ideas. Give students two minutes to share.

Team Project:

Creating Their Team Handshake

Have students create their team handshake. Let teams know that they can add a quiet sound to it if they choose. One rule is that all hands must touch at one point. Teams will have five minutes to come up with a team handshake that can be shared with the class. Ask if there are any questions. Turn the teams loose. As the teams work move around the room listening in on the conversations of the various teams.

Stand and Share:

Team Handshakes

After five minutes call time and ask teams to prepare to present their handshake within the next minute. Begin calling on teams to demonstrate their handshake. After each demonstration lead the class in applause.

Reflections & Affirmations

Pairs Compare:
Reflection Question

Assign each team two reflection questions to answer. Have **pairs** within each team discuss the same reflection questions. Give pairs a few minutes to discuss their responses. Have pairs come back together with their teammates. Now each pair **compares** their answers to the reflection questions.

Have two of the following questions written on an overhead or the board.

- How did members of your team participate in developing the handshake ideas?
- Who provided leadership?

- If anybody didn't feel included what could you do to include them next time?
- What could you do differently to help your team be more successful?

When teams have finished discussing the questions randomly, call on several teams to share their responses.

Roundrobin:
Affirmations on the Affirming Chair

Have students think about what kinds of affirmations they could give the other members of their team. Have each member of the team take a turn on the affirmation chair. For 10 seconds team members will give the student as many affirmations as they can. Those receiving can only respond with "thank you."

∼ ✾ ∼

esson 18 Alphabetical Roundrobin

Lesson-At-A-Glance

Goal: Teambuilding (Mutual Support)

Grades: 2-Adult

Time: 25-40 minutes, depending on the how well your students take turns, alphabetize, and if you do each step

Materials:
• Directions on the board or an overhead
• Goals (step 4) on board
• Posted list of affirmation starters

Outcome — Students will:
• Take turns in order.
• Demonstrate the knowledge of alphabetical order.
• Have fun.
• Show team support.

Structures:
• **Think-Pair-Share**
• **Roundrobin**
• **Brainstorming**
• **Team Discussion**
• **Roundtable**

Lesson Overview

This is a fun approach to reinforcing alphabetizing skills and creating mutual team support. It's a good early-in-the-year teambuilding activity.

Lesson Sequence

Think-Pair-Share:

Games Played on Trips

Ask students to think of games they have played while they were on trips with their parents. Now have students from same team form pairs and tell each other about the games they played while on trips. Have several students volunteer to share the car games they played with the class. Tell students you are going to teach them a new car game. This car game has to do with naming things in alphabetical order. It's very possible that you will have students who have played this game before. If so, ask these students to tell their variation. Thank the student for sharing, if one did, and go on to tell how your game is played.

Teacher Note: This activity should only be used with groups that are already good at alphabetizing. This is a team building activity. A Roundrobin activity is geared for high success, not frustration. If several students are having trouble alphabetizing, then I would use this after they have improved. Another option would be to use this as a developmental activity to assist students to learn to use alphabetical order. In that case this lesson would not be a teambuilding lesson.

Teacher Talk

A. Share Rules

"In your cooperative teams you will name as many different foods as you can with the first letter of the food being in alphabetical order. You keep going until you get to the end of alphabet. If someone gets stuck you can only help them after 15 seconds. Hints are OK after 15 seconds. The person whose first name starts closest to the beginning of the alphabet will start. You will have five minutes for this activity. If you get to Z before five minutes is up, start again and try to use different foods." Have students move into their teams.

B. Team Demonstration & Check for Understanding

Tell teams they will share in alphabetical order by first name. Ask all teams to determine who in the team starts first. Select one team to demonstrate for the class how this game would be played. Ask the team who is going first. (Eric) Ask why? (Because Eric comes before Joanne, Nadine, or Ted.) Now they will Roundrobin, one after the other. Ask the students to start naming foods in alphabetical order starting with A. (Apple, Bananas, Cheese, Donuts.....) Check for understanding by randomly selecting another two students to restate what their teams are supposed to do.

C. Explain & Post Goals

Explain that the goals for this lesson are to:
a. Take turns in order.
b. Name as many foods as they can in alphabetical order.
c. Have fun as a team.
d. Show team support.

Ask students if they remember what to do if they get to Z before the five minutes is up. (Start over with different foods.) Ask students to begin.

Roundrobin: Alphabetize Foods

As the teams begin, walk around the room and check to see that they are being successful with the task. If teams are having trouble try to determine why. Intervene only if necessary. Give students time to solve any problems they run into.

Brainstorming:
Different Ways of Alphabetizing

Ask teams to think of other ways they could play this game by alphabetizing things other than food. Have teams select roles (and brainstorm the different items to alphabetize. Give teams one-two minutes to come up with a list. Have teams quickly share one idea each. [Note: Refer to brainstorming section and review the brainstorming rules with your students.] Read Brainstorming Structure p. 1:1 for roles.

Reflections & Affirmations

Team Discussion:
Reflection Questions

At five minutes, check to see that everybody is on task. If students are on task allow them another minute or so. If not, ask students to finish up the word they are on. Ask students to review the posted goals and direct the teams to discuss how well they implemented the goals which you posted.

Give students only a minute or so to discuss this in their group. Ask for teams to tell how successful they were with the goals.

Simultaneous Roundtable:
Affirmations

This activity should only be used if students are already grounded in using affirmations and do not use put-downs with one another in class. Students write their name at the top of the paper. They then pass their paper to their teammate to the right. Students then write one affirmation for the student whose name is at the top of the paper. Students then pass the paper again to the student to their right. This process is repeated until each team member gives a written affirmation to each teammate. They keep passing the paper until you direct them to stop. Return the papers to their "owners" to read their affirmations.

esson 19 Castle Building

Lesson-At-A-Glance

Goal: Teambuilding (Mutual Support & Synergy)

Grades: 3-Adult

Time: 30-45 Minutes

Materials:
- 30 sheets of scrap paper for each group
- One or two rolls of masking tape

Outcomes — Students will:
- Use non-verbal communication skills among team members
- Develop team synergy

Structures:
- **Formations**
- **Team Project**
- **Roam the Room**
- **Three-step Interview**
- **Brainstorming**

Lesson Overview

This lesson is designed to have students work together building a castle out of scrap paper and masking tape. Students will have only 8-10 minutes to complete the task. Students will not be allowed to talk to one another or write messages. Students can only communicate non-verbally with body language or eye movement.

Lesson Sequence

Team Formations: Basic Shapes

Ask teams to form the shape of a circle, then a square, triangle, and rectangle without talking. Explain that they will be using these shapes in the task to be assigned now.

Team Project:
Construct Castle without Talking

A. Teacher Explains Directions

Explain the task. Tell students they will have only 8-10 minutes to complete the best castle they can design and build. The only materials students can use are paper and tape. It must be free standing and cannot be attached to something else. Remind students that they cannot talk or write.

B. Make Castle

Hand out paper and tape to each team and call "Go." Monitor as they begin the task. Gently remind any teams which are talking about the ground rule of no talking. The teams almost always come up with outstanding castles. Many will be unique in their own way.

Roam the Room:
Viewing Student Accomplishments

When the teams have completed their castles or the 8-10 minute time limit is up, it's time for students to take a look at what each group has accomplished. It's important for the teams to see the variety of approaches to accomplishing the same task.

Note: This lesson is also a great energizer for creating a sense of inclusion among team members. It's a good way for students to experience working together in a positive, non-verbal manner. It can help teams develop closer working relationships. Often, if teams are experiencing communication problems, this lesson can help them understand these issues by pointing out the conflicts and the need for further work. It also provides a teambuilding experience which helps the team pull together to collaborate and create.

Reflections & Affirmations

Three-Step Interview:

Reflection Questions

Have teams divide into pairs for this activity. Pairs will interview each other on reflection questions.

Step One: Person One interviews Person Two.

Step Two: Reverse the process.

Step Three: Roundrobin paraphrase - partners response.

- What was difficult about not talking to one another?

- How would the task be different if you had been able to talk to one another?

- How did you decide what to do?

- What is one thing you learned in doing this task?

- How might you change the way you made your castle if you could do this activity over again? How?

Brainstorming: Affirmations

Have teams brainstorm affirmations appropriate to them as a team. They will need a recorder for this task.

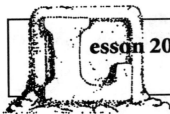

Lesson 20 Gallery Brainstorming

Lesson-At-A-Glance

Goal: Teambuilding (Valuing Individual Differences)

Grades: 3-Adult

Time: 20-45 Minutes

Materials:
- Several sheets of butcher paper posted around the room
- Colored dots (red, blue, and yellow) for each student. (available at office supply stores.)
- One set of colored pens with a different color for each team
- Timer, bell, or other method to gain attention so teams move together
- Post reflection questions and affirmation starters

Outcomes — Students will:
- Practice brainstorming several issues simultaneously.
- Learn how to use a weighted prioritizing system.

Structures:
- **Brainstorming**
- **Color-Coded Prioritizing**
- **Numbered Heads Together**
- **Think-Pair-Square**

Lesson Overview

This is a great method to gain student input on various classroom issues. Students will learn how to brainstorm solutions to several issues simultaneously in teams, using a weighted point system to determine which issues they believe are the most important.

Assign Students to Teams

This is a teambuilding activity in which long-term teams are most appropriate. It will have more of an impact if students are going to stay with this team for at least several weeks.

Lesson Sequence

Class Discussion:

Issues of Class, School, or Community

Choose several topics students could have some say in deciding. These could be issues in the classroom, within the school as a whole, or in the community.

Examples of classroom issues:
- How can we ensure the room is clean enough when students leave?
- How might we deal with late homework?
- What should we do when students talk and disrupt learning?
- How can we get everyone to participate in their team assignments?
- How could we establish a pen pal program?

Examples of school issues:
- How could we ensure the playground is kept free of litter?
- How might we deal with bullying on the playground?
- How can we ensure students honor playground rules?
- How might we make the cafeteria food more appealing to students?

Examples of community issues:

- How can we better promote substance abuse awareness in our community?
- How could local businesses help our schools?
- How might we have more of our school activities reported by our local newspaper?
- How can the community help us provide more afterschool activities for students?
- How might the community and school create more summer activities for students?

Narrow the focus of this discussion to issues within the classroom, around school, or in the community which you have already posted at the top of the pieces of butcher paper on the walls. Do not show favoritism toward one issue over another. This should be a discussion of the issues in general.

Teacher Talk:

Explain Gallery Brainstorming
(Have Sheets of Butcher Paper Posted)

Direct students that their team will go to one of the sheets of butcher paper posted on the wall. (There should be one sheet posted for each team). You have identified an issue at the top of each piece of paper, (e.g. Keeping The Room Clean, How To Have More Homework Turned In, or How To Reduce Put-downs At Lunch). Explain to students that they will have to select a recorder. Ask recorders to raise their hands. Each team's recorder will have a different color felt pen. Teams will have two-three minutes at each piece of butcher paper. Review the 4 S's of brainstorming (Structure 1:2). Remind teams they will have only two minutes at each sheet of butcher paper to come up with as many solutions for the issue as they can. Each team will be at a different sheet of butcher paper and will simultaneously be brainstorming issues.

Brainstorming:

Teacher Monitors, and Teams Rotate on Signal

Ask students to begin brainstorming. You need to be monitoring responses in the different groups. Take some notes for discussion purposes. At the end of two-three minutes, give the signal for teams to switch. This signal could be a timer, bell, lights on and off, or whatever you prefer. Keep switching until teams have had an opportunity to brainstorm on all issues.

Teacher Talk:

Point System Explained

Explain to teams that it is sometimes easier to reach a decision when everyone has input to the decision. This point system involves everyone in the decision making process.

Review with teams the point system they are to use.

Blue	=	25 Points
Red	=	15 Points
Yellow	=	5 Points

Have the point value posted on the wall, on the board, or overhead for students to refer to. Give teams blue, red, and yellow stick-on dots so each team member will have one set (blue, red, & a yellow dot) for each issue. If there are seven issues each student will have seven sets of dots. They are to place the dots on the three solutions they feel the strongest about, placing the blue by the solution they feel is the best, red on next best, and yellow as their third choice. Check for understanding by randomly asking a few students to explain what they will be doing with the dots.

Note: You can also use a set of colored pens (a blue, red, & yellow) for each team if you do not want to invest in the colored dots. I recommend you try the dots if you haven't used them before. They create a different feeling than the pens. Try it both ways.

Color-Coded Prioritizing:
Teams use Point System and Rotate

Direct students to begin using their dots on an issue by taking turns within teams. They are to place their dots on the solutions they feel are best for solving the particular issue. Monitor for any problems. Have teams rotate when you give them a signal (timer, bell, etc.) as you see teams are completed. Ask some teams to speed-up if they are holding up other teams. Teams need to rotate simultaneously on your signal.

Teams Report: Tally The Totals

When teams are at the last sheet of butcher paper, direct students to complete placing their dots and then to add up the points for the top three point winners on the sheet. Remind students of the point values. When teams have computed point scores have them report to the class. Star or circle the top solution on each sheet.

(I first heard of this concept from Trudy Schoneman, Principal of Fox School in Belmont, CA. Trudy uses this approach at her faculty meetings to involve her staff in school decisions. I've also used it with our staff. It works!)

Reflections & Affirmations
Numbered Heads Together:
Reflection Questions

Step 1: Number off.

Step 2: Teacher presents a question.

Step 3: Each team puts heads together to discuss.

Step 4: Teams share with the entire class.

Choose the questions from below which are most relevant to your students or create your own.

- How do you feel about the solutions the class came up with?
- How important are these issues to resolve?
- If they were resolved, how would our class, school, or community improve?
- How well did your team work together during brainstorming?
- How might you have improved your working relationship?
- How did you feel about using the point system?

Think-Pair-Square: Affirmations
Think:

Have students Think of an appropriate affirmation they could give to each of their team members. Remind students that they can use the affirmation starters which are posted if they run into difficulty.

Pair:

Students now Pair with one of their teammates and share what their affirmations were for their teammate and the other team members.

Square:

Team members now take turns Sharing the affirmations for each team member. Team members' response to receiving affirmations should only be "thank you."

Affirmation Starters:

Great job recording, _____ .

I like the way you were supportive _____.

Thanks for your help, _____ .

~ ❋ ~

Lesson 21 Team Roles Review

Lesson-At-A-Glance

Goal: Teambuilding (Mutual Support)
Grades: 3-Adult
Time: 45-90 Minutes
Outcome—Students will:
- Learn the roles of Checker, Gatekeeper, Recorder, and Praiser.
- Practice each of the roles .

Materials:
- Role definitions on a poster or chart paper
- Handout of team roles, one per team
- Pairs questions written on the board
- Overhead projector for Stand and Deliver
- Reflection questions, and affirmation starters posted

Structures:
- **Pairs**
- **Numbered Heads Together (Stand and Deliver Format)**
- **Choral Response**
- **Team Discussion**
- **Roundrobin**

Lesson Overview[1]

This lesson is designed to teach students four roles and how to perform these roles in their team. Students will use Partners to learn the duties and the **Stand and Deliver** format of Numbered Heads to review these roles.

Getting Ready

Assign Students to Teams

Students can be assigned to permanent or short term teams. However, the teams should be together long enough so that the lesson can be repeated, allowing each student an opportunity to practice each role presented.

Lesson Sequence

Pairs:

Same Roles Meet Review Roles

Have a poster, chart, or overhead with the team roles (you can enlarge the roles handout following this activity if you have a poster maker in your Instructional Materials Center) and one handout of team roles per team. Have teams count off one to four. Assign each person on a team a partner from another team who has the same number. (2 from Team "A" will pair # 2 from Team "B", etc. Have all the # 1's meet with their partners in one corner of room. Have the other numbers meet in pairs in the other corners. Let students know they can ask others who are studying the same role for assistance if they need it.

This way if they have questions or the teacher needs to provide added instruction about a specific role it can be accomplished easily. Discuss with the total class what the purpose of each role is and how that role helps the team be successful.[2]
- # 1's will discuss the role of Checker
- # 2's will discuss the role of Gatekeeper
- # 3's will discuss the role of Recorder
- # 4's discuss the role of Praiser/Affirmer

---

1. Special note: Stand and deliver should be practiced on something easier before used with this lesson.

2. An excellent resource for assuming roles is the "Role-Cards Packet", published by Kagan Cooperative Learning.

Pairs Discuss Role Questions

Remind students they will soon be practicing the role and need to teach it to their other team members.

Pairs now review the role and discuss the following questions which are written on the board:

• What is difficult about this role?

• What makes this role important?

• What are some ways you might teach this role to your team members?

Monitor the pairs. If you find you need to review a role with more than one pair then it's a good idea to review it with all the pairs studying that role. <u>Give pairs five to seven minutes to discuss the questions above.</u> When time is up have them thank their partners and return to their teams.

Teacher Talk:

Explain Stand and Deliver

Stand and Deliver is a variation of the Numbered Heads structure. The teacher poses questions or situations to the students. Teams are to put their heads together to discuss possible responses and choose the the best one. Next, call on the students to respond by calling out a number 1 - 4. The person who has that number on each team will respond by standing. An incentive to stand up fast is if you usually call on the first person standing. *This structure is explained in detail in Part II, 1:1.*

Ask the following questions of the teams one at a time. When you select a student to answer the question, you can have them answer only part of the question and ask them to stop. Thank them and then ask another student standing to answer the next part. This way several students can provide answers and you'll have more participation. Many teachers using "Stand and Deliver" use an overhead to keep track of points they

award to teams. The key in doing this is to keep the team standing as close as possible so that one team doesn't pull too far ahead allowing the others to become discouraged and quit trying.

Numbered Heads Together:

Stand and Deliver Questions

a. What is the one duty of the Checker? Another?

b. What is one responsibility of the Praiser? Another?

c. What is a role of the Gatekeeper? Another?

d. What is a role of the Recorder? Another?

e. How do you tell if everybody understands the task?

f. What is one example of affirmations the Praiser might use? Another?

g. What kinds of problems might a recorder have? How could you help your recorder?

As students answer questions record points on the overhead for each team. The points do not have to necessarily be used for anything. Some teachers use them for extra credit or bonus points. Again, the important aspect is to keep all the teams close in point totals.

Choral Response:

Review and Practice

Explain Choral Response and tell students you will be using Choral Response to review. Ask all students to respond at the same time (refer to Part II, 2:1 for more information on Choral Response). Show students your hand signal. I usually hold my right hand palm forward, up high, so all students can see it. Explain that you will ask a question, while you have your hand raised. They are to think of a response. After a few seconds you will lower your hand straight down. When you do this students are to respond in unison. If students do not respond in unison, repeat the procedure until they do. When they can do it consistently praise the class.

Choral Response: Questions

1. The person whose job it is to write down information needed in the group is _____.

2. They ask team members if they understand the task. Their role is _____.

3. They try to make sure no one student dominates the team. Their role is _____.

4. They refer to the Affirmation starters on the wall. They are the _____.

5. They make sure each person participates. They are the _____.

6. They do the writing for brainstorming. They are the _____.

7. They keep track of how many Affirmations are given in the team. They are the

_____.

8. Might ask a teammate to explain how they got the answer. They are _____.

Reflections & Affirmations

Team Discussion:

Reflection Questions[3]

Have one handout of the following questions for each team. Have the gate-keeper on each team read the questions. The students will continue in their roles (gate-keeper, checker, recorder, and praiser. The recorder will write down team responses to each question.

---

3. As the teams are working on these questions, move around the room listening to various teams. This reminds teams that you expect them to be on task. After about five minutes, randomly call on teams to answer the different questions. This provides accountability for being on task.

- ❧ What was difficult about this activity for your team?
- ❧ What more do you need to know about the roles?
- ❧ Which of these roles will be most difficult for you?
- ❧ How might you help team members be successful in their role?
- ❧ How will knowing each of these roles help your team be more successful?
- ❧ How might you practice using these roles?

Roundrobin: Affirmations

Have teams do a Roundrobin of affirmations by having them start with person #1. Other team members will give as many affirmations as they can to person #1 in thirty seconds. The teacher needs to be the time keeper. Tell teams when to switch. Remind students they can use the affirmation starters if they need to and have the ones below posted if you do not have a class list.

Affirmation Starters:

_____ , thanks for doing such a good job.

_____ , you were fast on your feet.

Way to go, _____ .

Team Roles

Checker

It's important for team members to know if everyone on the team understands the task and the reasons behind the team's answer.

Job Responsibilities:

1. Ask team members if they understand the task. Have them explain the task to the team.

2. Check if team members understand the process of the task by asking them to give an example.

3. Be sure all team members can give reasons for solutions of decisions.

Gatekeeper

The Gatekeeper equalizes participation in the team. If one member is talking too much the gatekeeper "shuts the gate," and asks others for their responses.

Job Responsibilities:

1. Monitors that all team members have an equal opportunity to participate.

2. Asks others for input if they are not participating.

Recorder

This person's job is to do any writing required by the team for group projects. Other members may assist with spelling or suggestions. The recorder does the writing.

Job Responsibilities:

1. When one paper is expected from the team, the recorder will do the writing for this paper.

2. Do all writing for brainstorming and other note taking.

Praiser

Giving Affirmations is a valuable skill for team members to develop. The praiser is designated as the person who gives Affirmations to all team members. It's important for the praiser to be sincere and real when giving Affirmations. If the praiser needs assistance, other members can make suggestions.

Job Responsibilities:

1. Give Affirmations to fellow team members when they do something helpful, correct or make a good effort.

2. Refer to Affirmation chart for suggestions.

3. Keep track of how many Affirmations you give in an activity. Spread the Affirmations among all team members.

Role Cards

Checker

Gatekeeper

Praiser

Frontview

backview

Praiser   Make sure each teammate feels good.

Gambits:

1. "Great job Johnny!"
2. "You always have an interesting opinion, Sue."
3.

4.
5.
6.

"The Role-Cards Packet" is available from Kagan Cooperative Learning.

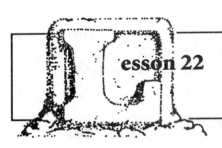

Lesson 22 Blocks to Active Listening

Lesson-At-A-Glance

Goal: Relationship Skills (Active Listening)

Grades: K-Adult

Time: 40-55 Minutes

Outcomes — Students Will:
- Begin to recognize how non-verbal active listening skills can enhance communication.
- Experience blocks to active listening.
- Practice non-verbal active listening.
- Share their feelings about the experience.

Materials:
Overhead, handout, or chart with description of blocks to active litening and with steps of active listening.

Structures:
- **Pairs**
- **Choral Response**
- **Pair-Share Together**
- **Numbered Heads (Stand & Deliver)**
- **Three-Step Interview**

Lesson Overview

Students will learn about "blocks" to active listening and will experience these "blocks" as both sender and receiver. Students will learn the basics of effective, active listening and will practice using these non-verbal active listening skills as both sender and receiver. It's important to complete both parts of the lesson on the same day so that students who have experienced "poor" listening can immediately contrast it with "active listening."

Lesson Sequence

Teacher Talk:

Discuss Blocks to Active Listening

Share with students the blocks to active listening. Use the attached handout which describes the blocks and/or uses as an overhead or chart. Put-downs could also be discussed as blocks to communication. Discuss how these different blocks impede effective speaking and listening.

Note: If you are adapting for a younger group, you might concentrate on put-downs as blocks to active listening rather than using the roadblocks listed here.

Pairs:

Choosing Pairs & Numbering Off

Place students in pairs. Tell students that this lesson will allow them to practice communication skills. Ask students to decide in their pair which one of them will be #1 and which one will be #2. Ask all students who are #1 to raise their hands to check that all pairs have made a choice.

Choral Response: Review Rules

A. Rules for the Talker

Explain that in this lesson there will be two roles, the talker and the listener. The talker will be talking about something they enjoy doing. It might be a hobby, sport, going to movie, taking a vacation, or whatever they choose to share. Remind students, if you need to, that is must be appropriate to share in class.

Choral Response prompt: "What do we call the person speaking?" Two seconds of wait time. Hand signal. Choral Response from the class. "TALKER."

B. Rules for the Listener

The listener's task during this part of the lesson is to use some of the blocks to active listening (or put-downs) which are listed on the handout, chart, or overhead. Review the roadblocks and role play for students that you want students to exaggerate the blocks as thier partner is talking and keep it up until time is called. The rule is no physical contact or vulgarity.

Choral Response: Choral prompt: "Which role uses the roadblocks (or put-downs)?" Two seconds of wait time. Hand signal. Choral Response from the class. "LISTEN-ER."

Pair-Share: Final Rules and Start

Remind students that this exercise is an opportunity to experience blocks to active listening and to do their best in their roles as talkers and listen-ers. Talkers will have one minute to share their interest. Listeners will practice using blocks to active listening. Talker and listener should be sitting facing each other squarely without anything

between them. (if possible). Their knees should be within an inch of each other's. Have two students demonstrate sitting appropriately.

Choral Response: Choral prompt: "How much time will the talker have?" Two seconds of wait time. Hand signal. Choral Response from the class. "ONE MINUTE."

*Note: The use of Choral REsponse can be a powerful classbuilder. It involves 100% of your students and gives you direct feedback on whether they understand your directions. The hand signal and wait time need to be practiced. Practice CHoral Response in other lessons where you want direct feedback which will involve all of your students. Review the rules for Choral Response in Part II, page 6: 7, before doing this section of the lesson.

Talker Begins

Ask the Talkers to begin. Remind Listeners to use the blocks to active listening. Walk around the room monitoring the pairs. At the end of one minute ask talkers to stop. I may stop at the end of thirty seconds if students are really getting into it. I find that one minute can be too frustrating for some groups.

Switch Roles and Teacher Monitor

Ask students to swith roles. (The person who was the Talker will become the Listener and vice-versa). Ask the Talker to think of what they would like to talk about. Remind the Listener to use the blocks to active listening. Make sure they are still facing one another. Ask Talkers to start again. Walk around the room monitoring the pairs' interaction.

After one minute ask Talkers to stop. Tell students to hold on to any felings they have about this lesson until a little later when they will have time to share. Students stay in their pairs.

Choral Response

A. Review Activie Listening

Introduce the ground rules for active listening from the handout or overhead at the end of this lesson. Explain to students that we will only be using the non-verbal aspects of active listening for this lesson. These include eye contact, nodding and leaning forward. We will not practice paraphrasing of reflective listening. In non-verbal active listening, the listener doesn't say anything. She/he keeps eye contact, can nod and lean forward appropriately. Discuss how non-verbal active listening means that the listener does not talk.

CHORAL REPONSE: Choral prompt: "The Listener in non-verbal active listening maintains eye _____." Two seconds of wait time. Hand signal. Choral Response from the class. "CONTACT."

CHORAL RESPONSE: Choral prompt: "The Listener in non-verbal active listening does not _____." Two seconds of wait time. Hand signal. Choral Response from the class. "TALK."

B. Rules for Talker and Listener for Round #2

During this round the person who spoke first last time will speak first again. Try to share the same information as before. The Listener's job is to use the non-verbal active listening skills discussed. They are to be good active listeners by using eye contact, appropriate nodding and leaning forward, and not talking. Tell students they have one minute; Talkers begin. Walk around the room monitoring the interaction. At the end of one minute, ask Talkers, to stop.

Pair-Share

Switch Roles and Complete Round #2

Now ask the Talker and Listener to switch roles. Remind the Talker to talk about what they shared last time. Remind listeners to use thier non-verbal active listening skills. Tell students they have one minute; Talkers begin. At the end one minute, ask students to stop.

Note: This activity was adapted from *Tribes: A Process for Social Development and Cooperative Learning* by Jeanne Gibbs with further refinements by Robert Rudholm of California State University, Stanislaus.

Reflections & Affirmations

Numbered Heads Together (Stand and Deliver):

Debrief and Reflections

Have pairs join another pair to form teams of four. Have teams number off 1-4. Review rules for Stand and Deliver. You will be giving teams a minute or two to discuss each question. Teams call out a number. The students with that number will stand to represent their teams. Call on several teams to share their answers. See Numbered Heads Together, page 6:25, for more information on this structure.

A. Debriefing and Discuss Talker's Role (Choose one or two)

- Who would like to share what they experienced differently as a Talker during Round 1 and Round 2?
- How did Talkers feel when the blocks or put-downs were being used?
- How did Talkers feel when the Listener was using non-verbal active listening skills?
- Do others ever use some of these blocks when they talk with you? (Your parents, teachers, friends?) Which would you prefer, blocks/put-downs or active listening?

B. Debrief and Discuss the Listener Role (Choose one or two)

Have a few students share with the class how it felt to be Listener using the blocks. Ask students to tell how they felt using non-verbal active listening skills.

- Listeners, how comfortable did you feel using the blocks or put-downs?

- How did the Listener using the blocks hinder good communication?

- How could using non-verbal active listening help communication?

C. Reflection Questions
(Choose one or two)

↝ How could you use your knowledge about blocks/put-downs to help you discover why your communication with someone isn't working?

↝ How could you use active listening to improve your listening skills?

Three-Step Interview:
Affirmations

Ask students to think of appropriate affirmations they might give their partner (Step 1). THen have students pair with a different person on their team and share those affirmations as they are being interviewed (Step 2). For Step 3 their partner will paraphrase to the team the affirmations they chose. Post the ones below or others for students to refer to if needed.

Affirmation Starters:
Thanks for.....
I appreciate the way you....
You were great when you.....

Blocks to Active Listening

Ordering: You must...

Threatening: If you don't, then...

Preaching: You should...

Lecturing: Do you realize...

Providing Answers: What I would do is...

Judging: You are bad...lazy!

Excusing: You'll feel better...

Diagnosing: I know what you need...

(Permission to reproduce for classroom use)

Active Listening

- EYE CONTACT

- NODDING
- PARAPHRASING
- REFLECTIVE LISTENING

- LEANING FORWARD

(Permission to reproduce for classroom use)

VANSTON SHAW: *Communitybuilding in the Classroom*
Publisher: Kagan Cooperative Learning • 1 (800) Wee Co-op

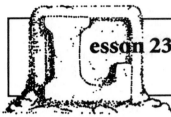

Lesson 23 Pairs Share and Listen

Lesson-At-A-Glance

Goal: Relationship Skills (Active Listening)

Grades: K-Adult

Time: 15-30 minutes depending on their communication skills

Outcomes — Students Will:
• Share personal experiences.
• Use non-verbal active listening skills.

Materials:
Directions on the board, chart, overhead, or as a handout for each pair
Posted non-verbal active listening skills

Structures:
• Brainstorming
• Numbered Heads Together
• Role Play
• Pairs
• Think-Pair-Share

Lesson Overview

This lesson provides a model for non-verbal active listening and an opportunity for students to practice with each other. Students begin with Brainstorming indicators of non-verbal active listening strategies. Students will role play non-verbal active listening

Note: You are also welcome to reproduce the previous page with the drawings and use this as an overhead or handout.

Lesson Sequence

Brainstorming:

When is a Person Listening

Ask students how important it is to be able to tell if someone is listening when you are talking. Ask students to brainstorm in teams how they can tell when someone is listening even if the other person is not talking.

Class Chart

As you call on students representing various teams to share their teams brainstorming results write on a class chart or overhead some of their suggestions. One way to equalize participation is by having each team Roundrobin share one idea at a time. Using this approach the first two teams called on don't have the lions share of ideas.

Numbered Heads Together:

Responses from Teams

Students in each team will number off 1-4. Ask students the following questions one at a time and receive feedback from each team as you call on the numbers (refer to Numbered Heads Together in the Structures Section).

1. What is one way to show you are actively listening using your eyes? Be prepared to demonstrate.

2. What is one way to show you are actively listening using your head? Be prepared to demonstrate.

3. What is one way to show you are actively listening using your body? Be prepared to demonstrate.

4. What are some other ways you can demonstrate active listening? (Answers will vary; accept reasonable responses.)

Record appropriate responses on the board or overhead. Use student responses and your own suggestions to write the following criteria on a chart:

Eye Contact

Nodding

Leaning Forward

Tell students that today we are going to practice using non-verbal active listening skills. You will need to remind them the difference between verbal and non-verbal.

Student Role Play:
Use Non-verbal Active Listening

Ask two students to model the non-verbal active listening skills of eye contact, nodding, and leaning forward. One student will be the Listener and the other will be the Talker. The talker will share something they did last week that was fun or interesting. The Listener will use non-verbal active listening skills. Have the two students role play for one minute.

Note: If students are unable to model the listener role appropriately, you may model that role.

Ask the class if the Listener used all three of the non-verbal active listening skills. Thank the students who modeled the activity.

Teacher Talk:

Pairs Number off

Tell students they will now have an opportunity to practice using this skill. Have students form pairs (either random or preassigned) and ask each pair to number off one and two. Ask for a show of hands of all the number one's. All the number two's raise their hands. Number one will be the Talker. Number two will be the Listener.

Pairs:
Choose Topic to Share

Students choose from the following, depending on the age and interests of your students, or make up your own:

a. Something interesting that happened the past week.

b. Your favorite TV program.

c. Your favorite family vacation

d. What you like to do best on a Saturday afternoon

(The key to topic choices is to make the introductory lesson as easy as possible. We are not searching for deep truths, only non-verbal active listening.) Pairs should quickly tell their partners the topic they chose.

Teacher Talk:
Check for Understanding

Once you have explained directions to students, it is important that you check to see if they understood. There are several approaches to doing this. One sequence I recommend is:

1. Ask for a volunteer to paraphrase the directions. If the student is correct, go to step 3.

2. If volunteer is incorrect, give the directions again, and repeat step 1.

3. Ask that one volunteer in each team paraphrase the directions within the team.

4. Randomly call on a student to paraphrase the directions. If they are incorrect, ask a volunteer from each team to paraphrase the directions.

Never leave this step until you are certain students understand the instructions.

Pair-Share:
Students use Active Listening Skills
Round One

Inform talkers they have one minute to talk. Remind Listeners to use those non-verbal active listening skills. Talkers begin. (As you time the students, walk around the room observing on task behavior, and use of appropriate speaking and listening skills.)

At the end of one minute, raise your hand and ask students to stop talking.

Note: If students are not using the active listening skills, do not interfere yet. Students may not yet understand, and they may catch on by the next round or others may give these students a model of how to do it correctly on the next rounds. Remember this is an introductory lesson.

Round Two

Now explain to the class that they will switch roles and person number one will become the Listener and use non-verbal active listening. Person number two will become the Talker. Tell students they have one minute and begin. As you time the students, again walk around the room and monitor. As you see good examples of active listening, make a mental note or jot these down to share later. At the end of one minute, raise your hand (or use your own signal to gain attention) and ask your students to stop talking and give you their attention.

Teacher's Note: With older students or adults you can mention that sometimes people need to share without being interrupted. Some of us tend to block communication with our need to interject. Good listeners are intent on what the

speaker is saying and are not making up responses as the person is sharing. Not many people use effective communication skills all the time. This is an introduction into active listening. Now you and your students need to practice with each other and at home.

Reflections & Affirmations

Pairs: Reflections

Have students stay in their pairs. Give the pairs a few minutes to discuss the questions from below or others you create.

- Why might it difficult to use non verbal active listening behaviors?
- Why might it be difficult not to talk?
- Was it difficult to talk for one minute? Why do you think so?
- When was the last time you spoke without being interrupted for a full minute?
- Did you enjoy talking or listening more? Why?
- Why do you feel it's important to use non-verbal active listening?

Think-Pair-Share: Affirmations

Ask students to think of a way to thank their partner for talking and listening. Give students one minute **think** time. Have students **pair** with the partner they have been with and **share** one affirmation with this partner. Monitor this by randomly asking students to share the affirmation they received. This shows students they are accountable for participating.

Lesson 24 Affirmation, Put-Down Brainstorm

Relationship Skills
• Affirmations

Lesson-At-A-Glance

Goal: Relationship Skills (Affirmations)

Grades: 3-Adult

Time: 30-45 Minutes

Outcomes — Students Will:
• Use brainstorming.
• Distinguish between affirmations and put-downs.

Materials:
• Paper for students to use during brainstorming
• Written reflection questions and affirmation starters posted

Structures:
• **Line-Up**
• **Think-Pair-Share**
• **Brainstorming**
• **Team Discussion**
• **Roundrobin**

Lesson Overview

This lesson gives students an opportunity to distinguish between affirmations and put-downs in a fun, fast method. Students will brainstorm affirmations and put-downs and discuss how each affects us.

Lesson Sequence

Line-Up: Form Pairs[1]

Ask students to line up by birthday, (month and day) and group the students together in pairs.

---

1. You can also form random groups by counting off. If you have 32 students in your class and you want groups of four, have students count off by eight. This way you'll end up with eight groups of four. If you have less or more then have one or two groups of three or five.

Think-Pair-Share:

Discuss Affirmations

Discuss with students that affirmations are compliments, comments, or encouraging statements which make people feel good. Ask students to **think** of a comment another person made which made them feel good. Have students **pair** with another student and take turns sharing the affirmation they received. Randomly select students to **share** the affirmation their partner recalled. Record these on the board, overhead, or chart.

Brainstorming:

The Four S's, Roles and Affirmations

Have two pairs form groups of four before explaining Brainstorming.

Share the Rules for Brainstorming: Four S's

Speed - Quick sharing of ideas. (1-3 minutes)

Suspend Judgment - Defer judging ideas, no comments

Silly - Off the wall ideas are encouraged. All ideas are OK

Synergy - Build on ideas of others
(See brainstorming structure summary for a page with the Four S's which can be used as an overhead master.)

Groups Select Roles and Brainstorm Affirmations

Announce that there will be four roles on each team for the brainstorming task. The roles are:

- **Taskmaster** (keep everyone on task)
- **Recorder** (write down what the group brainstorms)
- **Speed Captain** (monitor the time; keep the team going quickly)
- **Encourager** (keep the team going)

Ask all recorders to raise their hands and hold up the pencil or pen and paper they are going to use. Direct teams to come up with as many affirmations as they can. The recorder will list the affirmations. Teams only have three minutes. Have teams start. Monitor the groups and intervene if a group isn't functioning. Stop the groups after three minutes.

Count the Number of Affirmations

Ask each group to count the number of affirmations they listed and write that number on a sheet of paper, so you can see it from where you are when you give the signal. Total the number of affirmations for the class. If your students did a good job, congratulate them.

Teacher Talk:

Discuss Put-downs with Class

Ask students what we call the opposite of affirmations. Give them think time. Students may come up with "put-downs" or something similar. Ask students to give a few put-downs they have received and tell how they felt receiving them. Discuss that put-downs can come from family, friends, classmates, teachers, or anyone.

Brainstorming: Put-downs

Keep students in their groups. Roles can stay the same or change - it's up to you. Ask students to brainstorm as many put-downs as they can in three minutes. These can be put-downs they have heard from students, parents, teachers, or anyone else. Remind students of the brainstorming rules. Ask recorders to hold up pen or pencil and paper to check that each group has a recorder. Tell students to begin. Stop groups after three minutes

Count the Number of Put-downs

Ask each team to count the number of put-downs their team listed, and write it on a large piece of paper. Have teams hold up their count simultaneously when you give the signal. Record the number on the chalkboard or overhead so the class can see how many. Write the total the number of put-downs next to the total number of affirmations.

Reflections & Affirmations
Roundrobin Team Discussion:
Reflections

Analyze the Difference

Look at the difference between the numbers of affirmations and put-downs listed by students. Usually, they come up with more put-downs than affirmations. Whatever the case use this as a springboard for team discussion. Have the following questions posted. Give the teams a time limit and ask for feedback.

Use Roundrobin Team Discussion to answer the questions.

1. Person #1 on each team chooses a question and asks it of the group. The group discusses the question.

2. Person #2 selects another question. The team discusses it.

3. If time allows, this process continues.

Reflections

- Why did groups come up with more put-downs than affirmations?

- Are put-downs used more often than affirmations? Why?

- How do you feel when you give a put-down? When you receive one?

- How could you use more affirmations when you interact with others?

- How could you use more affirmations in your personal life?

- What kinds of affirmations could you use in class?

Roundrobin: Affirmations

Ask students to give one another affirmations using Roundrobin. The recorder starts by giving an affirmation to the person to his/her right. The person receiving the affirmation can say only "thank you". Students each take a turn giving an affirmation to the person to their right.

Affirmations

- Way to go!
- Great!
- Wow!
- Cool!
- Good job!
- Fantastic!
- Nice job!
- You know how!

Affirmation Starters:

I liked the way you ......

_____ you had great ideas.

You are great at ....

~ ✤ ~

esson 25 101 Affirmations

Lesson-At-A-Glance

Goal: Relationship Skills (Affirmations)

Grades: 3-Adult

Time: 30-45 Minutes

Outcomes — Students will:
· Develop a class list of affirmations.
· Follow Brainstorming rules.
· Become more aware of how to use appropriate affirmations.
· Practice using affirmations.

Materials:
· Affirmation lists from Brainstorming Lesson 24 (if available)
· Butcher paper or chart paper
· Colored pens

Structures:
· **Think-Pair-Share**
· **Brainstorming**
· **Roundrobin**
· **Team Discussion**
· **Roundtable**

Lesson Overview

This can be an extension of the previous lesson or a lesson of its own. The purpose of this lesson is to have the students start developing a list of at least 101 ways they can give one another an affirmation. You can modify the number you want to 40 or 60 or whatever you choose based on the age of your students, etc. Also included at the end of this lesson is a list of ways you can give affirmations to students.

Lesson Sequence

Teacher Talk:
Discuss Affirmations, Share One You Received

Discuss put-downs and affirmations with students. Ask for examples of each.

Now discuss with students the last time you (the teacher) received an affirmation, what it was, and how it felt. It is important to share yourself. This models for students a way for them to respond, and gives students information about you as a person, not only as a teacher.

Think-Pair-Share: Last Time
Students Received an Affirmation

Give students one minute to recall the last time they received an affirmation. Have students pair up and share the "last affirmation" they can remember receiving (2-3 minutes). Randomly call on several students to describe their last affirmations with the entire class (five minutes).

Brainstorming: 101 Affirmations

Now place students in teams of four, have students select roles, review roles and the four S's of brainstorming (Chapter Two). Pass out the butcher paper and colored pens, and ask students to brainstorm as many affirmations as they can. Explain the class goal will be to come up with at least 101 different affirmations which can be posted. These can be a single word, phrases or short sentences (five minutes).

Roundrobin:
Sharing Brainstormed Lists

After 5 minutes of brainstorming, have the teams show their lists to the rest of the class. One way to do this is have teams take turns telling one item at a time. Rotate the roles you call on so everyone in the class can share. As students speak, list their affirmations on butcher paper or the chalk board (five minutes). It's important to move this along quickly so students stay tuned in.

Post List, Count, Set Next Goal

Post the list which has been created, count the number of affirmations, and estimate how many students could come up with if given another opportunity. Calculate how far from 101 affirmations you are and establish a goal of 101. A homework assignment might be for students to come up with as many new affirmations as they can for their team and to report on them the next day.

Reflections & Affirmations

Roundrobin Team Discussion:
Reflection Questions

Write the following questions on an overhead or on the board.

Use Roundrobin Team Discussion to answer the questions.

1. Person #1 on each team chooses a question and asks it of the group. The group discusses the question.

2. Person #2 selects another question. The team discusses it.

3. If time allows, this process continues.

Call on each group to provide their response to at least one question. Remember, discussion and reflection questions are steps in the lesson which often promotes the most learning. Don't leave them out.

- Was it difficult to think of affirmations? Why?

- How well did your team follow the brainstorming rules? How could you improve?

- How comfortable would you feel using all of the affirmations on our list?

- Why is affirming others important?

Roundtable: Affirmation Starters

Ask students to use one sheet of paper and one pencil per team. The person who starts will write one affirmation (which could be for any other teammate), and passes it to the person to their right with the pencil. This person writes an affirmation and passes the paper and pencil. Give teams two minutes.

Affirmations Starters

_____ , thanks for the great ideas you came up with.

You are _____ .

Note: An extension on this activity would be to have students graph the number of affirmations they receive during a twenty four hour period. Bring this back to class and discuss it.

Partial List of Affirmations
Some Teachers Use

That's great!
Good job!
Way to go!
I like you.
GREAT!
Rad.
Wow!
Fantastic!
Beautiful!
Sweet.
You've got it.
That's the best.
You're the best.
That's good.
I appreciate you
for.......
Thanks.
Thanks for your help.
You're a lot of help.

You're tops.
Great smile.
You're a winner.
Good!
Better every day.
Good going.
Excellent!
Outstanding!
You're fun to be with.
You did that fast.
I think you're the best.
Way to go.
SUPER!
Terrific!
You did it!
I like it.
etc., etc., etc.

(Permission to reproduce for classroom use)

───────VANSTON SHAW: *Communitybuilding in the Classroom*───────
Publisher: Kagan Cooperative Learning • 1(800) Wee Co-op

Chapter 7: 94

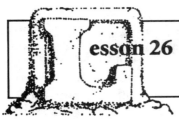

Lesson 26 Victory, Viper, Vulture

Lesson-At-A-Glance

Goal: Relationship Skills (Affirmations)

Grades: 4-Adult

Time: 30-50 Minutes (for each of three lessons)

Outcomes — Students will:
- Use non-verbal active listening skills of eye contact, leaning forward, and appropriate head nodding.
- Learn to recognize and signal when they hear affirmations, self put-downs, or put-downs of others.
- Demonstrate the use of this skill in class.

Materials:
- Directions on the board, overhead projector, or as a handout for each pair
- Affirmation starters posted

Structures:
Mini Lesson #1
- **Brainstorming**
- **Team Project**
- **Team Discussion**
- **Roundtable**

Mini Lesson #2
- **Think-Pair-Share**
- **Numbered Heads Together**
- **Roundrobin**

Mini Lesson #3
- **Pairs**
- **Inside-Outside Circle**
- **Numbered Heads Together**
- **Think-Pair-Share**

Lesson Overview[1]

These lessons teach students to recognize affirmations, self put-downs, and put-downs of others. We know how important it is for students to use affirmations and avoid put-downs of self or others. However, sometimes it is difficult to know when students have learned the lesson. In these lessons, you will teach students a strategy to demonstrate that they recognize the difference between these behaviors. The lessons have been arranged into mini lessons each no longer than 50 minutes. This should allow you to teach the lessons you feel are appropriate for your students in the sequence you choose.

Lesson Sequence

It may be important for your students to focus initially only on affirmations and put-downs and not go into self put-downs. Self put-downs are an important concept, but you can only teach so many concepts at one time. I would suggest teaching "victory for affirmations" first. After students have demonstrated mastery of this concept, move on to "vultures for put-downs." Once your students have demonstrated mastery of both victory and vultures, then you can introduce students to vipers. "Vipers for Self put-downs" is an especially important concept for junior and senior high school students, who are at an age where self doubts and self put-downs are at their height.

---

1. I first heard of Victory, Viper, & Vulture from Gordon Chan, a high school teacher in Modesto, California. He said he originally got the idea from Gail Dusa.

Note: An option would be to do Lesson 24 (brainstorming affirmations and put-downs) first and use this as the follow-up without repeating the brainstorming.

Modeling

It is important to model the use of the Victory, Vulture, and Viper on a regular basis and reinforce their use if you want your students to continue to use them.

Mini Lesson #1

Recognize Affirmations with "VICTORY"

Brainstorming: Affirmations

Discuss with students the kind of words schoolmates say to them that make them feel good (refer to Affirmation/Put-down Brainstorming, page 24:1). If students have already come up with another list and it is posted, refer to it. If not, have student groups of four brainstorm as many affirmations as they can in one minute. Have students report what they brainstormed and then add up the number for the class. Record the total on the board. Discuss the types of words teachers might use to make students feel good. Ask students to brainstorm these. Share these with the class. What kinds of words might parents use? Brainstorm and share with the class.

Teacher Talk and Demonstration:

Visual Cue for Affirmations

The signal to use when you hear an affirmation is a "V" finger sign, as used near the end of World War II by Winston Churchill and also used in the early seventies as a peace symbol. Demonstrate this for students. Ask for a volunteer and ask them to give an affir-mation to you or another student in class. The rule is that the affirmation must sound genuine and not phony. This may be difficult for students. However, it is important that students give genuine affirmations or others will know the difference.

Students Practice:

Affirmations and Teacher Monitors

Now, tell students you are going to test them by giving some affirmations. Your students' job will be to recognize the affirmation when they hear it and give the victory signal. You need to model genuine affirmations for your students. These affirmations should be specific to individual students to begin with. Some examples you might use are:

"Ryan, that drawing you did was excellent. I especially appreciated the colors you used."

"Kirston, in the story you wrote, I particularly like the way you developed your characters and made them seem alive."

Some examples of statements which are <u>not</u> affirmations are:

"Ryan, that was a good drawing. However, your colors were too bright."

"Kirston, in the story you wrote, I like your characters, however you didn't provide enough detail."

Monitor Student Responses

Monitor student responses and give teams feedback on their identification of affirmations. Pick out teams that have done an excellent job and give the team recognition in front of the class.

Team Project:
Role Play Practice

Now ask students in their groups to design role plays using real affirmations and phoney affirmations. Give groups two minutes to come up with one role play. Call on one team to role play while the rest of the class gives the affirmation "V" sign each time an affirmation is used.

Team Discussion:
Reflection Questions

Have the questions below written on the board. Direct groups to discuss the possible answers. Have them share responses with the class.

Discussion Questions

- ↝ Why is it important to recognize affirmations when you receive one?

- ↝ Why is it important to give affirmations?

Reflection Questions

- ↝ How do you feel when you give affirmations?

- ↝ Why might it be difficult for you to receive affirmations? How might you change this?

Simultaneous Roundtable:
Team Affirmations

Have each team member write their name at the top of a blank piece of paper. Then they pass their paper to the right. Team members are to write one affirmation for the person whose paper they have. It can be regarding the lesson or from another interaction. The following affirmation starters can be written on the board.

The affirmation I enjoyed the most was........

I appreciated ....

You were quick at ....

Mini Lesson #2

Recognize Put-downs of Others with "VULTURES"

Put-downs of others are endemic in most of the schools I visit, and teachers often ask me "What can we do about it?" I believe that to reduce their use of put-downs, students must first recognize what put-downs are. Secondly, students must consider how it feels to receive a put-down. Third, students need to have an alternative to giving put-downs. This lesson assists students to recognize put-downs and has students discuss how it feels to receive a put-down. (The victory mini lesson taught students to give affirmations as an alternative to put-downs).

Teacher Talk and Demonstration:
The Vulture Signal

When students hear a put-down (given to someone else or themselves) they are to use the "vulture signal". This is made by curling the first three fingers on the right hand and having them pointing down. It resembles a claw and thus the name vulture.

Student Practice: Vulture Signal

Ask for volunteers to come up and model using verbal and non-verbal put-downs with others. Ask students to give the vulture signal when they hear or see a put-down. Have students practice using the signal several times, and practice discriminating between affirmations and put-downs by using the correct signal. This practice is important. Remember to use the signals yourself after you practice using signals with students. Then your students will be encouraged to use the signals, and you will be able to tell which students know the difference between affirmations and put-downs.

Numbered Heads Together:
Discussion and Reflection Questions

Ask students to think about the following questions. Have students in teams number off 1-4. Ask one of the questions and give teams a minute to put their heads together and discuss it. Then call out a number 1-4. The students with that number either stand or raise their hands. Randomly select a person who has the number you called out and have them answer the question. Repeat the process.

- ☙ How do you recognize a non-verbal put-down when you hear one?

- ☙ How do you recognize a put-down when you see one?

- ☙ When was the last time you last received a put-down? How did it feel?

- ☙ What did you do when you received that put-down?

- ☙ How else might you handle put-downs?

Teacher Talk:
Receiving Affirmation

Share with students that it is important to know how to receive affirmations as well as give affirmations. Give a few affirmations to one of the students in class. Prompt students to use the victory affirmations signal. Ask students how it felt to receive the affirmations.

Roundrobin:
Receiving Affirmations

Students use the Roundrobin structure. and take turns receiving affirmations from their team. Each member will have thirty seconds on the affirmations seat. While sitting in the affirmations chair, teammates will give as many affirmations as they can. The student receiving affirmations can only respond by giving a "V" sign and saying thank you. If students need affirmation starters have those below posted.

Thanks for ....

I liked your ....

Note for Primary Age Children: Rather than use the terms "affirmation" and "put-down", you can use the transactional analysis terms "warm fuzzy" and "cold prickly" which may be more meaningful to young children.

MINI LESSON #3

Recognize Self Put-downs with "VIPERS"

Self put-downs are not usually dealt with in conjunction with cooperative learning. Many of us do not realize the amount of harm we do to ourselves by being self-critical. It's important for students to recognize negative self-talk, just as it's important to know when you are giving someone else a put-down. Give students examples of self put-downs: "That was stupid!", "I'm such a dummy", "I can't do anything right," etc.

Pairs: Blackboard Share

Ask students to put their heads together (in pairs) and see if they can come up with two more examples. Have them share their examples with the class by writing them on the blackboard. Remind students that self put-downs can become self fulfilling prophecies. An option is to ask themselves how they could improve next time. Kicking ourselves about poor choices doesn't stop us from making poor choices again. Making a plan on "what to do next time," will make a greater difference.

Teacher Talk and Demonstration: The Viper Signal

Every time students hear a classmate's self put-down, they are to use the viper signal which is an inverted "V" using the same fingers as for victory, only pointing down.

Whole Class, Students Practice: Viper Signal

Ask students to use the viper signal whenever they hear someone use a self put-down. Give yourself a few self put-downs

such as:

"I'm a dummy, I should know how to do that," or

"I can't do this; it's too hard," or

"I hate myself" or "Nobody could love me."

Monitor student responses to make sure they are signaling correctly.

Inside-Outside Circle: Practicing Victory, Vipers, and Vultures

Divide your students into two equal groups. Have one group form a circle facing out. Have the other group form an inner circle facing in. Have the student facing each other pair up. Explain that you will be giving directions or asking questions. First, the inside circle will give their response or answer to their partners in the outside circle, and then the outside circle will give their response.

Questions:

1. Give an example of an affirmation. Partner responds with correct hand signal.

Now everyone move two spaces to your right. This means that both the inside and the outside circle are four students from where they started.

2. Give an example of a self put-down. Partners respond with correct hand signal.

Now everyone move one space to your right.

3. Name two people who have given you affirmations within the past week.

Now move three spaces to your right.

4. What was the last self-put down you heard someone give themselves?

Numbered Heads Together:

In pairs, or teams of two pairs together, have students discuss the following questions. Ask one of the questions and give teams (numbered off 1-4, see Numbered Heads Together in Structures Section) a minute to put their heads together and discuss it. Then call out a number 1-4. Randomly select a person who has the number you called out and have them answer the question. Repeat the process with the next question.

• How are vipers different from vultures?

• Why might vipers be more difficult to stop using?

• How could becoming more aware of affirmations, put-downs and self put-downs make a difference for you at home?

• How could it make a difference at school?

Think-Pair-Share:
Affirmation Starters

Ask students to **think** of affirmations they might give their fellow team members. Now have students **pair** with their partner and share the affirmations they might use. Next ask several students to **share** the affirmations they came up with. If they need affirmation starters you can list the ones below.

The affirmation I enjoyed the most was........

I appreciated ....

You were quick at ....

~ ❀ ~

> ### Note: Changing the School Climate
> Recognition of affirmations, self put-downs, and put-downs of others is the first step toward monitoring our own behavior and helping students monitor their behavior. Share what you are doing in the classroom with your administrator and fellow faculty. Let your colleagues know how important improving the climate of the school is to you. Perhaps some of your colleagues will want to be involved. Some schools have launched a "War on Put-downs" in their attempt to improve school climate. This is not an easy habit to break. Our use of put-downs of self and others is firmly ingrained. It may take months or years to change these behavior patterns. As you proceed with this process, be kind to yourself. It's not easy for you, your students, or your colleagues to make these changes quickly. If you persevere though, you may not only make personal changes, you will help change the world by making it a better place for all people.

Lesson 27 Charting Affirmations

Lesson-At-A-Glance

Goal: Relationship Skills (Affirmations)

Grades: 3-6

Time: Introduction: 30-45 minutes
Debriefing and sharing results
30 minutes

Outcomes — Students will:
• Monitor the number of affirmations and put-downs they receive during a day.
• Share results of observations with a peer by keeping a log.
• Become more aware of how to use appropriate affirmations.

Materials:
• Affirmation, Put-down Monitoring Worksheet for each student

Structures:
• **Brainstorming**
• **Paraphrase Passport**
• **Think-Pair-Share**
• **Team Discussion**
• **Three-Step Interview**
• **Numbered Heads Together**
• **Roundrobin**

Lesson Overview

The previous lessons on affirmations and put-downs brainstorming and Victory, Vulture, and Viper should have been completed by students before you do this lesson. Your students have been introduced to affirmations and put-downs and you believe they know the difference and can recognize them. This lesson is designed for students to use a time log to monitor the number of put-downs they receive in one day (or see on a TV program). Part of the discussion will center on how students may make changes in their environment to reduce the number of put-downs and increase the number of affirmations.

Note: I recommend that you try this lesson yourself before you have your students try it to see how difficult it can be. You can then give students feedback on how they may be more successful.

Lesson Sequence

Brainstorming:
Importance of Recognizing Affirmations & Put-downs

Ask teams to brainstorm why it is important to recognize put-downs and affirmations? Make sure they know the Four S's of Brainstorming (page 6: 3) and have a recorder. As students are brainstorming, walk around the room to monitor the teams. Note how each team is following the brainstorming rules. The most difficult rule is to suspend judgment. Take notes so you can give teams feedback. When five minutes are up, or when you feel teams have finished, ask the teams to finish recording their last statement.

Paraphrase Passport:
Teacher Records Responses

Inform teams of what you observed as you monitored the Brainstorming task. Give affirmations to those teams which were making good faith efforts. Ask teams to share their results. Explain that they will be using "Paraphrase Passport." Students who are called on will need to paraphrase what the student preceding them said before they give their own response. Call on teams randomly and select a team member who volunteers or randomly call on a student. Teacher records responses when the student paraphrases rather than from the original speaker. This supports student accountability for listening and the teacher not giving students a visual cue. Record several responses, at least one from each team.

Teacher Talk:
Discuss Research

Tell students how researchers find out what happens in the world. Breakfast cereal makers do research on what kind of breakfast food people like to eat. The television industry has the Nielsen Ratings which provide data on which programs people watch. Researchers rely on surveys and counting the responses.

Think-Pair-Share:
Student Search

Ask students to **think** of one kind of research we could do at school. Students then **pair** and discuss what they came up with. Next, students **share** with the class when called on. After several responses, if no one comes up with research about affirmations and put-downs bring it up yourself. Explain that as a class we can do research ourselves.

Teacher Talk:
A. Introduce Affirmations, Put-down Worksheet A or B

At this point you can introduce either of the worksheets A or B (Do not introduce both at the same time!)

Worksheet A: Affirmation, Put-down Diary

This is designed for students to record affirmations and put-downs they receive during the course of one day. Students begin the worksheet the next morning as soon as they wake up. Students are to record each affirmation or put-down they receive during the day. The method of recording can vary from recording the word or phrase to keeping a tally.

Worksheet B: TV Affirmations and Put-downs

This is designed to monitor affirmations and put-downs observed during a TV program. Students record what the affirmation was. They might write, "smiled, and said good to see you." For put-downs they might write, "Joke about how fat Roseanne was." This can be coordinated so that different teams choose different TV programs to watch to collect the data. Team # 1 might choose to do the "The Wonder Years" while team # 2 watches "Roseanne." It's important to give teams a choice. All members of a team should agree to watch the same program.

B. Hand Out Worksheet, Discuss How to Collect The Data

Hand out the worksheet you will be using with your students. Remind students that it's best to write just a word or two on the sheet to describe the affirmation or put-down. For example, if someone shoves you in line and it hurts your feelings, you might record on worksheet A, "shoved in line" next to the time it happened. Ask students what they would record if nobody gave them any affirmations or put-downs. Those areas would be blank. For the day they are collecting data it's important that they keep their worksheet with them at all times. If they can't, they need to be aware of the time and any events they want to record when they get their worksheet. Discuss how important accurate data is. Record only those things which occurred.

Note: A good way to practice doing the "TV Affirmation, Put-down Worksheet B" is to bring in a ten minute video tape of a TV program with has both put-downs and affirmations. The class can initially give the Victory and Vulture signals (Lesson 26). Then you could show another segment with students using their worksheets, and have them cross check each other within their team. Discuss how we see affirmations and put-downs differently and how this makes gathering accurate data difficult.

Team Discussion:
Why It's Difficult to Collect Data

Direct students to take the worksheet home and collect the data requested. Ask students to discuss in their teams why this research might be difficult to collect. Give students a few minutes and ask teams for feedback, for example students might find it difficult to remember to keep their worksheet with them all the time. If students are not sure something is an affirmation or a put-down they record a question mark by it. Draw out several student responses and discuss. Stress again the importance of accurate information. Some teachers ask teams to arrange to call one another once to see how the other is doing collecting the information.

Students Gather Data
Three-Step Interview:
Reporting Data Gathering in Team

Ask pairs within teams to use a Three-Step Interview structure to discuss the research data gathered. If you have four person teams the following would apply:

Step One: Pairs interview their partners as to what data they gathered.

Step Two: Switch role and reverse the process.

Step Three: Total team Roundrobin sharing of what each person said. Person one will share with the team what person two said. Person two will share what one said and so on.

Team Reports:
Reporting Class Data

This can be accomplished several ways:

Worksheet A: Affirmation, Put-down Diary

- Simple tally - Have teams add up the number of affirmations and put-downs received during the day. Record the team score then add these up for a class score. You could do this occasionally throughout the year for a check on how it's going for students.

- Integrate math into this lesson by having each team chart by time blocks when the most affirmations and put-downs occur. Have the teams come up with creative ways to chart their data. This could be bar graph, or pie chart, etc.

Worksheet B: TV Affirmations, Put-downs

- Tally - Each team records the number of affirmations and put-downs for the program they watched. Teams then can report this to the class.

- Per half hour or hour rate - Team could tally how many affirmations or put-downs occurred during a half hour or hour program.

- Cross Check - They could check for reliability. Did students categorize the same things as put-downs or affirmations?

Numbered Heads Together:

Reflection Questions

Have students number off 1-4 in their teams. Introduce the questions below one at a time and have teams discuss possible answers. They need to be ready to share on your signal.

- What was difficult about collecting this data?
- What helped you to do a better job collecting data?
- Did you improve in your ability to recognize affirmations and put-downs? How did you improve?
- How could you improve your gathering of data next time you do this activity?
- Why do people see affirmations and put-downs differently?
- What have you learned from doing this lesson?

Roundrobin:

Affirmation Starters

Have students take turns sharing affirmations with teammates. Students need to make sure each teammember has received one affirmation. Post the affirmation starters below for them to refer to if needed.

Affirmations Starters:

I like the way _____ shared about _____ .

Thanks for your ideas about _____ .

I appreciate your _____ .

~ ❀ ~

> **Note:** This would be a lesson which you might want to send a note home to parents explaining that your students are studying how affirmations and put-downs affect students. This could be sent before you begin or after the lesson has concluded. It's also a good idea to alert your principal to this project in case a parent questions what you are doing. The principal can then be supportive of you.

NAME_____   DATE _____

Affirmation, Put-Down Diary
Worksheet A *(Permission to reproduce for classroom use)*

Directions: Starting when you wake up in the morning record any affirmations and put-downs you receive at home and at school. Affirmations are those words or actions that make you feel good, encouraged, or supported. Put-downs are those words or actions which make you feel bad, or sad, are discouraging and are not supportive. Record your responses by either a descriptive word or two about the incident or a tally mark.

Affirmations

Put-Downs

Write Brief Descriptions or Tally Marks

6:00 am

7:00 am

8:00 am

9:00 am

10:00 am

11:00 am

12:00 Noon

1:00 pm

2:00 pm

3:00 pm

4:00 pm

5:00 pm

6:00 pm

7:00 pm

8:00 pm

9:00 pm

10:00 pm

NAME_____ DATE _____

TV Affirmations and Put-Downs
Worksheet B   *(Permission to reproduce for classroom use)*

Directions: As a team, select a TV program to view in the next day you could all normally watch at your homes. Record the affirmations and put-downs you observe on the program. Affirmations are those words or actions that make people feel good, are encouraging, or are supportive. Put-downs are those words or actions that make people feel bad, or sad, are discouraging and are not supportive. Record your responses with a descriptive word or two about the incident or a tally mark next to the character each time they give an affirmation or put down.

Program _____ Station_____ Beginning Time _____ Ending Time _____

	Character	Character	Character	Character
Affirmations				
Put-Downs				

Lesson 28 Inside-Outside Affirmations

Lesson-At-A-Glance

Goal: Relationship Skills (Affirmations)

Grades: 3-Adult

Time: 20-30 Minutes

Outcome—Students Will:
- Share supportive statements with each other.
- Practice using appropriate affirmations.

Materials:
- Lists of affirmations posted on the wall (from another activity, "Brainstorming Affirmations & Put-downs")
- Four signs with discussion and reflection questions posted around the room

Structures:
- **Three-Step Interview**
- **Inside-Outside Circle**
- **Corners**

Lesson Overview

Students recall the last affirmation they received and share that in pairs. Then students will form an Inside-Outside Circle. The outer circle will give affirmations to each person on the inner circle as they go around. Students will use a Corners structure for reflection questions posted in the corners of the room.

Lesson Sequence

Three-Step Interview:
Setting the Stage

Review with students the importance of giving affirmations and how it feels to give and receive affirmations. Ask students to visualize the last time they received an affirmation. Give students time to remember. Ask students to remember exactly where they were. Were they inside or outside? What time of the day was it? What was the weather like? What kinds of feelings did they have when they received the affirmation? Now ask students to think about the affirmations they have heard in class this year, and the positive things others in class have done for them. Direct them to form their teams of four and share using the Three-Step Interview structure. Pairs will interview one another (step one and two), then they will form their team of four and Roundrobin paraphrase what their partner said.

Note: There are times when your class has had smooth sailing for awhile and your students are honoring the class rules and being supportive of one another. Then comes a day when student teams get rebellious and don't honor all the class rules. This would be an appropriate time for this lesson, which focuses students on the positive and becomes a classbuilder as well as a relationship skill building lesson. This lesson should only be done towards the middle or the end of the school year when students have already had many opportunities to interact with one another and have mastered giving affirmations to each other.

Teacher Talk:

A. Purpose of this Lesson

Explain that students will now have an opportunity to give affirmations to half of their classmates in order to practice using affirmations and to create a more positive classroom atmosphere. Review the class rules of no put-downs and use of affirmations where appropriate. This will remind students to stay positive.

B. Form Circles

Ask one half of the students to form a circle, shoulder to shoulder, facing out. (It could be one side of the room or students whose names are in the first half of the alphabet). Now ask the remaining students to form a circle around the first circle of students facing inward. Both circles of students should be facing one another now. If you have an odd number of students, lets say 33, then have one circle with 16 and one with 17 students. One student in the larger circle will not be sharing at any given time (or they can pair with another and become a twin).

C. Directions on Giving Affirmation

Explain that students should describe one positive thing they've noticed during the school year about the person across for them. They may have received help or support, been listened to, or been encouraged by this classmate. It could be something positive they noticed outside the school

setting. The key is that it needs to be a sincere and positive affirmation. They will have only 20 seconds to give each affirmation

During the first round, the outer circle will be giving the affirmations, while the inner circle uses their non-verbal active listening skills. This means the inner circle can only nod or smile. In round two, the inner circle will have an opportunity to give the affirmations.

Explain how students will be rotating: have the outer circle rotate to the right one student while the inner circle remains stationary. It's important to give each student an opportunity to share with all students in the opposite circle.

Inside-Outside Circle:

Round One

Students in the outside circle give one affirmation to the student across from them. Inside students listen and can only respond with a smile or nod. Have a signal (bell, timer, or chime) to indicate when students rotate. At the end of 20 seconds have the students rotate and begin timing the next 20 seconds after they have switched. Depending on the sophistication of the class you may allow more time. Have students rotate until each student has given an affirmation to every student in the inner circle.

Round Two

Now the inner circle will be giving the affirmations and the outer circle will be using their active listen-

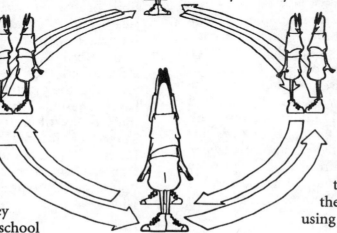

ing skills and can respond only with a nod or smile. Begin round two having students move every 20 seconds or as appropriate for your class.

Corners:
Reflection Questions

Choose four questions from those listed below and have them posted in different corners of the room. Point out the questions to the students and ask them to choose silently which question they would like to discuss. Have students write the first three words of the question on a piece of paper. Next, direct students to stand by the question they chose. Have students form pairs within the group at their corner and discuss the question with their partner. Tell

pairs they have only three minutes to talk before sharing with the entire class. Walk around the room listening to conversations to monitor if students are on task.

- ❧ What types of affirmations did you come up with? Could you give some examples?
- ❧ How difficult was it to think of affirmations to give? Why do you think so?
- ❧ Why might it be easier to give an affirmation than to receive one?
- ❧ Did you think of affirmations that you didn't use? What can you do about that?
- ❧ Do you most often receive affirmations at school or at home? Why?

Call on several students to share their responses.

∼ ❀ ∼

Affirmation Starters

- Thank you.
- You're great _____ !
- I like the way you _____ .
- One thing I like about you is . . .

esson 29 Affirmation Cape

Lesson-At-A-Glance

Goal: Relationship Skills (Affirmations)

Grades: 3-Adult

Time: 30-45 Minutes

Outcome—Students Will:
- Anonymously give supportive statements to each other.
- Increase their awareness of appropriate affirmations.
- Practice writing affirmations.

Materials:
- Lists of affirmations posted on the wall
- Scratch paper
- One piece of 8 1/2" x 11" construction paper for each student (only one side needs to be usable)
- Masking tape
- Reflection questions posted on the wall or overhead

Structures:
- **Roundtable**
- **Team Discussion**

Lesson Overview[1]

This is low risk way to involve students in giving affirmations. Students will meet in pairs and practice writing affirmations they might like to receive. Next, each student will have a piece of construction paper on his or her back. Fellow students will write affirmations on each other's back. They will continue doing this until the teacher calls time. This should be done only after students have demonstrated they can honor the ground rules.

---

1. I first used this activity while using *Tribes: A Process for Social Development and Cooperative Learning* by Jeanne Gibbs.

Lesson Sequence

Roundtable:

Practice Writing Affirmations

Ask team members to prepare for a Roundtable task. Students in a team face one another with all books and material off their desks. Students need a sheet of paper and one pencil or pen. The team's task is to write as many affirmation statements as they can within a three minute period. Each student is to write one affirmation on the paper and quickly pass the paper and pencil to the next student as quickly as they can.

Monitor

As students are doing their Roundtable, walk around the room to monitor their responses. Encourage those students who are doing a good job.

Stop And Reflect

Ask the teams to stop writing after three minutes. Select some teams to read some of the responses. Let students know you are looking for affirmations and give recognition to good efforts. Ask students how they would feel if someone wrote down certain affirmations about them. Have several students respond.

Teacher Talk:

Explain Affirmation Capes

Remind students that they have had opportunities to give affirmations to one another in various class and team settings.

Now they are going to share affirmations with one another in writing. Hand out construction paper and tape to all teams. Students should help each other place a piece of construction paper on each other's back between the shoulder blades. Students can use only pencils to write appropriate affirmations on as many backs in the room as possible.

Note: Have a student place a piece of paper on your back. As the teacher it's important you have a paper on your back and that you participate.

Find-Someone-To-Write-On:
Monitor and Participate
As students begin to write, you also participate by writing affirmations on students' backs. Write on as many backs as you can before you call time.

Stop
Stop the process when you have run out of time or students have finished. Ask students to finish the back they are writing on. Ask students to take their papers off and give them a few minutes to read them.

Team Discussion:
Reflection Questions
Have the two sets of questions posted or on an overhead. Direct students to discuss and

answer the questions. Remind students that after the teams have reviewed the questions there will be whole class sharing.

- How difficult was it to come up with affirmations? Why was it easy or difficult?

- Did it become easier as you went along? Why?

- Were you afraid what people might write? Why?

- Were you surprised at what is written on your card? Why?

- Why might it be just as important to know how to receive affirmations as to give them?

- To whom else might you like to write affirmations?

Note: Affirmation Cape is less threatening for some participants than the following Affirmation Circle. This is primarily because you never talk directly to the other person and the person you are affirming cannot see what you are writing. Also, in the other lessons you receive verbal affirmations. In this one you receive written affirmations, something you can take home with you.

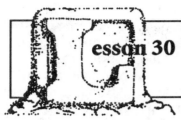

esson 30 Affirmation Circle

Lesson-At-A-Glance

Goal: Relationship Skills (Affirmations)

Grades: K-Adult

Time: 35-50 Minutes

Outcome—Students Will:
· Give affirmations to one another.
· Practice receiving affirmations.

Materials:
· Lists of affirmations posted on the wall
· One stool slightly higher than students' chairs. The teacher's chair is all right to use if students are sitting on the floor

Structures:
· **Roundrobin**
· **Community Circle**
· **Think-Pair-Share**

Lesson Overview[1]

This is an excellent way to end the semester or the year. This lesson is done only when students do not use put-downs and have demonstrated that they can use affirmations appropriately. Students should have already practiced doing this in their team setting during the year; see Team Practice below. This class affirmation circle can help cap off a year and have students walking away with positive feelings about themselves and the class.

Lesson Sequence

Roundrobin:

Students Share Their Last Affirmation

Ask students to form teams (this can be of three, four, or five members). Ask students to remember the last time someone said something which made them feel good. (PAUSE for 20 seconds.) Now ask students to share this last affirmation using Roundrobin, one at a time. Tell students they only have thirty seconds each. Monitor by listening to various teams. When two or three minutes have passed and you notice the level of talking starting to change, ask students to finish their thought and stop.

Teacher Talk:

A. Forming a Community Circle

Ask a couple of students to share their last affirmation. Comment on how important it is to know how to receive and to give affirmations. Have students form a Community Circle as quickly and quietly as they can. Once in the Community Circle, explain that students will practice giving and receiving affirmations with the entire class.

---

1. This lesson was adapted from *Tribes: A Process For Social Development And Cooperative Learning* by Jeanne Gibbs

B. Rules for Class Affirmation Circle

Each student will have an opportunity to sit in the affirmation chair. While sitting in the chair students' response to comments from classmates can only be "thank you". No other comments are allowed. Students will be giving affirmations to the person in the affirmation chair. The affirmations should be based on personal interaction or knowledge of the student. Each student will only have <u>one minute</u> in the affirmation chair.

Community Circle:

A. Model

Ask for a volunteer to show how to receive affirmations. Start off yourself with an affirmation for the student. Remember to monitor the time and cut it off after one minute. It will take another 10-20 seconds for transition to the next student and to get started it will take another 10-20 seconds. The others will catch on quickly. Whoever goes first, the next person can be the person sitting next to them, or you can have the person who finished choose the next person.

B. Practice

Each student takes a turn sitting in the affirmation chair. Check off student names if they are not going in seating order. Make sure you keep track of who has had a turn so everyone has an opportunity.

Note: Students Passing

You may have some students who prefer to pass on this activity and not participate. I don't usually mention this as an option. However, if there is a student who has strong feelings about this and doesn't want to participate, I would honor those feelings. They may learn a tremendous amount by watching the others. Always go back to a person who has passed and give them a second chance later on. They may feel safer once they've seen everyone else go through the lesson.

Think-Pair-Share:

Reflection Questions

Ask students one of the following questions. Ask students to **think** about their answer. Then have students **pair** with another student and share with that other student. Call on students to **share** and ask what their partner's response was. Repeat the process with the other questions.

- Which was more difficult: to receive or give affirmations? Why?

- How did you feel when it was your turn to sit on the affirmation chair?

- How did it feel to hear your class mates giving so many affirmations?

- How might this activity make it easier to receive affirmations from others?

- Will it now be easier for you to give affirmations to others?

- Why is it important for each of us to know how to receive affirmations?

Note: This activity works best when students have already had plenty of experience using affirmations. This is to finish a semester with, not begin one.

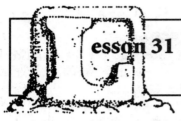

Lesson 31 Sharing About Conflict

Lesson-At-A-Glance

Goal: Relationship Skills (Conflict Resolution)

Grades: 3-Adult

Time: 30-50 Minutes

Outcome—Students Will:
· Share a personal experience with conflict.
· Write how they would like to change their personal experience.

Materials:
· Paper for students to use during Brainstorming and individual writing

Structures:
· **Brainstorming**
· **Three-Step Interview**
· **Think-Pair-Share**
· **Roundrobin**

Lesson Overview

Students need to be aware of the importance conflict plays in their life. Teams Brainstorm definitions of conflict to share with the class. Students then use Three-Step Interview to share a personal conflict in which they were involved. Students Think-Pair-Share about how they might want the conflict they described to end differently. Then students will individually write a paragraph about how they would have liked their conflict to end. During reflection, the class and teams will discuss why it might be a good idea to learn some conflict resolution skills.

Lesson Sequence

Brainstorming:
What is Conflict?

Review the four S's for Brainstorming listed below. Ask students to form their teams, with each student having a Brainstorming role (see Brainstorming in Structure 1:1 for information on roles).

Review the roles if students are not familiar with them. Ask students if they have ever been involved in conflicts. Discuss with students, "What is conflict?" Teams then brainstorm their own examples. After 3-5 minutes of brainstorming ask each team to share one example of conflict. Record it on the board or overhead.

Speed - Quick sharing of ideas.

Suspend Judgment - Defer judging ideas, no comments.

Silly - Off the wall ideas are encouraged. All ideas are OK.

Synergy - Build on ideas of others.

(See brainstorming structure 1:2 for a page with the Four S's which you can use for an overhead on structure 1:2)

Three-Step Interview:
Students Share a Conflict They Had

In pairs, within teams, students share a conflict in which they were personally involved. Interviewers are to ask appropriate questions to draw out information from the interviewee (refer to the Three-Step Interview structure in Chapter 2). During step three students will do a Roundrobin paraphrasing of what their partner shared.

Three-Step Interview:
Another Way to Resolve Conflict

Ask students to reflect on the conflict they shared in the last task. If they had an opportunity to change the ending of the conflict so that both sides could have walked away feeling better about the conflict, what might they do? Give students a minute or two of think time. Now ask students to interview their partner as to what they would prefer for a different ending to their conflict. (Keep this relatively short - two minutes each.) Roundrobin paraphrase in Step 3.

Individual Writing:
Students Write the Ending

Direct students to individually write a paragraph about their conflict and the way they changed the ending so that each person involved in the conflict felt better about the outcome. Tell students they will only have five minutes to write their paragraph. Monitor student involvement in this task closely by walking around the room and encouraging a good effort.

Think-Pair-Square-Share:
Reflection Questions

Ask students to **think** of how they would respond to two or three of the reflection questions listed below. Then have students **pair** and **share** how they would respond. Next, have two pairs form a square and share with the other pair their response.

- Why is it important to know how to deal effectively with conflict?

- What would be some good ways to learn about resolving conflicts?

- How easy was it for you to share about a conflict you were involved in? Why was it easy or difficult for you?

- How would learning about resolving conflicts help you at home?

Roundrobin: Affirmation Starters

Ask students in their teams to affirm one another using a Roundrobin structure. The recorder will start by giving an affirmation to the person on their right. The person receiving the affirmation can only say "thank you." Make sure every one has a turn.

Post affirmation starters such as:

I appreciate your sharing about..........

Thanks for what you said..........

esson 32 Types of Conflict

Lesson-At-A-Glance

Goal: Relationship Skills (Conflict Resolution)
Grades: 3-Adult
Time: 50-70 Minutes
Outcome—Students Will:
 • Recognize the three types of conflicts.
Materials:
 • Cassette tape deck and music
 • Handout on Types of Conflicts
 • Paper for students to use during quiz
Structures:
 • **Think-Pair-Share**
 • **Choral Response**
 • **Numbered Heads Together**
 • **Think-Pair-Square**
 • **Roundrobin**

Lesson Overview[1]

Students will be introduced to different types of conflicts and will begin to see how knowing about these different types of conflict can make a difference for them. The class will participate in a game of competitive and cooperative musical chairs. Using Think-Pair-Share students will reflect of how cooperative musical chairs differs from the way it is usually played. The teacher will then present a definition of conflict and information on the types of conflicts, resources, needs, and values.   Students will use Think-Pair-Share-Square to share their own examples.   The teacher will then lecture about why it's important to know about the types of conflict. Numbered Heads Together

_____

1. Information on Types of Conflict was adapted from *Creative Conflict Resolution* by William J. Kreidler. (Scott, Foresman, & Co. 1984.)

will then be used for students to review the types of conflict. Next, students will use Choral Response to practice matching the correct type of conflict with a situation.

Lesson Sequence

Cooperative Game:
Competitive and Cooperative Musical Chairs

Have students place their chairs into a tight circle facing out. Start the music and have students begin walking around the chairs. Let students know that when the music stops they will need to find a chair. The students who don't find a chair will have to stop playing and watch. As the music is playing remove a few chairs. Stop the music. Those students who didn't find a chair must stand away and watch. Do this for several rounds. Then ask the students to stop, replace all the chairs and tell them that now we'll try playing COOPERATIVE MUSICAL CHAIRS. This game will be different because rather than a student leaving the game when a chair is removed they must sit on someone's lap. Start the music, students walk around the chairs, remove a few chairs. This time when the music stops, students who do not have a chair must sit on another student's knee or lap. Pull out a greater number of chairs as the music is playing to make the game go faster. [2]

_____

2. I would only try this with 7-12 graders who worked well together on other lessons. It might be too much for some students. You decide, you know your students.

Think-Pair-Share:
Reflect on How Games Were Different

Ask students to **think** of which version of musical chairs might cause more conflict between students and why. Give students a minute of think time. Have students form **pairs** and **share** their responses.

Teacher Talk:
Types of Conflict

Use the information about the definition of and types of conflict (in Chapter 5:6 resources, needs, and values) to give a short Lecturette. Ask which of the types of conflict the musical chairs game might fit into. (It would be a conflict of resources because there are only so many chairs and, in the first version of the game, people were losers when they didn't find a chair.) Review examples of the different types of conflict.

Choral Response:
Review Types of Conflict

Ask students to respond as a class to the following questions. Review the Choral Response Structure information in the Structures Summary Chapter. Ask the students to respond together and only when you give the hand signal.

1. When two people have a conflict over politics it is a conflict over ....[think time]...It starts with a "V"..[hand signal] "VALUES"

2. When a group of people all want to listen to a cassette tape on the earphones, it is a conflict over...[think time]......It starts with a "R"...................[hand signal] "RESOURCES"

3. When students are competing in class for a grade it is a conflict over..[think time].. It starts with an "N"..[hand signal] "NEEDS"

4. If the conflict is about who has the power to make decisions for a group, it is a conflict about..[think time]...[hand signal] "NEEDS"

5. If two brother have a conflict about who will get the attention of their mother, it is a conflict about......[think time]...[hand signal] "RESOURCES'

6. Only so many girls can make the basketball team. This type of conflict is about...[think time]...[hand signal] "RESOURCES"

Numbered Heads Together:
Review the Types of Conflict

Have students in teams, or their last group of four, number off 1-4 (refer to Numbered Heads Together in Structures Chapter). Explain that you will ask the class a question and teams are to put their heads together to come up with the answer. Any student can be called on for an answer, so it's in the teams best interest to thoroughly discuss the answer.

Questions:

↪ Which type of conflict is it when you want a magazine someone else is reading and why?

↪ What is one example of a NEEDS conflict?

↪ Which type of conflict is it when two people argue about who has the best religion?

↪ Why are NEEDS conflicts more difficult to resolve than conflicts about RESOURCES?

- What are two examples of RESOURCES conflicts?
- Which type of conflict is it when someone gives someone else a put-down and why? (Needs, because put-downs effect self-esteem which is a need for all of us.)

Make up other questions you believe are appropriate.

Think-Pair-Square:
Students Think / Share Examples

Ask students to **Think** of the conflict shared at the beginning of the lesson, and which type of conflict it might be (resources, needs, or values). Ask students to **Pair** and share their thoughts. Then direct students to **square** (two pairs come together) and each pair share with the other pair.

Teacher Talk:
Why Knowing Types is Important

Explain how knowing why conflict occurs can help us avoid and/or resolve conflict. Refer to the information on cooperative conflict resolution on the next page for content for this lecturette. Draw out from students how knowing about the different types of conflict might make a difference for them.

Roundrobin:
Affirmation Starters

Ask students in their teams to affirm one another using a Roundrobin structure. Person number one will start by giving an affirmation to the person to their right. The person receiving the affirmation can say only "thank you". Take turns within teams. Make sure everyone has a turn. Post affirmation starters such as:

You are a good ....

 I like it when you ....

$\sim$ ❀ $\sim$

Three Types of Conflict

RESOURCES
A conflict occurs about resources when two or more people want something which is in insufficient supply.
- ATTENTION OF THE TEACHER
- A GIRL FRIEND OR BOY FRIEND
- USING THE ART SUPPLIES
- MAKING A SPORTS TEAM

These conflicts are often the easiest to resolve and are the ones most frequently encountered on the school grounds.

NEEDS
Students have the same basic psychological needs as adults.
- POWER
- FRIENDSHIP AND BELONGING TO A GROUP
- SELF-ESTEEM
- ACHIEVEMENT

Conflicts of needs are more difficult to resolve than conflicts over resources because the reasons are not as clear.

VALUES
The beliefs we hold most closely to us are our values.
- RELIGIOUS
- POLITICAL
- CULTURAL
- FAMILY
- GOALS

(Permission to reproduce for classroom use)

Lesson 33 Eight Modes of Conflict Resolution

Lesson-At-A-Glance

Goal: Relationship Skills (Conflict Resolution)

Grades: 3-Adult

Time: 50-70 Minutes

Outcome—Students Will:
- Identify eight modes of conflict resolution.
- Choose a situation from an appropriate mode.

Materials:
- Handout on eight modes of cooperative conflict resolution.
- Poster of Eight Modes of cooperative conflict resolution

Structures:
- **Three-Step Interview**
- **Team Discussion**
- **Numbered Heads Together**
- **Think-Pair-Share**
- **Talking Chips**
- **Roundrobin**

Lesson Overview[1]

Students will be introduced to eight modes of cooperative conflict resolution and begin to see the importance of knowing different ways to solve conflicts. The teacher will role play a simple conflict. Students will use a Three-Step Interview structure to develop solutions. Students will Think-Pair-Share the same problem. Numbered Heads

----

1. The eight modes are taken from *Cooperative Learning* by Spencer Kagan. Kagan Cooperative Learning, 1992.

Together will allow teams to choose one of the modes to resolve conflicts described by the teacher and why.

Lesson Sequence

Role Play:
Problem Situation is Acted Out

Ask a student to help you with this role play. You play the role of Suzi. The student plays the role of John (or vice-versa).

Suzi: "John, it's your turn to turn in the group's papers."

John: "I don't want to do it today. Buzz off."

Suzi: "John, you're obnoxious. Go turn the papers in - it's your turn."

John: "Suzi, I'm not going to turn in the papers."

Three-Step Interview:
How Would You Solve This Conflict

Ask students to get into pairs (if they already have work pairs, great). Review the process for Three-Step Interview (Refer to the Structures Chapter). Pairs interview each other on how they would solve this conflict between John and Suzi.

Step One: Student one interviews student two.

Step Two: Reverse the process.

Step Three: Students come together in a team of four. Team members take turns, Roundrobin, paraphrasing their partner's solution.

Teacher Talk:
Eight Modes of Cooperative Conflict Resolution

Use the information about the eight modes of cooperative conflict resolution in Chapter 5:7 to give a short lecturette. The eight modes make an acronym STOPHACC:

SHARE

TAKE TURNS

OUTSIDE HELP

POSTPONE

HUMOR

AVOID

COMPROMISE

CHANCE

Numbered Heads Together:
Review the Modes

Have students in teams of four number off 1-4 (refer to Numbered Heads Together in Structures Chapter). Explain you will ask the class a question and teams are to put their heads together to come up with the answer. Any student can be called on, so it's in the teams best interest to thoroughly discuss the answer. Students must refer to the Eight Modes of Cooperative Conflict Resolution.

Ask students to try to use a different mode for each problem they solve.

Questions:

1. You want a magazine someone else is reading. How could you resolve this conflict?

2. Another student crowds in front of you in the cafeteria line. Which mode?

3. A teammate makes a mess in your work area and is about to leave without cleaning it up. Which mode will you use?

4. Your partner and you both want to give your team report. How will you resolve this?

5. Your parents want you home by 9:30 p.m. You want to stay out later. Which mode and why?

6. You and your brother can't decide who gets to take their friend on the family vacation. There is room for only one friend in the car. How can you resolve this?

Think-Pair-Share:
Solve Role Play with Modes of CCR

Ask the students who role played John and Suzi to repeat the performance. Ask the class to **think** of which mode of cooperative conflict resolution they would use and why they would use it. Direct students to refer to the poster or hand-out. Give students one-two minutes **think** time. Then ask students to form **pairs** and discuss. Next ask for volunteers to **share** responses with the class.

Team Discussion with Talking Chips:
Reflection Questions

Ask students to think of how they might respond to two or three of the reflection questions listed below. Attempt to draw out the importance of knowing different modes of conflict resolution (refer to Team Discussion in Section II).

Using Talking Chips, one student gives their response to one of the questions and then puts his/her pencil/pen in the middle of the table. He/she does not talk again until everyone in the group has shared and placed their pencil in the middle.

Reflection Questions

↬ Which mode of conflict resolution do you use most often? Why?

- How might knowing different modes of conflict resolution help you deal with conflicts better?

- How might these modes help you at home?

Roundrobin: Affirmation Starters

Ask students to affirm one another in their teams using a Roundrobin structure. Person number one will start by giving an affirmation to the person to their right. The person receiving the affirmation can say only "thank you." They take turns within their team. Make sure everyone has a turn. Post affirmation starters such as:

You're really good at..............

Thanks for helping me..............

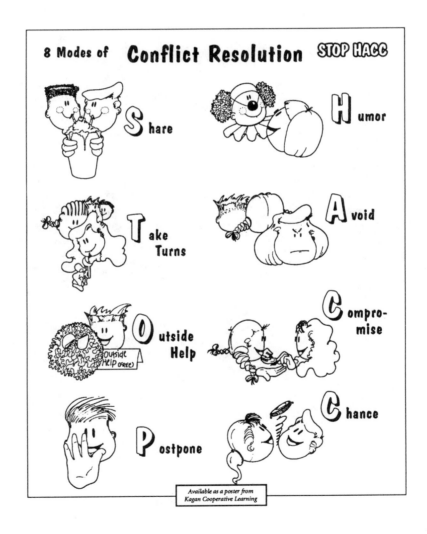

Lesson 34 Cooperative Conflict Resolution Projects

Lesson-At-A-Glance

Goal: Relationship Skills (Conflict Resolution)

Grades: 3-Adult

Time: Two class periods

Outcome—Students Will:
• Recognize the three types of conflicts.
• Identify eight modes of conflict resolution.
• Be able to develop a simple role play or skit, in writing, and act it out.

Materials:
• Poster of eight modes of cooperative conflict resolution
• Eight modes written on individual strips of paper - see handout

Structures:
• **Numbered Heads Together**
• **Think-Pair-Share**
• **Team Projects**
• **Inside-Outside Circle**

Lesson Overview

This lesson is intended to review the types of conflict and involve students directly with one of the eight modes of cooperative conflict resolution. It is intended to help students integrate their understanding of the mode through scripting and acting it out. Students will review the three types of conflict and the eight modes of cooperative conflict resolution through a Numbered Heads approach. Next, in Think-Pair-Share, students will share their personal experiences with the different modes. Finally, in pairs, students will be assigned to use one of the modes as the basis for a Team Project. Their Team Project will be to create a role play or skit using the assigned mode as the solution.

Lesson Sequence

Numbered Heads Together:
Review Modes of Cooperative Conflict Resolution

Have students in teams of four number off 1-4 (refer to Numbered Heads Together in Structures Chapter). Explain that you will ask the class a question and teams are to put their heads together to come up with the answer. Any student can be called on for an answer, so it's in the team's best interest to thoroughly discuss the question. Students must refer to three different types of conflict and the Eight Modes of Cooperative Conflict Resolution. The three types of conflict are resources, needs, and values. The eight modes of cooperative conflict resolution are: **S**hare, **T**ake Turns, **O**utside Help, **P**ostpone, **H**umor, **A**void, **C**ompromise, and **C**hance. Refer to Chapter 5:7 in Part I to review this information. Ask students to try to use a different mode for each problem.

1. Two brothers with only one TV set are arguing over who is going to get to watch their favorite TV program. Which type of conflict is this, which modes could be used to solve it?

   Possible Answers: Type of conflict - **Resources**, because viewing TV is a limited resource.

Possible Modes :

Take Turns: One watches their program for an hour, the other then watches his.

Compromise: Each has a different night.

Chance: Flip a coin to see who gets to watch what.

2. Jerry feels his partner on the project isn't doing her fair share. Which type of conflict is it? How might Jerry resolve this using one of the eight modes?

Possible Answers: Type of conflict - **Resources** if it's an issue of time spent doing the project.

Needs if it is an issue of achievement and feeling that his partner is keeping him from achieving.

Possible Modes :

Outside Help: Involve the teacher to have the partner do their fair share or dissolve the partnership.

Compromise: See if there is a reason the partner isn't doing their share of the work and make an agreement acceptable to both.

3. Jason and Maria are supposed to prepare an ethnic food for a world cultures class. Maria wants to cook Mexican. Jason tells Maria he doesn't like Mexican food. Maria's feelings are hurt. Which type of conflict is this? How might they resolve this conflict?

Possible Answers: Type of conflict - **Needs**, if either of the motivations is only for the power of the situation. **Values**, if Maria is hurt because of her ethnicity.

Possible Modes :

Take Turns: If they have more than one project, they could prepare Mexican food one time, and something else the other time.

Compromise: Perhaps make a dish which may not be either's first choice, but both will agree to.

4. Jeremy and Juan both want to sit next to the teacher on the field trip. Which type of conflict is this? How would you resolve this using one of the eight modes?

Possible Answers: Type of conflict - **Resources**, if it is an issue of getting the teacher's attention (which may be a limited resource) or **Needs**, if it is an issue of feeling important (power or self-esteem) because one is sitting next to the teacher.

Possible Modes :

Share: Perhaps they can have the teacher sit between them.

Take Turns: Jeremy can sit with her while going, and Juan can sit with her on the way back.

Humor: They could make up the best poem for the teacher and the winner sits next to her.

Avoid: One or both could decide that conflict is not worth it, and choose to avoid the conflict and not sit next to the teacher.

Chance: They could play rock, paper, and scissors. The winner sits next to the teacher.

Think-Pair-Share:
Students Share Personal Experiences

Explain to students that you will be asking them to tell about personal experiences they have had where they used one of the different modes of cooperative conflict resolution. Ask students to share only conflicts they feel comfortable sharing with the class. It's a good idea to model this for students. Relate a personal experience where you actually used one of the eight modes to resolve a conflict.

Think about a conflict where you used one of the conflict resolution strategies we have discussed.

Pair with a partner as directed by the teacher and discuss your experiences. You have only two minutes.

Volunteers **share** experiences with the class.

Teacher Talk:
Why is it Important to Know the Modes?

Use the information about the eight modes of cooperative conflict resolution in chapter 5:7 to give a short lecturette on why knowing and using different methods of conflict resolution gives us more choices. If we only have one choice every time a conflict occurs, it limits our options. The eight modes make the acronym **STOPHACC:**

> **S**HARE
> **T**AKE TURNS
> **O**UTSIDE HELP
> **P**OSTPONE
> **H**UMOR
> **A**VOID
> **C**OMPROMISE
> **C**HANCE

Team Project:
Pairs Develop a Conflict Scenario

The class will work in pairs to develop a one minute role play or skit using one of the eight modes of conflict resolution. Have the eight modes cut into strips. You'll need two sets of eight strips for a class of 32. Each pair chooses one of the modes to use as the basis for the role play or skit they develop. All projects must be written and acted out. The story must include the following: Introduction, what the conflict is, which solution was used, how it resolved the conflict and why. Students will need 15-45 minutes to develop this project.

Pair Inside-Outside Circle:
Acting It Out

Pairs who planned their conflict scenario partner up with another pair to form an Inside-Outside Circle. All students do this simultaneously. They take turns acting their scenario out for the other pair. Give them a one minute time limit for each team. At the end of two minutes, ask teams on the outside circle to move one team to the right. All teams shift at the same time. Teams again act out their conflicts for their new partners. Continue until pairs have shared at least three times.

Inside-Outside Circle:
Reflection Questions

Ask students to think of how they would respond to two or three of the reflection questions listed below. Attempt to draw out the importance of knowing how to use different modes of conflict resolution.

- What happens if you get stuck with only one way to approach conflict resolution?
- Why would you want to know more than one way to resolve conflicts?
- Who might help you resolve conflicts and how could they help you?

Inside-Outside Circle:
Affirmation Starters

Ask students in their pairs to think of a way to affirm their partner. The person receiving the affirmation can say only "thank you." Have them pair and share their affirmation.

Post affirmation starters such as:

You're really good at _____.

Thank for helping me...

~ ❀ ~

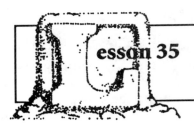

Lesson 35 Introduction to Assertive Communication

Lesson-At-A-Glance

Goal: Relationship Skills (Assertive Communication)

Grades: 9-Adult

Time: 45-60 minutes. (This could be split into two consecutive lessons)

Outcome—Students Will:
• *Become aware of four types of communication.*
• *Examine their own experience with each type of communication.*

Materials:
• Overhead of four types of communication
• Paper & pencil for each student

Structures:
• **Pairs**
• **Think-Pair-Share**
• **Choral Response**
• **Team Project**

Lesson Overview

This lesson introduces four different types of communication: Doormat, Bagging, Aggressive, and Assertive. Pairs share their own experiences and practice identifying each type.

Lesson Sequence

Teacher Talk:

Explaining Concepts

Explain to students the goal of this lesson is to teach them to be able to identify four types of communication.

Pairs: Forming

With high school students I ask them to do this activity in <u>boy/girl pairs.</u> I find this activity works much better in mixed gender pairs. If you end up with some girl/girl or boy/boy pairs, that's all right, but don't have the majority of your groups like this. (It's interesting how some teachers will say that their students won't work in mixed gender pairs. My experience is just the opposite. They may say they don't want to. However, when I make this the norm, I find students go along with it.) If students can't find a partner, I find one for them. If you are already working in teams of four, then you can have the partners pair up.

Teacher Talk:

Explain Passive "The Doormat"

Use the information from the section on Relationship Skills (Chapter 5:13) and an overhead which shows the different communication styles listed, review the relevant information about Doormat. Stress that this is when we let someone walk right over us and *we do not respect our own rights.* We accept the other person getting their way and do not respond. It may not feel quite right, but we don't know what else to do. We don't necessarily hold a grudge, but we know we should be doing something differently. *Give an example of yourself where you've felt like a doormat or share about someone else if you don't have a personal experience.* This is important. If you can't share with students you can't expect students to share this type of information with you.

Think-Pair-Share:

Students Share A Doormat Experience

Have students think about a time in their lives when they felt like a doormat. Give students a minute or so to think about it. Ask for a few responses to see if students understand. Clarify if needed.

Ask students to **pair** and discuss their experience with their partner. Give students only one-two minutes to share. (At first, a short time is better than too long. It lets students know that they need to start sharing immediately). Ask for volunteers who would like to **share**. After a few volunteers, call pairs who have not shared.

Teacher Talk:

Explain Passive "Bagging"

Explain the behavior called bagging (refer to Chapter 5:13). Remind students that it has to do with letting small annoyances build into big ones. Give an example from your personal life as a parent or teacher where you were bagging, letting things build up and then exploded inappropriately. Ask if students can have any personal examples. It's best to get at least one or two examples from students before you move on. Ask for a student volunteer to define bagging.

Think-Pair-Share:

Students Share A Bagging Experience

Have students **think** about their experience with bagging. Perhaps it happened to them, a sibling, friend, or family member. Give students one minute of **think** time. Ask students to **pair** with their partner and share the experience they came up with. Give pairs two minutes to share their experience. Randomly call on students to **share**.

Teacher Talk:

Explain Aggressive Communication

Share your own experience with aggressive communication. Refer to Chapter 5:14 on aggressive communication. Aggressive communication is where one person tries to intimidate the other, for example, by yelling or threatening. Being aggressive usually means the person wants their way and isn't willing to listen to the other person. Ask students to tell the class about any experiences they have had with aggressive communication.

Think-Pair-Share:

Students Share An Aggressive Communication Experience

After a couple of students have shared, then ask students to **think** of an a time when they have experienced aggressive communication at school, in their family, or with friends. Have students **pair** to discuss their experience. After two minutes, ask for volunteers to **share** their experience. Call on a few students.

Choral Response:

Review Bagging, Doormat, and Aggressive

Tell students you will be using Choral Response to review. (Refer to chapter two for information on Choral Response). Show students your hand signal. I usually hold my right hand palm out, up high, so all students can see it. Explain that you will ask a question while your hand is raised. Students are to think of a response. After a few seconds you will lower your hand straight down. When you do this students are to respond in unison. If they do not respond in unison, repeat the procedure until they do. When they do respond in unison, praise the class.

The Questions For Choral Response

On an overhead or on the board have Doormat, Bagging, & Aggressive listed. Students can refer to these for this first round.

1. **The first type of communication we reviewed today was?** (Think Time) and then [Signal] I often will say "thinking..." students will know not to respond while I am holding up my hand. Drop your hand. Student response should be **"DOORMAT."** If the response is ragged or you don't have 100% participation, repeat the procedure until you do. Once students see you are serious about their responding they will participate.

2. **The second type of communication we reviewed had to do with stuffing your feelings. It was?** (Think Time) [Signal] Giving hints such as the sound of the first letter of the answer is often appropriate in the initial stages of learning new information. Student response should be **"BAGGING."** Again, if students are not 100% correct or not responding 100% ask the class to repeat. Praise the class for participation.

3. **The third type of communication we discussed which had to do with the "fighter" was?** [Signal] Think time for students [Drop your hand]. Students respond, **"AGGRESSIVE."**

4. **Which type of communication style had to do with holding onto feelings until and later letting them out inappropriately?** [Signal] Think time [Drop your hand]. Students respond, **"BAGGING."**

5. **In which communication style is one person trying to intimidate another?** [Signal] Think time [Drop you hand]. Student response, **"AGGRESSIVE."**

6. **In which communication style do people let others walk all over them?** [Signal] Think time [Drop your hand]. Students respond, **"DOORMAT."**

Team Project:
Pairs Create Short Dialogue

Each pair will develop a short dialogue for either Doormat, Bagging, or Aggressive communication styles, which should be a short interaction between two individuals and as an example of the communication styles listed. Pairs will be expected to hand in their written dialogue. Two pairs will be randomly selected to act out their dialogue in front of the class. Let students know they will have 10 minutes to complete the assignment. While students are working, walk around the room monitoring how pairs are doing. Intervene as necessary to give support. Let pairs know when they have two minutes left. Have a couple of groups read their dialogue. Have two groups act theirs out. Papers should be handed in from all groups. This is an assignment which can be graded if you need to.

Pairs: Reflection

Have some of the following questions written on an overhead or on the board. Ask pairs to spend one-two minutes discussing at least two of the questions.

- Which of the communication styles is the easiest for you to understand?

- If you used Bagging often what would happen to you?

- Which type of communication style of these three do you use most often?

- Which of these communication styles do you see your friends or family use most often?

- What could you and your partner do to improve working together if you work together again?

✤ How might you be able to recognize these communication styles when you see them?

✤ What could you do to avoid using them?

Think-Pair-Share:
Affirmations
Have these written on the board.

Thanks for sharing about...

I liked the way you...

Have students **think** of one positive aspect their partner has shared with them today. Ask partners then to **pair** and share this with one another. Ask several students to **share** one affirmation they used with the class. Call on students randomly.

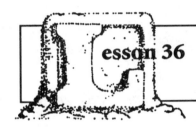

esson 36　Creating I-Statements

Lesson-At-A-Glance

Goal:　Relationship Skills (Assertive Communication)

Grades:　3-Adult

Time:　45-60 minutes. (This could be done in two consecutive lessons

Outcome—Students Will:

• Practice creating "I-statements."

Materials:

• Handout #1 for 3-6th grade, Handout #2 for 4-12th grade, Handout #3 for 7-12th grade and pencils
• Group discussion questions

Structures:

● **Brainstorming**
● **Pairs Compare**
● **Roundrobin**
● **Numbered Heads Together**
● **Pairs Share**

Lesson Overview

This lesson helps students develop and practice giving "I-statements," and provides students with the support of team members as they learn this skill. Pairs of students will be given several short scenarios and asked to create an appropriate "I-statement" in response.

Lesson Sequence

Teacher Talk:

Teach "I-Statements" And Review Feeling Words

Teach The Concept of "I-Statements"

Using the information in chapter 5:14 explain the concept of "I-statements." It is usually best to begin with the first two parts of an "I-statement",

"I feel _____" and "when you _____."

This will facilitate students using "I-statements" immediately, rather than having to master all four parts. Stay with only these two parts with younger students. When older students master these, you can add the other two elements as appropriate. The next activity will extend to all four parts of an "I-statement."

Form Pairs:

Have students form pairs in any manner you choose. I find that there is usually more on task behavior with mixed gender teams. Ask pairs to choose a recorder to be ready with paper and pencil. Have the recorder hold up their pencil. Review the Four S's of brainstorming, if needed. (Review Brainstorming in Section II of this book.)

Brainstorming:

Basic "I-Statements"

Once students are ready to brainstorm introduce the "I feel _____" portion of the I-statement. Give an example of a feeling word. "I feel sad or happy." Ask students to share a few feeling words. Now ask pairs to brainstorm as many feeling words as they can within one minute. Walk around listening in on pairs as they brainstorm. At the end of one minute, ask students to stop. Call on each team to give at least one feeling word. Using an overhead projector or the chalk/white board record responses as students give them.

Note: For more information on "I-Statements" and more ideas on introducing them refer to Chapter 5:13.

Teacher Models:
Give Model for "I-Statement"

On the chalk/white board, or overhead projector write a situation with a partially completed "I-statement." Show students how they might create an "I-Statement."

A. Another student cuts in front of you in line on the playground.

(Elementary)

I feel _____

when you _____

B. You ask a friend to help you with a difficult math problem. They tell you to "do it yourself."

(Intermediate)

I feel _____

when you _____

because _____

C. Someone makes a joke about a class mate which makes most students laugh. The student who it was aimed at cries because it hurt her feelings.

(Secondary)

I feel _____

when you _____

because _____

and what I want is _____

Explain to students how "I-statements" can be used to solve conflicts which arise. It's very important to use "I-statements" when the conflict is small (mouse size) rather than waiting until it has gotten larger than an elephant. Small size conflicts can be solved much more easily with "I-statements" than large sized conflicts.

Pairs Compare:
Use Practice Sheet To Form "I-Statements"

There are three worksheets following this lesson, designed to be used with various grade levels.

Worksheet A. Elementary grades 3-6

Worksheet B. Intermediate and secondary grades 4-12

Worksheet C. designed for Secondary grades 7-12

Remember to review the questions and use those appropriate for your class.

Tell your students to imagine being in the following situations. They are to develop an "I-statement" they could use to respond to each situation. Give one sheet to each pair. Give students a few minutes to complete the sheets, depending on the age of the students. (A variation is to have students work individually in this section. Pairs assist students who are unsure of how to apply this skill. As the teacher, it is your choice.)

Roundrobin: Read Responses

Assign pairs to meet with another pair. If you have teams of four, then have each pair within the team reform into the original team. Ask teams to use Roundrobin sharing for each one of the pair to read one "I-Statement" each. Listen to how the other pair responded.

Roundrobin:
Reflection Questions

The questions below are to be handed out to each team. Teams Roundrobin each question.

✤ What was the most difficult part of the "I-statement," the "I feel..." or the "when you......." part?

✤ Does everyone on your team understand "I-statements?" How can you tell?

✤ If someone didn't understand, how might you explain it to them?

Numbered Heads Together:
Reflection Questions

Once the team has discussed the questions, then it's time for class discussion and reflection. Review with the total class the team reflection questions. Use the Numbered Heads format for teams to share some of the answers they came up with in their teams. Draw from students how using "I-statements" might help them in school.

Using Numbered Heads Together format, have students in teams number off 1-4 (refer to Numbered Heads Together in the Structures chapter). Explain that you will ask the class a question and the teams are to put their heads together to come up with an answer. Any student can be called on for an answer, so it's in the team's best interest to thoroughly discuss their answers.

✤ How could "I-statements" help you with your friends, family, teachers?

✤ What are potentials risks if you use an "I-statement?"

✤ Where would be the easiest place for you personally to begin to use "I-statements?"

✤ How can "I-statements" be empowering?

Pairs Share:
Affirmation Starters

Ask students to think of affirmations they might give their team members. They can refer to the posted Affirmation Starters or make up their own. Have students pair up with one of their teammates. Each person gives an affirmation to their partner and other teammates.

Affirmation Starters:

• I liked it when you...................
because.................and I want you to..............
• Thank you for............made me
feel..............because................please...........

Note: Some of these questions were adapted from material in *Conflict Resolution: A Secondary School Curriculum*, from The Community Board Program, Inc. San Francisco, CA.

Create an I-Statement
Handout #1

Creating "I-statements" is considered risky business for many people. They may be afraid that if they use an "I-statement" the other person may become angry with them. Often, just the opposite is the case. If we let small problems go without venting our feelings, those feelings build and build. Pretty soon a small problem grows out of proportion and becomes a big issue. Most people receive"I-statements" in the manner they are given. If you can use an "I-statement" without being angry, then chances are the other person will not respond with anger.

Instructions: Complete the following "I-Statements" with your partner:

1. Another student cuts in front of you in the lunch line. You don't like it. Give her/him an I-statement.

   I feel _____

   when you _____

2. One of your friends makes fun of you in front of others. It hurts your feelings. Give him/her an I-statement.

   I feel _____

   when you _____

3. Your parent yells at you and it scares you. Give your parent an I-statement.

   I feel _____

   when you _____

(Adapted from *Conflict Resolution: A Secondary School Curriculum,* 1987, The Community Board Program, Inc.) (**Permission to reproduce for classroom use**)

Create an I-Statement
Handout #2

Creating "I-statements" is considered risky business for many people. They may be afraid that if they use an "I-statement" the other person may become angry with them. Often just the opposite is the case. If we let small problems go without venting our feelings, those feelings build and build. Pretty soon a small problem grows out of proportion and becomes a big issue. Most people receive "I-statements" in the manner they are given. If you can use an "I-statement" without being angry, then chances are the other person will not respond with anger. Risking anger may be worth clearing the air with a small concern rather than having that concern grow into something larger.

Instructions: Complete the following "I-Statements" with your partner:

1. You see a classmate take a pencil from your desk without asking.

    I feel _____

    when you _____

    because _____

2. You are playing in the yard when another student runs by and knocks you down. They do not stop. They keep running and are laughing.

    I feel _____

    when you _____

    because _____

3. The teacher yells at you when you make a mistake in math, while you are working at the chalk board.

    I feel _____

    when you _____

    because _____

(Adapted from *Conflict Resolution: A Secondary School Curriculum*, 1987, The Community Board Program, Inc. **(Permission to reproduce for classroom use)**

Create an I-Statement
Handout #3

Creating "I-statements" is considered risky business for many people. They may be afraid that if they use an "I-statement" the other person may become angry with them. Often, just the opposite is the case. If we let small problems go without venting our feelings, those feelings build and build. Pretty soon what was a small problem grows out of proportion and becomes a big issue. Most people receive "I-statements" in the manner they are given. If you can use an "I-statement" without being angry, then chances are the other person will not respond with anger. Risking anger may be worth clearing the air with a small concern you have rather than having that concern grow into something larger.

Instructions: Complete the following "I-Statements" with your partner:

1. A friend wants you to lie to your parents about where you are going tonight. You don't want to lie.

   I feel _____

   when you _____

   because _____

   And what I want is _____

2. The hall supervisor has mistakenly blamed you for writing graffiti on the lockers.

   I feel _____

   when you _____

   because _____

   And what I want is _____

3. You forgot your lunch, and do not have any lunch money. Your friend offers to share their own lunch and buy you a soda.

   I feel _____

   when you _____

   because _____

   And what I want is _____

(Adapted from *Conflict Resolution: A Secondary School Curriculum*, 1987, The Community Board Program, Inc.) **Permission to reproduce for classroom use**

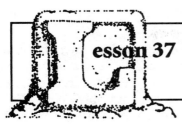

esson 37 Weaving Connections

Lesson-At-A-Glance

Goal: Classbuilding (Synergy)
Grades: 2-6, adults
Time: 30-40 Minutes
Outcome—Students Will:
• Share feelings with entire class
• Give and receive support.
Materials: One ball of yarn
Structures:
• **Think-Pair-Share**
• **Community Circle**

Lesson Overview[1]

This is an excellent end of the semester or end of the year lesson which allows students to share some final thoughts about their time together and to create a physical connection by tossing a ball of yarn to another student across the circle after sharing. This lesson works best when there is a high degree of support among students. That's why I recommend it be done at the end of the semester or year when a sense of inclusion, influence, openness, and community have been experienced by the class.

Lesson Sequence

Teacher Talk:

Strong Circles

You will need an open space for this lesson. Ask students to stand and form a large circle

---

1. This lesson is adapted from *Tribes: A Process For Social Development And Cooperative Learning* by Jeanne Gibbs.

sitting on the floor or on chairs.

Now ask students to consider which is stronger and why:

(Write this on the board or overhead)

• A circle where individuals are not connected, or

• A circle where individuals are all holding hands?

Think-Pair-Share:

Discussion Which is Stronger

Ask students to **think** about the question posed above. Now have students form **pairs** and discuss with their partner what they feel is the answer. If you are concerned about students being left out when partners are formed you can have the students number off 1-2, 1-2 before you ask the question. If you have an odd number of students, then there will be one triad. Give the students a couple of minutes to share. Then ask a few pairs to **share** their answers with the class. Discuss how connections between people make them stronger. Ask students to **Think-Pair-Share** where they might have noticed people being stronger when they are together. Answers might be: sports teams, band, singers, gangs, Indian tribes, etc.

Community Circle:

Students Share and Toss Yarn

Have students form a circle facing in toward the middle. Share with students your own feelings about the time you have spent together and ask students to share a word or

---

sentence about how they have felt in class this year. Start by saying something positive. You will be holding the ball of yarn. While you speak, you will be unwinding some of the yarn so that when you toss it, it will make it the entire way across the circle. When you finish speaking, hold on to the end of the yarn and toss the yarn across the circle to one of the students who you are certain will have something to share. Do not name who you are throwing it to. Wherever it lands, that's the person who speaks next.They will respond while unwinding more yarn, hold on to yarn and toss the ball across the circle to another student. This continues until all students have received the yarn, shared, held on to their place on the yarn and tossed it on.

Note: Have students pull the yarn tight as it goes around the circle.

When everyone has had a turn, have the students pull the yarn tight and hold it over their heads. Point out the interconnectedness of everybody within this class. Point out that we are all connected even when we are not holding hands or have a piece of yarn between us. On the count of three ask the students to all let go of the yarn at the same time. One, two, three, everyone lets go of the yarn.

Note: When you are finished have one student rewind the yarn before it is moved. Don't move the yarn before rewinding it. If you gather it up without rewinding it first you'll end up with numerous knots and need to do surgery on your yarn.

Toward Community and the Inclusive School

Chapter 8

When I first started using cooperative learning I used very few structures and saw it strictly as a tool for academic achievement. That was my end goal and that was enough. After a few years I discovered students made more academic progress when I stretched and made my students stretch. This stretching had to do with my beginning to feel that students needed more than the content I was teaching through cooperative learning. Students needed to learn how to relate more effectively if they were going to become truly cooperative teams in a collaborative classroom. Along with relationship skills came classbuilding and teambuilding. My students needed to experience stages of group development to enhance their ability to function well as class and team members. This book is about a process of helping students experience these stages and to give you, the classroom teacher, lessons and structures for accomplishing this.

Cooperative learning can be one of the tools we use to restructure the way we teach students. I visualize classrooms where we are consciously aware of the social dynamics and use them to empower our students and ourselves. I imagine cooperative learning as a process which unfolds over a number of years and that we are patient with ourselves as we learn to use it well. Cooperative learning, like all instructional approaches, doesn't work all the time. I believe cooperative learning, when used well, works more often than many other approaches and reaches more of our students.

I see the use of classbuilding, teambuilding, and relationship skill building merging with the issues of group development and creating an opportunity for a genuine sense of community to develop within our classrooms and schools. Our task will be to help the students we are teaching change the world in the next century. We must help students to foster a sense of community within their towns they live in, our state, our nation, and our world as a whole.

Faculty Building

I propose that we apply the cooperative learning principles of getting acquainted, building identity, experiencing mutual support, valuing individual differences, and synergy outlined in chapters four and five to our faculty and administration. Major issues facing American education today include stress, burnout, and a sense of isolation experienced by many of us at different times in our careers. We often experience these issues alone. Many of our colleagues have left the teaching profession because of these and other issues. I propose that we make a concerted effort to create an environment for collaboration to take place.

Getting Acquainted

We can structure opportunities for teachers and administrators to become better acquainted outside the scope of the faculty room and the staff Christmas party. What if we use some of the classbuilding, teambuilding, and relationship skill building lessons with our colleagues? This could be during a faculty meeting or as part of an ongoing program to build a school team. We know how important it is to build trust and a working relationship among our students. If it's important for our students to get acquainted, perhaps it's even a better idea for us to know each other at a deeper level. We need to model the collegiality among our staff that we want students to develop.

How could you promote a getting acquainted process in your school?

Building School Identity

Building a school identity involves all teachers, support staff, administrators, students, parents, and community members. Site-based planning approaches promoted in our schools must have an identity-building aspect if they are to be successful. What if we were to invite all parents, teachers, support staff, administrators, and students to an identity building day? This might be a day where part of the task would be to set goals for the school, or perhaps create a vision of what you want your school to look like in the year 2000. The possibilities are there and people are doing it.

How could you promote building a school identity in your school?

Experiencing Mutual Support

How important is it for adults to feel supported? I know that when I feel supported by my colleagues and

administrator I have a better attitude about the work I do. Excellent managers in corporate America make it a point to provide support and recognition to employees. Excellent schools recognize efforts by students, support staff, teachers, and parents. This recognition might be in the form of a thank you note, special certificates, or recognition parties or dinners. Some of these efforts might appear small. None of them go unnoticed, except by their absence. As educators we need to develop support systems for ourselves as well as our students.

How could you develop mutual support systems for yourself and your colleagues?

Valuing Individual Differences

Is it important for us to appreciate the individual differences among those with whom we work? How do we provide opportunities to express our differences and have our colleagues express their support or appreciation of our differences? As teachers, we all bring something a little different to the students we serve. Wouldn't it be exciting to acknowledge the differences we bring to our students and to each other? Some of us bring different values to our students. Some of us inspire different types of students. How often has it happened that a student you were not able to connect with, goes onto the next grade level into the room of a teacher you may not like, and he/she is able to connect with this student and make a positive difference in her/his life. How often does this happen and we may not even realize it?

How can you promote ways to value individual differences within your school?

Synergy and Issues of Group Development

If we are able to seriously approach the aspects of school building mentioned above, we are on our way to creating a school which has a positive effect on its students and the adults who work within it. How powerful could a school be if not only the students had a support team within a supportive classroom, but the teachers had a support team within a supportive school?

For this school building approach to be more effective, it's important to be aware of the stages of group development mentioned in Chapter One. Inclusion, influence, openness, and community occur as the process described above unfolds. It's important to note that this will not happen by itself. It must be intentionally created and cared for if it is to thrive. The principles which allow this process to flourish in classbuilding and teambuilding apply to school building as well. It takes vision and commitment to help make it happen, the same ingredients needed in any classroom.

How can you help move your school towards synergy?

Team Teaching

Another direction emerging in schools across America is team teaching. Teachers are pooling their resources and talents and working together to create cooperative classrooms. The advantage to this structure is that teachers have their own built-in support system. They plan together and at times co-teach a lesson. Two colleagues of mine, Nanci Navarro and Sara Valentine of Osborn School in Turlock, California have team taught two special day classes for learning handicapped students. They both started off collaborating on curriculum and sharing materials. Eventually they began to share more and more. They decided cooperative learning could work well with their students.

They both attended one of Spencer Kagan's five day cooperative learning trainings. The fall after they were trained in cooperative learning, they began using cooperative learning structures as a primary mode of academic and social instruction within their classrooms.

Nanci is stronger in reading and language arts so she soon began preparing these lessons. Sara's strengths are in math and science so she did the preparations in these. Their team teaching took several forms. One had them each teaching students from both classes in their chosen content area. While one teacher would deliver whole class instruction the other would use questioning strategies with small groups. This combination of students and teachers cooperating has led to impressive academic and social growth for their students.

Nanci and Sara would be the first to tell you that team teaching is their preferred style of teaching. They both indicate that to team teach you need to find a partner whom you can enjoy working with. Team teaching is like a marriage. To make it work, you both must be committed. What makes their style of team teaching so powerful is the combination of team teaching and cooperative learning. They model what they are teaching their students.

Restructuring

I see communitybuilding as a very appropriate process for assisting schools in their restructuring efforts. All the aspects of class-buiding, teambuiding, and relationship skill building are needed as a school attempts to take on new challenges and new path. Restructuring has been a buzz word more than a reality in most school districts because we are so caught up within the current educational system we're involved in that real change seems impossible.

Meaningful change must occur when we feel in our hearts and guts that we must change for the good of our children and ourselves. Making this leap comes form exploring the issues of what is excellent education? How do children learn best? What are the most effective teaching methods?

To make restructuring more than a buzz word we will need to consciously work toward building true learning communities within our schools. This process can help move us in the direction where administrators and teachers study research on learning and teaching, look at which models are proven most effective and make choices for themselves about what needs to change in their schools.

To make this change takes trust in ourselves and in one another and the knowledge that the change makes sense and is necessary. How can we develop this type of trust and knowledge without some type of community building process? If we use Community-building in our classrooms because our students need the classbuilding, teambuilding, and relationship skill building, then we need it as much among ourselves as we deal with the issues which face us in a new millennium.

The Three R's

I envision that in the twenty-first century the three R's will take on a new meaning: Relatedness, Respect, and Responsibility will become as important as the more traditional three R's. Educators will come to the realization that relationship skills are as important a process as teaching academic skills. Students must know how to relate to others, whether peers, adults, or different cultures. As our global, cultural, and economic lives become more interdependent, the ability to relate effectively becomes imperative, rather than just a "neat" idea.

Students and teachers will discover that respecting each other and themselves is the bedrock of self-esteem. Without self-respect there can be no respect for others. Teachers will begin to see cooperative learning as one process for teaching students about self-respect.

Teaching about responsibility for oneself, society, and the global environment will be an expected norm in schools throughout America and the world. The realization will begin to dawn on educators and governments throughout the world that we are all responsible for one another. If one of us in the human community suffers, we all suffer. When we feel this connectedness and sense of community, then the future possibilities shared here will become our present reality.

What we are engaged in here has the potential to change not only our classrooms, but the world.

> *I am a teacher;*
> *I touch the future.*
> *--Christa McAuliffe*